The Plus-One

The Plus-One

Getting By on Good Connections in the Analog Age

By David Klein

Cover, illustrations, and book design by Christopher Williams, Plastic Flame Press

ISBN: 979-8-218-47451-5
Printed in the United States of America
First 7/21 Books edition 2024

Published by 7/21 Books
Iamthefly.org

For Alison,
Nathan,
and Daniel

CONTENTS

The Plus-One

Chapter 1

Peppermint Lumps

Every story has to start somewhere. This one begins with a tight closeup behind Courtney Love's left ear.

I first noticed the clear-spot Band-Aid—that's what those little round ones made expressly for zits are called—at the after-party, while waiting to use the facilities. And I empathized, having utilized them before. Sensing my presence, Courtney glanced over her shoulder, saw that I was nobody, and turned back around. A moment later, the powder room door opened and out popped a bald, weirdly beautiful somebody: Billy Corgan, before a few extra pounds dulled the glam part of the Glam Uncle Fester equation. Their handshake produced a faintly perceptible sound of crinkling cellophane.

The after-party for the 1997 MTV Video Awards took place in the Ty Warner Penthouse Suite of the Four Seasons, the priciest hotel room in America. Perched seven hundred feet above the city, with floor-to-ceiling windows and a 360-degree view, the palatial digs were oversaturated with famous rockers, actors, and industry people. In the master bedroom, Leonardo DiCaprio lounged on an emperor-size bed with as many lady friends as its frame could accommodate. His pal David Blaine was nearby, pulling cards out of places cards aren't supposed to be. In another room, the Counting Crows guy, or somebody who looked a lot like him (possibly Jamiroquai) held court. In the main space, my cousin Noni, Winona Ryder, whose star my one was plussed to, was talking intensely with a rapt Dave Grohl.

Around here is where Courtney Love's Friend's Friend Who Has an Extra Hit of Ecstasy came into view, and Noni and Dave and Dave's mom slipped out, accompanied by assorted entourage members.

Hours later, in merciless morning light, there it was again—Courtney's clear-spot—when she leaned forward and whispered to her friend in the front seat of the limo, "Got any coke?"

Pushing tepidly through the revolving portals of a luxury hotel located somewhere between Midtown and Chelsea, I sensed I wasn't the only one on the wrong side of a pill. The prevailing mood was that awful squinchy come-down feeling. We followed Courtney into and out of an elevator, and when she stopped at the end of the corridor and rapped on the door, we all lurched to a collective halt behind her. After an extremely long minute, the door opened. And, as another David—Byrne—had prophesied, I did have to ask myself...

Well, how did I get here?

The moment is at least partly traceable to a rare April snowstorm that oc-curred fifteen years earlier, one that closed down the schools in New York's tristate area for days and forced our visiting relatives from the West, Mike and Cindy and their kids—Winona, ten, the very same Winona who would, years later, keep Dave Grohl in thrall, and Yuri, six—to extend their visit for several days. Much to the chagrin of my mother, who had played the good host for almost a week and was, quite honestly, ready to see the backs of them. As for me, I couldn't believe my luck. My little sister was on an extended sleepover engagement with her own coterie of pals. My older brother was off at Sarah Lawrence, having reluctantly agreed to attend the country's most expensive private college while continuing to play bass in a new wave band called the Method. So I had the Horowitz clan all to myself.

Uncle Mike's family was laid-back and loving in a way we were not, and having them around made normal life better. One night, as we all nestled *Simp-sons*-like on the basement sofa for *SNL*, Noni at one end, her feet in Cindy's massaging hands, I thought how absent this tactility was from my nuclear fam-ily relations. We Kleins weren't much for snuggling.

I'd always loved the company of young kids, and I was studying psychology at Vassar and thinking a lot about child development. At ten, Noni had prodi-gious levels of charm and sophistication. She was mad about Monty Python, and had the dry, absurdist wit and love of wordplay that went with it. We'd listen over and over to my Python cassette culled from *Matching Tie & Hand-kerchief*. A bit called "A Minute Passed" in particular: "A further minute passed quickly, followed by another minute, when suddenly, a different minute passed, followed by another, different minute…"

On the eve of the Horowitz's departure, the radio could not have been clearer about predicting a major snowstorm, but Mom refused to believe it. Partly because it was April already, mild and sunny to boot, and partly because she didn't *want* to believe it. And yet the following morning, there it blindingly was: sheer whiteness everywhere you looked. Uncle Mike, who had studied meteorology before earning a master's in English and American literature from NYU, was in heaven. A dedicated snow lover, he hadn't seen the stuff in years and couldn't wait to get out in it. Neither could the kids, who, having spent most of their lives on a commune called Rainbow, in Elk, California (pop. 208), had only observed the snow phenomenon in viewings of *Miracle on 34th Street* in Rainbow's converted barn-cum-movie house.

Rainbow meant living with six other families according to an aesthetic that was half hippie rejection of middle-class values and conformity, half futuristic experimental community.

"We consider it to be a space colony," Uncle Mike wrote at the time, "a self-contained, self-selected small community that could exist at L5 or somewhere like that." The arrangement lasted a few years, until the tribal leaders began advocating polyamory.

As Mike rummaged through the garage and retrieved a couple of neglected snow saucers, Cindy and I bundled up the kids in what we could find that fit them, and off we trudged toward a nearby house on a hill, known as Capitani's. It was a perfect sized hill for novices and gangly snow enthusiasts alike. Mom stayed home and fretted.

By Day 2 of the layover, Noni had had her fill of sledding. She was clearly an indoor type, happier to rewatch her VHS copy of *West Side Story* or comb through old copies of *Rampart's* magazine that Mike (she called her father Mike) kept stashed in the attic than to romp around in the snow. So we headed to my room for more Monty Python, and eventually she started sifting through my tapes.

My cassette collection was my most prized possession. I kept them numbered and maintained a master list in a hardbound blank-paged book. The mixes I treasured most consisted of songs culled from the airwaves. They might lack first verses or end with a segue into another track or DJ talk, but that was OK. I gave them fanciful names like "Scattered Showers" and "Assorted Poodles" and spent inordinate hours illustrating the narrow rectangular panel on the paper insert that lined up with the tape's spine.

"Let's try 'Peppermint Lumps,'" Noni said.

"Peppermint Lumps" was a good place to jump in. The tape was named after the first track, a one-off single[1] put together by Pete Townshend and spoken/sung by a little British kid named Angie. It was many of the things I loved: catchy, childlike, strange, and obscure. From there, one gem followed another, and over the next few days we got to "Assorted Poodles" and "Scattered Showers," and "Labor Daze '81."

Peppermint Lumps

PEPPERMINT LUMP – ANGIE

ANOTHER GIRL, ANOTHER PLANET - THE ONLY ONES

STARRY EYES – THE RECORDS

TOO COOL TO CALYPSO – KLARK KENT

TEARS OF A CLOWN – THE ENGLISH BEAT

WHO DOES LISA LIKE? - RACHEL SWEET

BOYS DON'T CRY- THE CURE

COMPLEX - GARY NUMAN

GIRL OF MY DREAMS – BRAM TCHAIKOVSKY

BROKEN DOLL – WRECKLESS ERIC

SHOES – TOMORROW NIGHT

TEN FEET TALL – XTC

THE LIGHTER SIDE OF DATING – THE MONOCHROME SET

STRAIGHT LINES – NEW MUSIK

BLACK AND WHITE – THE DB'S

PASSIONATE FRIEND – THE TEARDROP EXPLODES

EMOTIONAL TRAFFIC – THE RUMOUR

IT'S NOT MY PLACE (IN THE 9 TO 5 WORLD) – THE RAMONES

REASONS TO BE CHEERFUL (PT. 3) – IAN DURY & THE BLOCKHEADS

NEW TOY – LENE LOVICH

ALCHEMY – RICHARD LLOYD

DOT DASH – WIRE

As a college sophomore, I considered tape-making my most refined skill. My habit of inscribing Elvis Costello lyrics in the margins of my notebooks instead of taking useful notes earned me B's and C's and the occasional dress-

---

1. The proper title is "Peppermint Lump."

ing down from my professors, but among my peers I was at least known for my music collection, as the sort of guy with the wherewithal to break out Karl Denver's insane version of "Wimoweh" at a debauched townhouse throwdown that ends with a toga-clad dude pissing atop a flaming mattress. I would lay tapes on people. When a friend of mine underwent a bone marrow transplant during junior year, he awoke from the procedure and asked for his Walkman, which had a "Kleiner mix" all cued up.

The first time I made a tape—and I do mean a tape; nobody called these things mix tapes until much later—I pressed the RECORD button on my portable Panasonic unit, placed it between two cheap speakers, and tried to be as quiet as I could while Yes's *Time and a Word* played. My cassette game experienced a sea change once I got my first decent tape deck. Sometimes I would just spin the radio dial and record snippets all mashed together. This must have been how young Brian Eno felt when he held his first synthesizer.

It's now Day 4 of the extended blizzard encampment, and Mom is ready to start a small pillowcase fire just to clear the premises. Her brother's lackadaisical West Coast departure nearly does her in.

With the suitcases stowed, the family showered, and the car idling in the driveway, Mom is about to let out a huge sigh of relief, perhaps even fix herself an early cocktail, when one of the car doors flops open and out pops little Yuri, who's forgotten his Dodgers cap. Mom locates the cap, guides him gently but firmly out the door, and is on the verge of emitting a hallelujah when Uncle Mike reappears. He has to pee.

Mike pees, gives Mom a final hug that she practically shrinks from, and exits.

And they go. *Finally.*

Seven minutes later, Mom's downstairs in the laundry room, deep in the Zen of folding Dad's tube socks, when she hears it: the car pulling back into the driveway. After a beat, the sound of the side door opening, followed by a light, clambering footfall.

Enter Noni, waiflike. [And... ACTION]

"Oh my *gosh*, Joan. I almost forgot *West Side Story!*" she says, doe eyes wide, selling it. Noni retrieves the tape from the VCR, emits the cutest little "whew" and eyeroll you've ever seen, and scoots elfinly back up the stairs.

Dec 23, 1982

Dear Jonny

David said the Method were recording new material last fall; Joan said you're getting excellent grades and writing and publishing poetry. Wonderful!! Music, poetry, studying with some great writers, and three times as many girls as boys, hey, isn't it great to be an American college student? (If they try to send you to some fucking war to pay it back, tell them to fuck off.)

I swear, there is a line of writers in this family. And each generation gets better. Send me copies of what you feel is your best poem or two. Noni is amazingly good. She writes, nowadays, 6-page Sherlock Holmes-type stories – little movies of her imagination. But her strongest point is satire. She has a really sophisticated sense of humor. She's been watching Saturday Night Live (reruns) and gets like 95% of the jokes. She met Steve Martin last summer, through a friend. In fact, she could have gone to S. Martin's New Years' Eve party next week in LA, but – cool Scorpio that she is – she turned it down to spend the holidays with her best friend (who still lives on the Mendocino ranch).

Then there's me and Cindy. Our book[2] is so beautiful – receiving it, seeing for the first time (having no idea of layout, etc.) was the greatest moment I've had as a writer. It's in all the Bay Area bookstores, selling quite well, prominently displayed (in one shop, in the window between Jimmy Carter's Memoirs and The G-Spot!)

Love,

Uncle Mike

We weren't an "I love you" family. Everybody was fair game, and anybody could outstay their welcome, even Uncle Mike. But I never doubted I was loved. Whenever I started choking on something at the dinner table and Mom offered me her palm and said "spit," I knew I was loved. When Dad would tuck me in for the night and say "Goodnight, old bean" before closing the door, I knew I was loved.

Mom was almost four years older than her brother. They had grown up digging the Brooklyn Dodgers, J.D. Salinger, sci-fi novels, New York radio, and sneaking out of the family apartment on Empire Boulevard, in Brooklyn's Crown Heights neighborhood, for French fries after my grandmother's bland dinners. By 1965, both were on societally approved paths. Mom was married to a Jewish doctor, living in a well-appointed suburb, and raising three kids.

---

2. *Shaman Woman, Mainline Lady: Women's Writings on the Drug Experience,* Cynthia Palmer, Michael Horowitz editors; William Morrow & Co., 1982.

Michael, a voracious reader who loved the smell of old books, was working at his dream job in the books department of Parke-Bernet, the nation's premier auction house. While Mom had her hands full, Mike was living free and easy in a $100-a-month pad in the West Village—and having a high old time of it. Through a convoluted series of events, he'd managed to avoid some of his Army duty. As long as he kept his crew cut military grade and showed up at a city battalion for bimonthly troop meetings, he was at liberty to partake in the full swath of counter-culturalism.

On a typical weekend, Mike and his girlfriend, Bev, would smoke some tea with their friends John and Cindy, then catch a midnight showing of a French New Wave flick or a samurai movie at the New Yorker Theatre on upper Broadway. There was a thriving acid culture, too, only NYC and LSD made for a volatile mix. The city was just too clangorous and unpredictable to deal with on acid. Police sirens, especially, were a massive bummer. Mike and Bev and their friends learned to venture outside only when coming down. In June 1965, they and several members of their cohort rented a farmhouse in New England and spent that steamy summer imprinting their minds with revelatory new wiring.

John and Cindy soon relocated to San Francisco and began relaying tales of how you could take acid and walk out in the world and be met with warm vibes and knowing smiles. Every phone call or letter from the Bay Area seemed to add to the feeling of missing out on the California Gold Rush. As 1966 came to a close, "Good Vibrations" edged out "Mellow Yellow" at the No. 1 spot on the Billboard chart, and Bev, who had no real job, flew west. Mike waited until Christmas vacation rolled around before making the same journey. Anxious for him to experience the San Francisco phenomenon in proper fashion, his friends welcomed him with a much stronger dose than he'd ever had, powerful enough to conjure Frank Zappa's "Suzy Creamcheese" forth from the stereo, embroidered by a choir of Zen monks. When it felt right, they walked to Golden Gate Park, their feet barely touching the ground, and it was true, everyone they saw seemed to be in the same blessed state.

Not long after that peek through the doors of perception, Mike stood in the frigid vestibule of his apartment, gazing at Issue #4 of the SF *Oracle*. On the cover of the Haight-Ashbury neighborhood's psychedelic newspaper was a bearded, third-eye-emblazoned shaman in magenta-and-black tones, framed in spidery script that announced "A Gathering of the Tribes for a Human Be-In." This now-iconic happening had already happened—three weeks ago, and John and Cindy had been there. Though he wasn't quite ready to start packing, the notion that his life's path led westward began to assert itself.

In June of 1967, Mike and Bev drove off in a '54 Oldsmobile Super 88 that belonged to my grandparents. Five days later, they crossed the Bay Bridge, going west at sunset with "Light My Fire" heralding their arrival, and made their way to John and Cindy's place in the neighborhood known as Japantown. There they found a handwritten note taped to the door, announcing that their friends were in jail in Napa.[3] Fortunately, other friends—Staten Island friends—had a pad on Haight and Ashbury. Once he and Bev got settled, Uncle Mike sent me a postcard:

> Dear David,
>
> Do you still like Indians? There are some on the other side of this card. Indians are very popular out here. Last week a whole bunch called North American Indian Unity Caravan came to town and met with the hippies who dress like them and wear feathers and beads. Some of my best friends live in tee-pees!
>
> Love, Sgt. Pepper

Postmarked October 1967 and ostensibly an announcement for three shows by Quicksilver Messenger Service at the Avalon Ballroom, the postcard pictured a goddess on horseback, rendered in a psychedelic American flag palette of silver, red, and blue. The buzz I caught off it went way beyond the hypnotic visuals. Here was a voice addressing me, a five-year-old kid, in the language of the times. I was no mere little brother or child in Uncle Mike's eyes. I was a receptive young soul with a brain and a heart. And hippies were everywhere: in the news, in *Laugh-In* sketches, in my beloved *Mad* magazine. Having a certifiable hippie uncle was almost like having a celebrity in the family.

Inspired, I grabbed a few of Dad's freebie notepads from a pharmaceutical company hawking a new antibiotic (*"Keflin: Potent enough for the most severe infections, yet exceptionally well tolerated"*). I made pencil drawings of bell-bottom-clad hippies wearing fringed vests over bare skin, peace signs dangling. They weren't just acid freaks, though; they were freaks of nature, with arms of different sizes and legs that went straight into torsos. Abetted by sunglasses and scars, my male hippies were passable. But the women—grinning, bouffant-cropped, come-hither types—presented a much greater challenge. Mine were rendered in extreme one-eyed profile, breasts cantilevered at angles abhorred by nature. Undeterred by my tenuous grasp of human anatomy, I persisted, stoked by mind-blowing commix sent by Uncle Mike that intro-

---

3. It was the first cultivation bust in California.

duced me to Fritz the Cat, the Fabulous Furry Freak Brothers, and other rebels who spoke up to the Man and dispatched uptight squares with deadpan cool.

Despite being extremely left-wing, Mom was no hippie, or even much of a hippie sympathizer. The one time Uncle Mike tried to share the wonders of a good reefer with Big Sis, they smoked a joint and listened to *Let It Be*, and lo and behold, when "Dig a Pony" came on, a song Mom knew inside-out, this time it was *like wow*, man. Suddenly she detects this astounding beauty she'd never picked up on before. But when Mom comes down, she feels… hood-winked? Bamboozled, maybe. *Cheated* by the evil weed. Falling in love with "Dig a Pony," which isn't a great Beatles song by any stretch, was proof positive that pot messed with your critical faculties. And Mom liked to keep hers numbered in case of an emergency.

That's not to say she was square or conventional. I would say she was practical. As an undergrad at Brooklyn College, where most of her female classmates were working on education degrees, Mom shuddered at the thought of life as a teacher. Facing an endless stream of unruly kids, year in and year out, was her idea of a nightmare. Instead, she parlayed her English degree into a reporter job at *The American Weekly*, a Sunday supplement published by the Hearst Company. That's where she was in the spring of 1959 when she met Dad, who, as fate would have it, was about to become Jimi Hendrix's personal physician.

Chapter 2

Screaming Eagles

I've told this story at countless dinner parties and several first dates, and it's almost certainly not true, but six months after marrying my mother, my father found himself stationed at Fort Campbell, Kentucky—the home of the 101st Airborne Division, known as the Screaming Eagles. As clinic physician, one of Dad's major responsibilities was conducting re-up physicals, or what he liked to call "examining the assholes of assholes." Fifteen guys at a time would line up naked in a brightly lit room, and Dad would go around checking their equipment and adjacent areas for anything and everything: VD, inguinal hernias, you name it. But even if Dad had possessed some rare form of clairvoyance and knew that one of those assholes belonged to the twentieth century's most influential electric guitar player, it wouldn't have made much of a difference. Dad was a devout Charlie Christian[4] man, you see. More to the point, had the wind itself purple-hazed from Jimi's low end and cried "Mary," Dad would have been too miserable to notice.

With one year to go in his medical residency, my father enlisted in the Army, the better to get his mandatory two-year commitment over with. Other than the "infiltration course," where you crawl on your stomach as live ammunition is fired a few feet above your head, Dad didn't find basic training all that nightmarish at the relatively plush Fort Sam Houston, in San Antonio, Texas. So not

---

4. Christian, who died impossibly young at twenty-one of hard living and consumption, played elegant, clean-toned runs with the Benny Goodman Big Band in the 1930s, transforming the guitar from a rhythmic component into a lead instrument and profoundly influencing successive generations of players.

awful, in fact, that my brother Jonny was conceived there, in early 1960. Dad managed to avoid an overseas assignment thanks to some recent legislation, but having not completed residency, he was deemed by the Army draft board a non-board-qualified physician, which meant he'd be the junior of two doctors overseeing the medical clinic at a Kentucky army base.

Ending up at Fort Campbell, the butt of a cruel barb at his expanse, he quietly simmered as he went about his appointed rounds. Dad had always excelled. Even as a young teen, when he wanted to be a soda jerk to earn some pocket change, his parents said no, you're too smart, it's beneath you. They were right about this much: their first-born son, Richard, was made for medicine. That was apparent early on; at age four, he began swabbing the ears of the family dog, Nellie, a spitz, and rigorously attended to a subsequent pair of chronically symptomatic Old English Bulldogs. As a medical student and beyond, his instincts and diagnostic skills earned him the respect of his mentors.

Then came Fort Campbell. Military drab, permanently overcast, seemingly soulless, its population consisted mainly of grunts, which, as my parents saw it, greatly reduced the odds of striking up a meaningful conservation. What they resented most was an absence of culture. The nearest movie theater—where Mom and Dad took in *Psycho* and *La Dolce Vita*—was fifty-five miles away, in Nashville. As for music, Dad had to mail-order *Blues for Night People*, by ace guitarist Charlie Byrd, and its much-delayed arrival was a rare cause for celebration. Mom and Dad would pass the evenings listening to the Grand Ole Opry on WSM, and since sound waves travel in utero, I listened to a lot of country music in the womb, much of it of the high-and-lonesome variety. One night they ventured out to Nashville to catch the Opry in-person and got caught up in a hellacious snowstorm on the way back. After that, they stayed closer to the base, resigned to their fate.

To maintain her sanity, Mom found a friend, another medical wife with an infant about Jonny's age. Mom and Shirley would wheel the kids around in bulky strollers amid patchy grass and featureless brick housing units, under a sky that was often dotted with people. The babies would gaze upward, rapt at the sight of the down-drifting paratroopers, blissfully unaware that in five years or so, one of those human shapes would transfix the nation by setting fire to his hand-painted black Fender Stratocaster.

For a million reasons, notably his long-standing resentment of authority, Private James Marshall Hendrix was not made for the military. He was induced to enlist in May 1961 to avoid a likely jail term, either for auto theft or possibly just for riding in stolen cars. Yet he craved a Screaming Eagles patch, and the prospect of earning one likely provided him with a crucial bit of incentive to get through basic training.

Hendrix turned out to be a better-than-average paratrooper. By early January 1962, he had completed twenty-five jumps and earned that coveted patch. He was also playing frequent gigs with the Kasuals, the band he'd formed with his fellow Screaming Eagle and bowling pal, Billy Cox. But using borrowed instruments—or worse, items checked out from the on-base service club, the Eagles' Roost—had become intolerable. He desperately missed his guitar, a red Danelectro with the name of his high school girlfriend written on it. Early in 1962 he wrote a desperate letter to his father, saying, "I really need it now." Al Hendrix, a strict disciplinarian, had been disgusted by his son's delinquency and thought the Army might do him some good. But he was also familiar with Jimi's misery, from a previous letter that described jump school as hell, and the old man obliged him.

Factoring in a few weeks for the six-stringed parcel to travel from Seattle to Kentucky via the U.S. Postal Service, it could very well have arrived by the middle of February. Thus I contend that on the day I entered this world, Monday, February 19, 1962, as my mother held me in her arms for the first time, Jimi was mere miles away, curled up in his bunk with Betty Jean clutched in his huge hands.

If that sounds fanciful, it's no stretch to assert that Jimi and I shared something very concrete: a May 31 release date from the Army. Dad's tour of duty ended on that very day, while Jimi still owed Uncle Sam a few years and would have to incur a bit of self-sabotage to finagle an early departure. Most sources agree that, despite the damning assessments of his superiors, which started to multiply in February, doubtless exacerbated by that crucial mail order, and despite his resulting demotion in rank, it was an ankle injury sustained in an airborne jump (his twenty-sixth) that led to Hendrix being discharged, honorably, on the last day of May—one year after he enlisted in the Army.

A good deal of documentation from Jimi's army days has come to light in recent years, including those damning accounts, like that of Lt. Louis J. Hoekstra, who wrote, "His mind apparently can't function while performing duties and thinking about his guitar," and Lt. Gilbert Batchman, whose Request for Discharge asserted that Jimi had "no known good characteristics." To my knowledge, though, details on Jimi's ankle injury have not surfaced. But assuming he did sprain an ankle in one of his landings, he would have gone to the medical clinic to get it checked out. After all, he had previously availed himself of the Army's dental clinic, so he was not one to shun basic self-care. And *had* he come to the clinic with a twisted ankle, who would have looked him over? Why, Dad, of course—low man on the totem pole, checker of assorted low-grade maladies, resenter of assholes.

So, is it possible my father laid hands on Jimi Hendrix? More than a half-century later, Dad, ever the medical man, refuses to entertain such a hypothetical.

On the last day of June 1962, Dad takes his last salute at the sentry post and drops his discharge papers in the mailbox just outside—a joyous moment. With the light green Nash Rambler loaded and ready to roll, he glimpses Fort Campbell in the rearview for the last time, then heads on a northeast diagonal path, endpoint: Elmhurst, Queens. Mom does crosswords while Jonny, nineteen months old and thankfully a good car rider, lies untethered on a mattress placed over the backseat and watches in fascination as the world whirls by. Somewhere between Tennessee and Virginia, they catch a corny song on the radio and are content to leave it on. When the chorus hits (*"Oh, Johnny get angry / Johnny get mad"*), they share their first really solid mutual laugh in months. Because Jonny, like Fort Campbell itself, has been overcast most of the time. When they couldn't get him to stop crying, they would place him in a bassinet facing the radio. It helped a little. The song finishes, and when the singer is identified as Joanie Sommers, they laugh again. For Joanie is what Dad calls Mom, and summer's just beginning, and sometimes the radio is singing your life.

Here, I catch a break. On account of my extreme youth, I'm flying the friendly skies of United, nestled in the warm embrace of Celeste, a woman in the employ of Mom's friend Shirley, who agreed to convey me, like Moses in the wicker basket, into the arms of my grandmother.

"The first time we met was at Kennedy Airport," Grandma would often say. "A lovely little boy was put into my arms, we looked at each other, and it was love at first sight." Sounds a little corny in print, but neither of us ever grew tired of returning to this event. She would alter the wording in her retellings; sometimes it ended with "And we've been in love ever since."

As an origin story, being whisked by Celestial means into the embrace of Grandma, who loved me without reservation, sure beats the tale of being hatched in joyless, culture-deficient Kentucky.

Meanwhile, Dad, Mom, and Jonny spend a night in historic Luray, Virginia, home to the Great Stalactite Organ, before continuing past the hallowed halls of justice in Washington, D.C., and then due north to Queens. Grandma and

Grandpa have found us a nice two-bedroom apartment on Justice Avenue, suitable to our needs for the time being. In a few years, we'll make our way to the Jersey suburbs.

Chapter 3

Schmuck!

In dreams, I still return to the home where my family settled at the end of 1965. Located along the outer ring of an orderly circular block, 5 Sherwood Road stood pleasantly removed from car traffic and most random passers-by. But inside, wherever you happened to be—be it bathtub, basement, or at-tic—you were always aware of the physical presence of whoever else was there. The scrape of Dad's chair as he rose from the kitchen table, the staccato cadence of Mom's footfalls on the staircase, were inescapable.

Coming from a one-story garden apartment in nearby Englewood, the new house felt gigantic to me. My sense of direction has never been good, and at age three it barely existed. Mom learned to remain on alert for my muffled cries issuing from the basement, an upstairs bedroom, or wherever I'd managed to end up.

Mom and Dad were in the main bedroom overlooking a green grass lawn with a horse chestnut tree at one end of it. Jonny and I shared a room down the hall, and my sister—born Elizabeth but always known as Liza—slept across the hall from the folks' room in her crib.

Adjacent to the kitchen was Dad's den. This is where I watched *Romper Room*, seated on the floor against the couch to be closer to the screen. The show was hosted by Miss Louise, an affable, teacherly type who presided over a group of kids known as "Do Bees," after the show's moral-dispensing apiary mascot. (There was also a Don't Be, who was, according to the jingle, "a food fussy," "a car stander" and "a match toucher." These are now all subcategories on your less savory dating apps.)

Miss Louise regularly broke the fourth wall by peering out at the TV audience through her "magic mirror," as if she could see us. This confused me to no end. One time Miss Louise was doing a thing about the seasons.

"Who can tell me the name of one of the seasons?" she asked.

"Winter!" piped up one little Do Bee.

"Fall!" called out another. A third came through with summer, but then the Do Bees were stumped.

"There are *four* seasons," said Miss Louise, turning now to look out at us—at me. "Does anyone know what this other season is called?"

"Spring!" I cried. *"Spring!"*

"Do you know what?" said Miss Louise, with a look of authentic wonder. "I think I heard someone say it out there at home. That's right, boys and girls. It's spring!"

It would take some time for me to grasp that the people I watched on TV couldn't see me, that the music being played on the radio was not being performed by the band at the same moment, that alkaline batteries had nothing to do with Al Kaline of the Detroit Tigers, that the word "application" had nothing to do with apples, and that Mr. Noviello, the man my parents hired to paint our house, was not named for his trademark hue. For years, when Dad would ask my mother if the Record had come, I thought he was talking about the delivery of a record album, not the evening newspaper. But as for my unshakable belief that I was being watched and listened to at all times, by someone I knew well, I was on firmer ground.

She seemed to know intuitively when I'd neglected whatever business was at hand, whether it was drying between my toes or finishing my milk. Could my mother read my thoughts? Unsure of the limits of her power, I decided to test it.

One bright, frigid afternoon, after Mom told me to go outside and play, I pulled the strings of my parka hood so tight my whole head was enclosed in a warm, muffled cocoon. Pausing at the end of the driveway, just as far from the front door as I could be without standing in the street, I glanced left and right, then, moving my lips apart minimally not unlike a ventriloquist: "Shit," I half-whispered.

No lightning. No Mom materializing out of thin air. I was emboldened now.

"Fuck," I said, fully out loud this time. And again, nothing—glorious nothing.

The epithet I'd saved for last was one I often heard bandied around the kitchen table when Grandma and Grandpa came out from Brooklyn. Grandma would even say it, so it couldn't be as bad as the first two, but it sure sounded like a curse word: "Shmuck."

Like I'd been saying it all my life.

"*Shmuuuuuuck!*"

Right up the road was a narrow asphalt path that led to a vast lawn fronting a somber Tudor Revival mansion. The Cotswold, as it was known, could almost be taken for a mirage at first glimpse. With its steep roof of dusky stone, tall brick chimneys, and soaring stained glass, it was an intimidating structure no matter how many times you viewed it, even more so when you had to get close to it when cutting through the rear car park to reach Serpentine Road. Somewhere on the inside was an apartment that had belonged to Glenn Miller, the trombonist and big-bandleader who was America's premier hit-maker during World War II. He was living at the Cotswold when he halted his golden career to join the Army. And this is where his wife and two adopted children heard the news, in late 1944, that his military plane—en route to Paris for a Christmas broadcast—had disappeared over the English Channel.

We could not have settled near a less Hendrix-like spectral presence. Pale, politically conservative, uninclined to set fire to his chosen instrument even if it were possible, the bespectacled Midwesterner was as gung-ho to join the military as Jimi was to escape it. A full twenty years before the master guitarist abased himself to get drummed out of the Army, Miller—long in tooth at thirty-eight—had to entreat the draft board to let him join the war effort. Having already been rejected by the naval reserve, he stressed his morale-boosting band-leading abilities to the Army brass and was granted acceptance in fall of 1942. Miller made good on his pitch, infusing leaden Sousa marches with the jaunt of his popular hits and, in the process, shaking up some military squares ("goddamn idiot officers" he called them) who refused to get hip to his trip.

So maybe he and Jimi weren't so far apart after all. True, Hendrix represented a new sound and vision, while Miller's genius was giving marching orders straight to the mainstream sweet spot, but both figures embodied popular music at a momentous historical juncture, and each man became legendary through his shocking demise.

Tenafly had its share of hit-makers who were very much alive. Lesley Gore, who'd grown up in Tenafly but attended nearby private schools, was at her peak when we arrived in town. Gore would seem to share little in common with Glenn Miller, but she too was internationally famous when she put her career on the back burner.[5] The country singer Jimmy Dean, a Texas transplant and a bona fide star by mid-decade, had made his way to Tenafly's East Hill in the late fifties.

Marked by opulent showboat homes and multi-acre spreads, this geographically vertiginous zone had an aesthetic that was nothing like the rest of the borough, which was named "ten swamps" by a disdainful Dutchman. Unlike our neighborhood, where streets had humble arboreal names like Oak and Elm, and across the tracks, where roads were named for regular Joes, like George, Norman, and Franklin, up on the Hill the names had a pronounced haughtiness to them. The major roads—Essex, Churchill, and Kent—seemed inspired by gout-riddled English lords, reaching for the next pudding spoon, nonetheless.

In 1957, the teen idol Paul Anka bought a large home up there for his mother after receiving his first monster check for "Diana." Fittingly, he and *la famille* settled into a vast spread on the very pinnacle of the East Hill, Woodland Street, beyond which the land levels off briefly in anticipation of the Palisades Interstate Parkway and the Triassic-era Palisades themselves, which tower over the Hudson River for miles and miles.

Roughly a century earlier, George Coppell, a New York City financier who'd gotten stupendously rich overseeing railroad bankruptcies, had gazed across the same expanse from the Manhattan side and dreamed a dream. He built himself a sumptuous manor replete with statuary and fountains on a fifty-acre plot in Tenafly and called it Birchwood Knole. Eventually it passed to his son Herbert and his wife, who first enlarged the mansion to sixty-eight rooms, then grew tired of it and had it torn down and replaced with a slightly smaller version of itself—the Cotswold. This wouldn't be half as meaningful had Coppell not been born in Liverpool. The air was rich with musical phantasms.

Flash-forward to November 1986: Jonny's a producer at MTV News and he's assigned to interview Ringo Starr. Now, Jonny frequently interacts with well-known and even famous musicians in his work, but this is different. This is meeting a Beatle (a real Beatle!), albeit a Beatle who hasn't put out an album in several years, not since 1983's *Old Wave*, which tanked. Jonny gives considerable thought to what he'll wear for the occasion. Deeply into his vin-

---

5. Like my mother, the former Lesley Goldstein was a Jewish girl from Brooklyn, and like my brother, she attended Sarah Lawrence, where she didn't win any friends by complaining about the food.

tage tab collar shirt look at the time, he dry-cleans his favorite—a royal blue number—and arrives at Ringo's hotel on light feet. But as he's getting the man set up for the interview, placing a mic on Starr, the drummer recoils. He gives my brother a bitter, owlish look, and in his inimitable Scouse accent, says:

"Ooh la, that's the ugliest *fookin'* shirt I've ever seen in me *life*."

Fighting back tears, Jonny manages to get through the interview. But just barely. The idea that a Beatle has actually taken the time to insult him—his taste, his mojo—is almost too much to bear. Ringo, with his puppy dog eyes and plummy sing-alongs, had been the Beatles' gentlest spirit. We'd seen the dark side of John, who would rather see her dead, little girl, and George, in his lacerating hate note to the Taxman. Paul, too, had shown himself a bit of a cad with the cutting kiss-offs he added to "I'll Follow the Sun" and "I'm Looking Through You." Surely, the last of the Four you'd expect meanness from was Ringo. Peace and love, right? Peace and love?

A year or so later, in 1988, Ringo entered rehab and eventually kicked the alcohol habit that had come to consume him. He's since said that many of those besotted years are completely gone from his memory.

"He probably didn't mean to be so cruel," Jonny said later. "And that shirt *was* uglier than shit."

Chapter 4

Genius Jonny

In Tenafly parlance, the obviously smart kids were known as brains. As in, "Seth Leibowitz? Kid's a total brain." Being a brain meant your hyper-developed intelligence had externalized itself—you had become your thinking organ, pasty complexion and all. And if you had the smart disease, that was it. Brains were fated to consort exclusively with other brains. Being anything else—popular, for instance—was out. No one called my brother a brain. Bro was in another, much cooler category. Classmates called him "Genius Jonny," an alliterative accolade that mere brains would never acquire.

He was mostly self-educated. He could spend the entire afternoon on a couch devouring a book. An early favorite was the quietly subversive *The Teddy Bear Habit*, about a would-be rock star with an embarrassing fixation. I was far too restless to ever spend an afternoon reading (unless it was *Charlie and the Chocolate Factory*). At eleven, Jonny was a current events hound. He wrote letters to a catholic assemblage of public figures: Ernie Banks of the Chicago Cubs, Frances O. Kelsey, the FDA official who kept Thalidomide from being available in the U.S., Gunnar Jarring, a Swedish diplomat who attempted to broker peace in the Middle East. And his requests weren't childlike and gushing; rather they were sophisticated, and peppered with questions not everyone was willing to answer. FBI kingpin J. Edgar Hoover, for example.

February 8, 1971

Dear Mr. Klein:

Mr. Hoover received your card on February 2nd.

While Mr. Hoover would like to comply with your request, it has become necessary for him to forego [sic] autographing material in view of his heavy schedule; however, he wanted you to have the enclosed photograph. In connection with your other inquiry, Mr. Hoover does not comment on material other than that prepared by personnel of this Bureau.

Sincerely yours,
Helen W. Gandy
Secretary

And, man, could he write. At thirteen, my brother was a fully formed critic. Here's an excerpt from Jonny's review of *Lucas Tanner,* an insipid dramatic series that premiered on NBC in 1974, for the Tenafly High School student newspaper:

> Every once in a while, a series appears on television that is so asinine, so inane and so sickening that a humanitarian reviewer is obligated to advise those who have not made the mistake of watching to continue following their wise path…Tanner is a teacher who becomes personally involved with a different mixed-up (but well intentioned) student each week. He gets assistance in this Herculean task from his young next door neighbor, a blonde, squeaky fella named Glendon, who lives with his grandmother until she dies in what I consider by far the best episode.

My parents recognized Jonny's precociousness and curiosity, and began having grown-up conversations with him about politics and literature and the state of the world when he was still in single digits. Jonny's teachers raved about him, sometimes to the point of poetry, citing his level of insight and the natural intelligence that came gushing forth in his words and writing.

As for me, getting a laugh from my classmates was the ultimate affirmation. There was nothing quite like it in the school day, when the other kids rewarded you with a flood of laughter. Making Mom laugh had the same joyous effect. It felt like a standing ovation. And positive reinforcement was something I desperately desired. Many aspects of life on Planet Earth continued to vex me. Baseball for instance.

One night, I'm in my usual spot in front of the little black-and-white TV in Dad's den, where the Yankee game is just beginning. Dad's fixing himself a gin and tonic in the kitchen. He calls to me, "David, who are the Yankees playing against?" I have no clue, but at that moment the announcer seems to come to my rescue, saying something about tonight's umpires. That must be it.

"The empires?"

I hear Dad crack up. When he comes in, he explains to me what the umpires do.

Being a sort of genius, Jonny was well aware of the power he derived from his superior mental apparatus. Sometimes he would amuse himself at the expense of others. After the 1967 World Series, when I asked him for help writing a letter to Cardinals pitching ace Bob Gibson, he intentionally riddled it with spelling errors of the most pathetic variety. One time I woke up next to him on the bus back home after day camp, and he convinced me I'd emitted a stream of rude Freudian gibberish in my sleep that I'm ashamed to recount here. He was keenly attuned to my mental lapses, misunderstandings, and naivete. Even singing along to a gentle Beatles ballad like "And I Love Her" could result in a harsh wake-up call.

"She gives me everything / and tender leaves..."

" 'And tender *leaves*'? You dope, you think that's why he loves her—because she brings him salad?" I even repeated the food-related mishearing of a Beatle lyric on "Come Together" (*"Come together / Right now / All the meat..."*).

But sometimes Jonny used his power to do good things.

He once cured me of the fear of death.

Miss Pearce must have jumped three feet in the air when she came across *Ghost Ballads*. Actually, when I try to picture that moment—Miss Pearce, my school's music teacher, flipping through rows of vinyl in a record store or a Salvation Army thrift shop, or Miss Pearce jumping, for that matter—it's impossible. I cannot picture Miss Pearce outside of a school building. A broad-shouldered woman with bright red lipstick, emphatically drawn-on eyebrows, and a hair helmet of fierce vermillion, she seemed to exist in Technicolor, like one of the townspeople in *The Music Man*.

Miss Pearce's devotion was to seasonal songs and traditional ditties pulled from a perverse past, only we sang the cleaned-up versions. We sang *"Ding dong dell, Kitty's in the well,"* about a would-be cat drowner named Little Johnny Thin—only in the original it was "Pussy's in the well." Around St. Patrick's Day, Miss Pearce would lead us through the bowdlerized version of "Has Anybody Here Seen Kelly?" in which the unfortunate lass who loses her man in the big city avoids the ignominious fate depicted in the original 1908 version. (*"She got among the suffragettes who chained her to the grille."*)

Naughty double-entendres might have been verboten, but by introducing us to songs about casual violence, Miss Pearce was simply maintaining an age-old tradition. Whether it's chopping off the tails of blind mice or the implied bodily trauma of "Rock-a-Bye Baby," songs for kids have always traded in dark subject matter. The first song I knew all the words to was a murder ballad called "Josie," which Ed McCurdy recorded in 1957, the same year Dean Gitter recorded *Ghost Ballads.*

Gitter was an in-house producer for Tradition Records, a small label based in the West Village that was financed by some Guggenheim or other and run by Paddy Clancy of the Clancy Brothers. After helming Odetta's acclaimed 1956 debut—the one Bob Dylan said inspired him to go folk in the first place—Gitter put out a record of his own, on the venerable Riverside jazz label. Featuring a spooky haunted-house cover by the great Charles Addams, *Ghost Ballads* consisted of twelve "supernatural"-themed songs from the public domain. It wasn't a big seller, and one imagines that by the late sixties the only people still playing it were public school music teachers like Miss Pearce, who needed content for Halloween.

Gitter based his version of "Skin and Bones" on the rendition by folksinger and folklorist Jean Ritchie, one of hundreds of songs she sang with her family in hardscrabble Kentucky and subsequently helped preserve. Ritchie wrote that she and her siblings would take a wicked delight in singing the song for kids who had never heard it before and weren't ready for the little surprise at the end. But had Miss Pearce owned a copy of *Jean Ritchie Singing Traditional Songs of Her Kentucky Mountain Family* [1952] and played us *that* version, it would have produced a mild shock and nothing more. On the other hand, Dean Gitter's rendition of "Skin and Bones" is like a Shirley Jackson story set to music.

This tale of an emaciated old woman who takes a walk through a bone-laden graveyard and enters an old church house in need of sweeping unfolds with unsettling dream logic—and ends with an auditory ambush.

"She opened the door and..."

And Gitter emits this awful, jagged scream that sounds like it was torn out of him.

I almost fell out of my chair. Stunned, embarrassed, trying to collect myself, I noted that no one else appeared the least bit traumatized. In fact, most of the other kids seemed to have enjoyed the shock. In my defense, the liner notes of *Ghost Ballads* affirm that in recording "Skin and Bones," Gitter's final *geshray* "ruined a very expensive microphone in the studio."

And almost ruined me.

Months earlier I had been moved into a bedroom of my own, but that night I slept in my brother's bed, and continued to do so for weeks afterward. I didn't want to be alone in the dark, ruminating on that scream all by myself. Jonny was stronger, and he frequently pinned me down and did the classic older-brother tortures—the hanging spit, "Indian burns," and innovations of his own, like the steady breastbone punches he called "tom-toms." But early on we made a pact not to jump out and scare the other guy. Neither of us thought the shock was worth it. And in that spirit, as we lay in bed one night, Jonny convinced me that I didn't have to worry. Scientists were at that very moment working on a pill that would keep you from dying, and by the time I was older they would have it perfected. The story was plausible and he sold it well, and I found genuine comfort in the thought of an anti-death pill.

The front cover of *Meet the Beatles*—four faces suspended in a haze of silvery blue and black—was mesmerizing. Each visage stood up to intense inspection, but I often fixated on John on the far left, specifically the sideburn that was visible in the dramatic half-lighting. While the 'burns of the other three Beatles were tapered, John's looked impossibly thick and lush, edible almost. "One day, I will have sideburns," I snuck outside to whisper.

The arrangement—John-Paul-George on top, Ringo at lower right—suggested that Ringo existed on a slightly lower plane from the other three. The photographer Robert Freeman, who also took the cover shots for *Rubber Soul* and *Help!*, confirmed that the placement was deliberate: In Freeman's words, "He was the last to join the group, he was the shortest and he was the drummer." So perhaps it was appropriate that, while none of the faces confronted you with a smile or even a pleasing glint, only Ringo's mug held a splash of sadness.

The copy my brother and I shared was well-used and crudely repaired with masking-tape on two sides. On the back cover I made check marks next to the record's seismic moments ("I Want to Hold Your Hand," "I Saw Her Standing There," and "All My Loving") as well as two deep cuts: the wiry proto-power pop confection "Hold Me Tight" and "Not a Second Time," the dour closer. "I Wanna Be Your Man" had no checkmark. Not even the most rabid Beatle fan would call it especially memorable. In fact, the song's origin story is the most notable thing about it.

One fantastic day in London, in 1963, Andrew Loog Oldham, manager of the fledgling Rolling Stones, was out for a walk and ruminating on the follow-up to his band's debut single when he spotted John Lennon and Paul McCartney and asked if they happened to have a song to spare. You know, like bumming a cigarette. The two Beatles agreed to join Oldham and the Stones at a rehearsal studio, and Mick and Keith watched in amazement as a rudimentary melodic crumb was transformed into a full-fledged song. They came away with more than just a tune for the Rolling Stones' first LP. They'd been taught an object lesson in how a musical partnership works, and it was a revelation.

"I Wanna Be Your Man" was a revelation for us too. After Jonny discovered that one of the Beatles lets loose with an ecstatic bark just as the song fades out, it became a ritual for us to hover, heads close above the spinning record, in delicious anticipation of the final *I wanna be your man* before erupting with *"Woof woof!"* in perfect brotherly unison.

In lesser rotation were various U.S. releases on Capitol: the *Help!* soundtrack, *Something New*, *Beatles '65*, and *Beatles VI* ("Beatles vee eye" we called it.) These came to us courtesy of a tragic benefactor, whose mark appeared on the upper left corner in thick-lined pencil. Steve Silva was in his late teens when my father treated him for leukemia. At some point, he gave Dad his Beatles records to give to us, knowing that he would never get to go home and play them. I would think of S. Silva during "No Reply," the dark-tinged opener on Side 1.

By 1966, the Beatles were in the kids' basement collection with our cheap portable record player. Dad may have liked the harmonies and the wit of the early Beatles, but he was never a rock 'n' roll guy. I'm pretty sure he never let his backbone slip, and likely had medically sound reasons at the ready to discourage anyone else from attempting it. But with *Rubber Soul*, their genius became undeniable, and when he came home with a copy of the U.S. version—the only time the songs were better on a stateside release—that sealed it. Dad was back on board. He loved *Revolver* even more.

From then on until *Let It Be*, the arrival of the new Beatles album was the best day of the year besides your birthday. Things were never quite so paradisiacal as on that Saturday in spring when a New York radio station would play every single Beatles song, and the house was full of Beatles from morning till night. Hearing the songs in alphabetical order but out of context was a strange thrill, as was hearing songs you didn't even know.

All of us loving the Beatles felt like true kinship, like rooting for the same sports team or being members of the same religion. One day the folks packed the three of us into Dad's big red Dodge and we drove to Westhampton out on Long Island. Liberated from the confines of the back seat, Jonny and I ran around on the beach as the sun set. Mom called out, "Wave to the Beatles, kids!" and we leapt up and down at surfside, waving our arms wildly toward the Atlantic and calling out the names of our heroes, who were surely out there somewhere, beyond the horizon and as far out of reach as Pluto.

Then, one night after dinner, a hairline fracture appeared in that rare instance of familial unanimity. Mom, Dad, and I were in the den, listening to Benny Goodman's famous Carnegie Hall concert of January 1938. "Sing Sing Sing (With a Swing)" was one of Dad's favorites. It opens with an almost scarifying vamp, like every musical color you can imagine happening all at once, and then the bottom drops out, leaving just this menacing jungle-drum cadence.

"That's Gene Krupa," Mom says with quiet awe. "The greatest drummer. Wouldn't you say, Rich?"

Dad nods.

"Better than Ringo?"

"Uch," says Mom. "Ringo's not even in the same league."

Now this is heavy. One minute we're all united on the Beatles, like they're the Yankees of music, yet here's Mom, dissing Ringo like he's the relief pitcher who's been getting shelled lately. Anyone—even a Beatle, it seemed—could outstay their welcome.

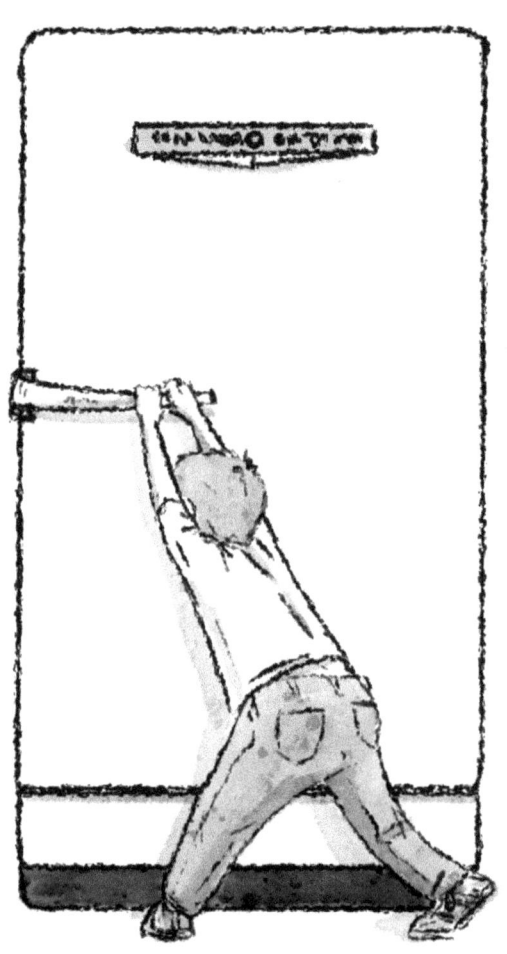

Chapter 5

Route 4

Every object in the basement of 5 Sherwood Road had been left behind by the home's previous owners, the Santinis. At the bottom of the dimly lit staircase was a reptilian, vinyl-covered trundle-bed that Dad called a glider, in which no one ever sat. In the far corner was a work table replete with a pair of vises—one metal, one wood—cabinets worthy of Caligari, and a lingering redolence of 3-in-1 Oil and man-sweat. Filling the recess beneath the narrow staircase was a hulking, eggshell-hued General Electric freezer. Easily the most notable leave-behind was the pool table.

Positioned between two unpainted support columns, atop a linoleum tile floor dulled to a pearlescent sheen from decades of foot traffic, the pool table dominated the room. The Santinis left plenty of cues and chalk behind, but we had no use for the finer points of billiards. Jonny, older by sixteen months, was fast and agile. He would chase me around the table, or we'd whirl the balls into the holes or into one another, just to achieve that satisfying thwack. With the addition of the Wilson girls from across the street, our games became twice as noisy and twice as exciting. Kasey, taller and a year older than Jonny, had a blond pixie cut; Kim, freckled and brassy, was my first crush.

The Wilsons' house was the block's largest and most impressive spread. Partially obscured by tall shrubbery, the grounds included a handsome rectangular swimming pool, protected by a pointy-topped chain-link fence. In the tar-black driveway nestled a neat white Mercedes coupe and a wood-paneled Ford station wagon, a pairing that combined opulence with suburban utility and a touch of retro "his-and-her" Rock Hudson/Doris Day-movie vibes. The pool alone imbued the Wilson home with a special glow. On weekends, their invited guests seemed to be families from out of town. We belonged to the town swim club, so we weren't starved for chlorinated water or anything, but the Wilsons' pool felt like an exclusive private club, one whose enticing whoops and splashes teased us with visions of a Disney movie taking place just out of reach.

In the midst of a primal pool-table chase with the Wilson girls, Jonny was inspired to shout out "Route 4!"—the name of a local highway he must have heard our parents mention. It struck a chord. Pretty soon all of us were doing it, racing around the pool table chanting "Route 4! Route 4!" for all we're worth, for the pure rush of it. And things just escalated.

Jonny decreed that the next person he tagged would have to show us "theirs."

The chase resumed, and as I had expected, Kasey was swiftly tagged. The room grew hushed, and she complied. Reluctantly, but without protest. Perhaps out of shame, we shifted to a game of hide-and-seek with the lights off. With its dim corners, numerous nooks, and easily achievable darkness, the basement was made for it.

Kasey counted first. We scattered, and I found a place behind the glider, careful to keep it from creaking. I could sense that Kim had found a spot beneath the worktable, behind the vises. We amateurs didn't last long, but Jonny, always the innovator, was nowhere to be found. We all drifted back around the room, then traipsed upstairs and looked for him there, even though no one had heard him leave the basement. Well, he had to be somewhere. He'd just outsmarted us again. The other kids started to drift off, but I was feeling restive. Seized with the certainty that he *had* to be down there, I scampered back down the stairs and started easing myself around the perimeter, listening, pausing, considering feasible hiding-place possibilities. In seconds I made a swift and sudden beeline to the freezer and yanked the lever. And out he tumbled.

The Refrigerator Safety Act had been on the books for a decade, yet this kind of fatal carelessness endured long afterward. As late as 1986, an episode of *Punky Brewster* was dedicated to the subject of refrigerator death, with Punky and her pal saving the day by administering CPR to the unfortunate hider. There was no follow-up episode on the after-effects of accidental entombment, but in my brother's case, those minutes he spent trapped inside that freezer, taking shallow breaths and fully aware of the danger he was in, had to have left some kind of a mark. He wasn't outwardly changed, not in any way that I could see. He kept on being Jonny, and the incident was allowed to recede. But he was surely praying while he was in there, and it wasn't God who intervened. If his kid brother had been distracted by something (Kim Wilson's freckles, say) and dawdled before realizing something was amiss, he'd have been a goner. From then on, Jonny vehemently resisted anything that seemed to encroach upon him, or anyone who wanted more from him than he was willing to give.

As for me, that yank, the sight of him pitching forward onto the ground in a desperate sweaty heap, became mythic in my mind. It quietly affirmed something I had no words for: Following my instinct, I had known what to do.

The freezer stayed right where it was. Why waste a good freezer? No point in being superstitious. Eventually the folks cleaned it out, plugged the thing in, and, cautiously at first, began populating it with Keckeroni—Dad's name for the trays of pasta one of his patients, a Mrs. Keck, plied him with until shortly before her death.

It's tempting to conclude that my parents were horribly negligent in leaving a potential death trap in the basement. But they were hardly alone. There was a conspicuously casual attitude toward public safety in those days, especially where kids were concerned. We were in harm's way on a daily basis. Run over by Chryslers while crouching in roadside leaf piles. Taking high-speed headers off poorly designed Raleigh Chopper bicycles onto unforgiving pavement. And yes, suffocating in the unused refrigeration units that many tax-paying U.S. citizens considered too cumbersome for safe disposal.

My brother's near-fatal run-in with G.E. merchandise was down to the era's dangerous lack of supervision. My own ludicrous entanglement with a seemingly innocent product of American ingenuity was nobody's fault but mine.

Chapter 6

The Chair

On the first day of first grade, once we were all seated at one of the desks lined up in neat rows, the teacher told us to listen up and listen good. She paused for effect, or so it seemed, but the reason for her hesitation soon became clear. A yellowjacket, its thrumming wings riffing agreeably with the faint buzz of overhead fluorescence, was making a balletic descent toward her, the one person in the room who wasn't afraid of it. When finally the bee alighted upon the not inconsiderable forearm of Miss Godlewski, my teacher looked, from all outward appearances, unperturbed. Moments later, the buzzer took flight again, its bluff called, and she shooed it toward an open window.

"Now, as I was *saying*... Children, these desks that you're now occupying—they're pretty old fashioned. That much is obvious. In fact, some are thirty or forty years old, and date back to a time when students were taught to write using a pen and ink. On the underside of your desk are two circular spaces that students used to use to stow away the nibs of their pens. These holes no longer serve any purpose. They just happen to be the perfect size to accommodate the fingertip of an unthinking or overly curious child—and snugly, too. Believe you me. So keep *away* from these holes, children. You are *not* to explore these little holes with your fingers."

Something—a furtive movement, maybe a hint of wind, alerts me that a kid behind me is waving his hand and possibly hyperventilating.

Miss Godlewski, wearily: "Yes, Mitchell, what's your question?"

"Miss G, y'memba last year when Cliffie Beshears got *his* stuck? Y'memba?"

"Yes, Mitchell. I remember."

"An, an' Mr. Kissell had to come in with a fresh bar of Bab-O 'cause we didn't have any, and then you said, 'Mr. Kissell if I can't depend on you to keep fresh Bab-O on hand I'll have to report you to Mr.—'"

The sound of sobbing fills the room. I look behind me and immediately spot the crimson-faced sobber. Stuck in a perverse, hip-level double-thumbs-up, he's scored the daily double in record time, his upper body heaving laterally while the rest of him stays seated. Sighing, knees cracking, Miss Godlewski rises and heads toward the single-toilet restroom in the back to retrieve some soap.

Well, at least it wasn't me. Until, almost by providence, it was me.

During certain periods devoted to free play, we were allowed to go to the back of the room while Miss G stayed up in front at her desk. You could mess around, read a book, play Battleship. I was telling Tommy Morgan how the wife of Bill Robinson, the Yankees' right-fielder, was my dad's patient, and no, she was not gonna die, she just had some kidney problems. I was kneeling on the floor, leaning through the gap in the back of a chair, below the lower of its two slats. At some point as I talked to Tommy, my arms resting on the smoothly tapered seat, I found I was unable to dislodge myself. Simply reversing the movements that had led me into this awkward position should have done the trick, but I seized up in a slight panic and couldn't think straight.

Letting out a defeated sigh, I finally told Tommy, "Guess you better go get Miss G."

Only a few months into the term, the battle lines had already been drawn. Miss G had sniffed out the hippie-lover in her midst, and she had no tolerance for subversives, outside agitators, or any kind of lip. In me she detected all of those things—along with something else that I wasn't fully conscious of, nor had I the words to express.

I was a wiseass.

According to Merriam-Webster, the word "wiseass" didn't come into common usage until 1971, which was two years away, but it was already part of the language thanks to this once-ubiquitous line of hostile inquiry: "What are you—some kind of *wiseass*?" Or the imperative: "Hey, don't be such a wise-ass." At any rate, nobody liked a wiseass. And once you were perceived as one, everything you did or said had the potential to confirm your wiseass status. Like, a few weeks earlier, when Miss G made a joke that I didn't realize was a joke, she took it as a wiseass thing when it was really just a misunderstanding.

"Who knows the longest word in the English language?" she had asked.

Well, hallelujah—she'd finally hit on a truly interesting topic. I even knew the answer— *antidisestablishment...* something.

" 'Smiles,'" said Miss G. Then, a beat later, "Because there's a mile between the first and last letters."

"But it's not the longest," I sputtered, forgetting to raise my hand. "There are much longer words than 'smiles.' It's just—"

"It's just that *you* have no sense of humor," she said, giving me a withering look.

After a minute, Tommy was back.

"Well, what'd she say?"

He looked at me sheepishly. "Well..."

"Come on. What'd she *say*?"

He sighed. "She said 'Good.'"

A few minutes later, Ronald Mueller, the school's newly hired principal, strode into the room carrying a small handsaw. Trim, with a receding hairline and the alert expression of a salamander, Mueller had the air of a man who would choose action over deliberation every time. Perhaps I alone detected a hint of theatricality in the way he unbuttoned, then rolled up his shirtsleeves, like William Holden in *Picnic*, or the seeming relish he took in the brief pause between setting saw blade on the slat, mere inches from my left ear, and applying two manly pats to my right shoulder.

I winced at the first shriek of metal tearing into wood. After that I willed myself to keep as still as possible until the ordeal was over. With growing alarm, I noted the accumulation of feet at the edges of my peripheral vision, especially the deluxe-size PF Flyers of Scotty Moo, my first bully, which seemed to be smirking. I felt like a pilgrim in the pillory, gawked at and going nowhere, a piteous little jerk.

"Hoo-*eee*," exclaimed Mr. Mueller, once he'd made it through one side of the slat. "Now that is some thick and sturdy wood, Miss Godlewski. I'm gettin' in my Jack LaLanne over here!"

Miss G emitted a cluck. "They were made to last back then, Mr. Mueller."

I was famous around school afterward—the kid who got his head stuck in a chair. It didn't help that they kept the chair. But why waste a perfectly good piece of school equipment? Sure, it was minus one slat, but you could still sit your insignificant little ass on the thing, could you not? Besides, its presence served as a living reminder not to do extremely foolhardy things.

What Miss G really lived for was the rhythm band, a twice-yearly performance in the school auditorium that she orchestrated from behind an upright piano, her back to the audience like a maestro. It was a complicated enterprise that began with her assigning each kid a pair of rhythm sticks to bang, a maraca or a tambourine to shake, or a triangle to tinkle. Sticks were coveted because they were the loudest; maracas and tambos made an agreeable noise, so they were good, too. I'm pretty sure no one wanted to be a meek, tinkly triangle. She made me a triangle. Tommy Morgan got sticks, of course. (She loved Tommy Morgan.)

Miss G was devoted to buttoned-up contemporary music from the beginning of the decade. Along with seasonal chestnuts, she favored the work of Leroy Anderson, whose musical confections embodied a straight and orderly vision of American life that she cherished, and which seemed to be under attack in that chaotic era.

Anderson was like the second coming of my next-door neighbor Glenn Miller—an arranger, a composer, and a conductor who also played the trombone and was proud to serve his country. In 1942, the year Miller enlisted, Anderson was drafted by the U.S. Army. Initially sent to Reykjavik (he spoke six languages, including Icelandic), he landed stateside in 1945 at the Scandinavian desk. Anderson, who would later compose his "orchestral miniatures" in a custom-built, soundproof room in his Connecticut home, managed to pen "The Syncopated Clock," one of his biggest hits, while stationed in the nation's capital and rooting out bad guys for Uncle Sam. And I do mean miniatures: "Syncopated Clock" runs 2:23, the same length as "Territorial Pissings" by Nirvana.

We also did the easy-listening standard "Yellow Bird." ("*Yehhhhh-low bird / up high in banana tree…* "). This was the kind of banana Miss G liked. Oh, it was 1967, but she was having none of it. My man Donovan and his *elec-trical banana* could take a long walk off a short pier.

On the day of the rhythm band concert, we're grouped onstage according to instrument, on risers, and made visually uniform via green-and-red matching paper tunics. We open with "The Syncopated Clock," a song that ostensibly emphasizes odd pauses and offbeats. But make no mistake: Miss G has us emphatically banging, shaking, and tinkling strictly on the one-beat. Let's not get crazy. Unseen by the audience, she's right there with us every step of the way, cueing us in the fiercest of whispers:

"Sticks!"

"Tambour-iiiines!"

"*NOW, you jackasses!!!*"

Miss Godlewski is seated at the center of our first-grade class picture, smiling proudly. She wears a tan woolen sweater and a checked skirt that ends past her knees. There's a small gouge around her chin and the remains of a beard and moustache drawn in blue ballpoint. Some of the girls in the middle row have similar additions of facial hair, as do two of the cross-legged boys in the front row. Mitchell—placed among the seated because he's short and beaming away cockily because he knows the drill—is adorned with a goatee and shades. Next to him, Artie O'Day has been given a pretty sweet Fu Manchu. Tommy Morgan—no mustache, of course—is in the back row with the taller boys, me included, his thick brown hair combed forward in a wave above his eyes. He's in a red blazer with a black bow tie, as is a kid to his immediate right. Apparently, the movie usher look was in that year. To one side of me is Scotty Moo, or what's left of Scotty Moo. His head has been scraped away, as if by a ballpoint pen or other sharp object. All that remains is his red-turtleneck-clad shoulder, at roughly my eye level.

In her end-of-year report, Miss G had this to say:

"David's persistence should make him very successful in anything he undertakes. I hope it will be channeled in the right direction. He exhibits a good sense of security, but perhaps he has too much self-confidence for his own good. He does resent criticism of any sort, and shows it with his looks. I hope he will get over this and learn to face up to his own shortcomings."

The following year, Miss Fromm was no less adamant that I learn to wise up, simmer down, and get with the program.

"Sometimes he comes out with inappropriate, unrelated comical comments mainly aimed at getting attention," she wrote, in the fall of 1969. "I am trying to encourage David to use self-control. As he builds this, he will be able to discipline his impulses. I also hope to provide guidance in learning about other people so that he acquires an understanding, tolerance, and respect for their rights."

The Beast
by Sylvia Plath

He was the bullman earlier,
King of the dish, my lucky animal,
Breathing was easy in his airy holding.
The sun sat in his armpit.
Nothing went moldy. The little invisibles
Waited on him hand and foot
The blue sisters sent me to another school.
Monkey lived under the dunce cap.

Chapter 7

Emmets and Mollusks

Mom kept a Sylvia Plath poem called "The Beast" that she clipped from the *Times* scotch-taped to a kitchen cabinet. The language and sentiments of the poem frankly scared me, beginning with the opening lines: "He was the bullman earlier / King of the dish, my lucky animal."

What the hell? Who was a bullman earlier—Dad?

How much earlier?

Was there a bullman later?

What the hell is a bullman?

Other lines, like "The sun sat in his armpit" and "I've married a cupboard of rubbish," were almost too much to take in. The poem ends on a devastating note, which, despite something about snails ("I housekeep in Time's gut-end / Among emmets and mollusks"), felt like an unambiguous reference to Mom's dissatisfaction with her dual role as mother and wife: "Duchess of Nothing / Hairtusk's bride."

Tommy Morgan's mom also posted words in her kitchen, although her credo was shorter and slightly more comprehensible. Hers said, MY MIND'S MADE UP. DON'T CONFUSE ME WITH THE FACTS. Like my own mother, she was continually catching her son in various acts of wrongdoing, only Mrs. Morgan seemed to take a wicked delight in the gamesmanship. When she had him cornered, Tommy would do his best to come up with something—an outright lie, or its cousins, the deflection and the dodge—and she'd toy with him, like a cat with a mouse, until he was exposed utterly in a trifecta of guilt: of the original act, as a liar, and as a bad liar at that.

Both of our moms were hitters. Mom used a flailing open hand, while Mrs. Morgan preferred the hairbrush. This was not discipline so much as a venting of rage. When Dad gave you a spanking, you could always feel some combination of his inherent reluctance to inflict pain on anyone and him holding back. In my early teens, I caught Mom's wrist in mid-flail and held it there, and it was a supremely satisfying moment. But that was a long way off.

Hearing about Tommy's mother's hairbrush abuse, that it was normal around the neighborhood, at least for boys, to fend off some blows, was kind of a relief. Because there was no way Tommy's twin sister, Christina, was getting the treatment. The only hairbrush for her was the one she used to give her long, center-parted blond hair a hundred strokes before bedtime.

Pale, with a dainty nose and sky-blue eyes, she was the obvious girl to have a crush on, Becky Thatcher to your Tom Sawyer. But it wasn't just her all-American girl-next-door looks. Lots of girls defaulted to a kindly, deferential manner. Christina had a rare self-possession. You might even call it nerve.

For science they'd bring in an outside consultant named Mr. Corigliano, who was slump-shouldered, combed over, and very sincere about science. In one of Mr. C's "units," we all were supposed to plant a hundred grass seeds in a certain amount of dirt, under various light and watering conditions. This was so we could deduce what was most optimal to grass growing. To start, we would all have to count out a hundred grass seeds. I did this painstakingly. Grass seeds are very wispy. A week later, most of the terrariums were Deadsville; the emergence of even a few sprouts was a cause for gloating. All except for Christina's terrarium, which glowed a vibrant green. Where classmates had failed, hers was a miracle of lush, vertical, light-seeking stalks. How the hell had she done it? Had she watered it attentively or positioned it in the sun just so, or what?

"Nope," she told me. "I just threw in a handful of seeds."

Hold on. You mean when they tell you "A, B, C, or D," you can just say "E"?

It never would have occurred to me not to do as instructed. I broke rules, sure, but I tried not to, and that's different from breaking them on purpose without a second thought. People who thought this way were like another species, and I was surrounded by them. Mom was no seed counter. Neither was my brother. Both would have seen the task as a numbingly dull and employed Christina's methodology. Dad would have counted them out, but he'd have made them grow.

I met Tommy Morgan one morning on my way to kindergarten. Having just been let out of the early session, he was perched at the top of the steps leading up to his house, his chin supported by an upturned palm. I'd seen him there before. This time I waved.

"What's your name?"

"Tommy," he said, almost like a question, with a touch of Boston in it. "What's yours?"

"David," I said, before adding "Klein" in a softer voice.

"You got Miss Stolper too?"

"Yeah. You have her too?"

"Yeah."

Not much of a moment, but it was the beginning of something. By the following year, under the eye of Miss G, we were best friends. Eventually Mom gave the OK for Tommy to come over and play after school. I was especially excited to show him my latest plastic monster model by Aurora: The Forgotten Prisoner of Castel Mare, which was basically a skeleton chained to a stone wall.

We took our time getting there, bouncing a pink Spaldeen back and forth between us all the way down Oak Street. We started feeling raindrops as we crossed Engle Street, and by the time 5 Sherwood came into sight, the drizzle was steady and intensifying. Still, we were determined that our catch should continue. Separated by about twenty feet of asphalt, lobbing rather than bouncing, it became like a silent dare between us: Who'll be the first to say, "OK, this is just stupid."

Just as we're on the verge of getting soaked to the skin, both of us cackling madly, I feel, rather than hear, the thunder of Mom's rapidly approaching footsteps. And then: *"Get back in the house!"*

Once inside, as we're removing our sopping sneakers, Tommy spots a bright red emergency panel located high up on a white wall opposite the cellar door, and he can't suppress his curiosity.

"Hey, what's that switch do?" he says.

I've wondered about it too.

"Don't touch that!" Mom shrills from the kitchen, and we flee down the narrow staircase to the safe harbor of the basement.

Despite having accepted motherhood as her row to hoe, Mom never warmed to its trappings. She didn't fuss with how we were dressed on picture day at school, when most mothers dolled up their kids in their Sunday best, or at least stuck them in a jacket. She put minimal effort into things like Halloween costumes. One year she'd find a straw hat in the attic and secure your dungarees with a length of rope from Mr. Santini's work bench, and you'd be a cowboy. The following year, a colorful scarf, a snap-on earring, and a swipe of eyeliner would render you a pirate. For a class project of Jonny's, each child was responsible for submitting an international food recipe. Mom's solution was to follow a standard recipe for sugar wafers and fulfill the assignment by dubbing her creation "English High Tea Cookies." She didn't dote on us, was never the gentlest trimmer of toenails, and Mom did not believe in Mother's Day. She contended it was an invention of Hallmark Cards, which was convenient enough. Tarring the holiday with the taint of commercialism was in step with the times, after all, but the real reason we didn't celebrate Mother's Day was that Mom didn't view motherhood—or mothers, for that matter, her own included—as worth making a big deal about. She damn well did not want to be celebrated, personally, merely for being a mother. (We didn't celebrate Father's Day either.)

Mom found what she was looking for somewhere in the wake of Richard Nixon's election. Friends of hers had joined a group called Tenafly Women for Peace, which organized events aimed at electing anti-war candidates, and pretty soon Mom was writing newsletters, doing PR, and forging bonds with other women of a similar mind in Tenafly. It was good for her soul.

A current events discussion was always within easy reach at 5 Sherwood. When Grandma and Grandpa visited, heated political conversations around the kitchen table lasted for hours, with familiar refrains like "Is it good for Israel?" "That SOB Nixon," and, usually muttered in connection with another failed Middle East peace summit, "the *God. Damn. Arabs.*" In TWP ("tee double-ya pee," as Mom pronounced it, her Brooklyn sneaking out), she found an outlet for the intense feelings she harbored about the state of the world.

On May 4, 1970, six hours after four students protesting the U.S. bombing of Cambodia were gunned down at Kent State University by the Ohio National Guard, a candlelight march took place. Organized in part by Mom's group, the procession began at the Roosevelt Commons, an algae-rich pond in the center of town. From there, the procession made its way through the working-class blocks of Tenafly Road until we crossed the railroad tracks at Westervelt and took a hard right along the more upscale Dean Drive. At Elm Street, we headed toward the East Hill, Tenafly's hallowed higher ground. People kept joining the group along the way, like the Feffers, two long-haired brothers who sometimes acted as sitters for us. I can still see Mom flashing them the peace sign.

Perhaps a hundred-strong when the marching was done, the group fanned out along the expanse of Leroy Street, which runs along the base of the East Hill, overlooking the Smith School playground. Roofs of houses, a vague tree line, and a goodly expanse of the darkening sky were visible beyond it. Scanning the trail of lights of the still-approaching marchers, I suddenly felt my knees wobble at the evanescent beauty of it all. Replaying it in my mind as we walked home, I looked up at Mom and said, "Do you think we'll ever get to do that again?"

"Well, my God, David," she gasped, jerking us to a halt. "I *hope* not. And you should hope not, too. We should hope that this never happens ever again."

Clearly I had missed the whole point.

If there was any human enterprise whose point I did get, it was Little League baseball. It was the sole area of life where I had moved beyond the novice stage.

Getting ready for a game—slipping out of your day clothes, alone in your room with the radio and your thoughts—was a happy ritual. The knickers and button-up shirt were fairly humdrum, but when you added the stirrup socks, the long-sleeved T-shirt worn under your jersey, and the black cleats, you felt ready for battle. And being catcher meant being decked out in all kinds of cool protective gear: shin guards that covered your knees and ended past your ankles, a chest protector that was like an added layer of flesh, an ultra-heavy-duty padded face mask, and a mitt the size and shape of a Boston crème pie. Peering through the widely spaced metal mesh, especially with a song traipsing or stumbling or sailing through your head, was a magical feeling. You could see the whole field and what was coming.

Little League games started in the late afternoon and often ended at twilight. One day, as I was getting ready for a game against Citizen's National Bank,[6] my softball-shaped Panasonic transistor radio emitted the most beguiling sound, one that stopped me in mid-stirrup pull. Later, as I crouched behind the plate, admiring the slanting gold rays filigreed in the air above the ballfield, my mind kept circling back to the song's opening line: *"I remember finding out about you."*

---

6. By precedent or town edict, Little League teams were named for the businesses that sponsored them, which meant team names ran the gamut from blandly corporate (Control Associates, Inter-Travel) to vaguely patriotic (American Legion, County Trust) to downright unmanly (Francisco Nursery, Hofstetter's Bakery). This held until the league was forced to add an expansion club in 1974, and one Junius "Jay" Peake, who oversaw a notably non-Tenafly-based brokerage firm in Manhattan's financial district, stepped up to the plate. Peake was a staunch conservative, but rather than saddle his young charges with the clinical sounding name of his business, he thought of the animal symbols of Wall Street and named his team the Tenafly Bulls, upending the status quo, if only briefly.

Badfinger's "Day After Day," I'd decided, was about the singer discovering the existence of that unnamed "you." Not about the moment when he *met* this unforgettable someone, but when he learned that she simply lived in the same world as he did. Maybe he was passing by a store and saw her through the window. Maybe she was waiting at the bus stop. Even as the rest of the song makes clear that the singer is obsessing about a lover who dumped him, to me it was about the good kind of finding out, not the kind associated with loss or betrayal. You're not alone in your lonely gloom, it seemed to assure. Hell, the guy in Badfinger knows just how you feel. And maybe one day you'll find out about somebody too.

Chapter 8

Heaven on Their Minds

I firmly believe that if the Jewish liturgical canon had better tunes and better rhymes, some *hooks,* I'd be a more observant Jew. How is it that the most resilient, creative, scrappy, *critical* people in history have settled for such a downer songbook? There's not a single grabber in the entire service. And I always felt silly singing them. Every other word rhymes with *eemo-shee-aynu,* which—they really painted themselves into a corner with that one.

Hebrew school classes on Saturdays were especially grueling. Lasting all morning, taught by the non-charismatic, they were occasionally broken up by a visit from a congregant who would lead us in singing Israeli children's songs. There we would sit—all pasty faces, bad 1970s haircuts, and temple breath—singing "Shalom Chaverim" joylessly and off-key. I'd stew and sulk, and she found this hilarious. Poised over an admittedly fine-looking acoustic guitar, Music Lady would wiggle her eyebrows at me, in mid-"Zum Gali Gali," just to say, "Come on, frowny—sing a little! What's the big deal?" And I'd pout even harder.

She was pretty, too, like a Jewish Joan Baez. God, how I hated her.

God was very big in 1971. George Harrison's "My Sweet Lord" was No. 1 as the year dawned, and inspirational earworms like "Put Your Hand in the Hand" and Judy Collins's "Amazing Grace" would soon dot the charts. The biggest song that spring, "Joy to the World" by Three Dog Night, had nothing to do with Jesus, but its kumbaya feel and the title it shared with a Christmas song we learned in Miss Pearce's class struck me as Christian in sentiment. Jesus would even pop up on secular tunes, like Brewer and Shipley's "One Toke Over the Line" (sweet Jesus!) and "Fire and Rain." Elton John, who was shaping up to be my first significant post-Beatles musical fixation, was at his peak of Christian and gospel imagery. *"And Jesus, he wants to go to Venus,"* howled Elton. And Jesus, so did I. Sadly, though, amid all this talk of Jesus, I was always on the outside looking in, until 1971, when the original Broadway cast recording of *Jesus Christ Superstar* played in heavy rotation all throughout that Christ-y summer.

Jesus Christ Superstar was about as welcome in the Klein household as mayonnaise, which is to say, all but explicitly prohibited. Now don't get me wrong: the folks had nothing against Christianity, or Jesus, or even a musical based on His life. It's just that we were a *Godspell* family.

Godspell, which opened modestly in early 1971, drew raves for its musical retelling of the Gospel of St. Matthew. And what a retelling! With his clown nose, Superman shirt, and mime makeup, *Godspell* Jesus was nothing like the bearded man with faraway eyes depicted on Christmas cards and religious medals. Right-wing Christians found this sort of modification sacrilegious, but for us, these were the best parts. We *liked* a winsome song-and-dance-man Jesus. We thought substituting a chain-link fence for the cross was actually an improvement on the original. Mom especially warmed to "Turn Back, O Man," a burlesque-style number where the singer flirts with the audience and slips in saucy asides like, *"C'mere, Jesus, I got somethin' ta show ya…"* In a rare impulse buy, Dad picked up the original cast recording on the way out of the theater, and for months afterward, our demonstrably secular household reverberated with the sound of John the Baptist exhorting all within earshot to *"Pre-ee-ee-pare Ye the Way of the Lord…"*

In June, my brother and I were shipped off to Camp Greylock for Boys, a well-respected, almost-all-Jewish camp in the scenic Berkshires, founded in 1920. It was my first immersion in non-parentally sanctioned music, which is how I came to form a personal relationship with *Jesus Christ Superstar*. As Jews, we hadn't had the story of Christ's last week on Earth drummed into us, so we found it fresh and lurid and kind of sexy. And by all rights, it should have passed me by. The Klein household had room for exactly *one* original cast recording of a musical about Jesus Christ—and we were all set in that department, thank *Godspell*.

This approve/disapprove aesthetic dividing line—choosing *Godspell* over *Superstar*—was a familiar concept. *Godspell* was an intimate affair with a minimal set and a small cast that shared bread and wine with the audience at intermission. To Dad, *Jesus Christ Superstar* was a special kind of bad, a big, showy extravaganza that stood for vulgar displays in general. And if Dad hated anything, it was a vulgar display—it reminded him of his parents. Mom's harshest disparaging term was "pretentious," a word she practically spat out. She had no use for any artistic expression that struck her as self-serious, sentimental, or high-minded, although she did make an exception for Donovan's "Atlantis." To Mom, *Jesus Christ Superstar* was the P-word incarnate. And my parents were hardly alone in their antipathy. Evangelicals were furious that *Superstar* Jesus was depicted as more human than divine and that Judas had more lines than the big man Himself. Jewish groups feared that the film's sinister Jewish priests would stoke a wave of anti-Semitism. Pretty much everyone hated *Jesus Christ Superstar*, save for its millions of paying customers.

As with *Godspell*, the folks had been so impressed with *Hair* when they saw it at the 1967 New York Shakespeare Festival that they bought the album on the way out. We did not own the much more famous recording of the show's Broadway production, however, with the cover showing a pair of anemone-like heads in neon-green and red. This struck me as another example of the parental aesthetic: there's a good *Hair* and a bad *Hair*, and I wanted the bad *Hair*. Badly. Because, to gussy the show up for Broadway, the show's creators had excised a couple of obvious bombs from the off-Broadway version—like "Exanaplanatooch," which even I knew was a turd—and replaced them with a half-dozen gratuitously topical ditties, liberally dotted with curse words.

Tommy Morgan's big sister Amy had the curse-word version, and for months Tommy had whisper-sung me all the choicest lyrics during recess. We finally found our chance one afternoon, and into Amy's bedroom we crept to listen to "Hashish" and "Sodomy" and "Colored Spade," which reveled in the N-word. Amy walked in on us in the midst of "Abie Baby," a mock birthday tribute to Abraham Lincoln, *"the emanci-motherfuckin-pator of the slaves."* She rolled her eyes and left us to our thrills.

Dad's place at the head of the table was strategically arranged to include a wide-brimmed, bone-white cereal bowl and three adjacent boxes of what Mom called dry cereal: a crunchy one, which would go on the bottom because it could withstand milk; Cheerios, because Cheerios comprised the middle of Dad's cereal sandwich; and on top, something fluffy and effervescent, like Puffed Rice. Served with *The New York Times*. Always the *Times*.

On weekends, when he had time to linger, Dad would read bits out loud to Mom. Thus I was privy to the scathing hit piece on *Jesus Christ Superstar* that ran in the October 31, 1971, Sunday edition of the paper, in which writer Guy Flatley gave "the strutting, mincing, twitching, grinding, souped-up *Superstar*" a public flogging in the form of a mocking Q and A. Flatley alternates between sneering and leering—at Tim Rice, anyway, "the blonde and lanky bachelor who wrote the lyrics," who "shakes his shoulder-length blond hair and sighs." Rice doesn't merely stand; rather, he "rises to his full, impressive height." Meanwhile, his collaborator, Andrew Lloyd-Webber, is likened to "a hippie Buster Keaton," a cruel epithet in any era.

Other than to ask what "mincing" meant, I kept my head down. The revelation that some of the show's songs had taken root within my still-forming brain, or to admit to the trashy frisson I felt on hearing that riveting first cry of "Jesus!!!" in "Heaven on Their Minds" would have been an act of heresy. I was no iconoclast like my brother. Why break up our tenuous *Godspell* family unity?

Chapter 9

The Eye Incident

The word "dawdle" always sounded a bit like *Davidel*, the Yiddish diminutive of my given name that Grandma sometimes used. Dad familiarized me with the word and the concept because it suited me so well. True to form, I dawdled over lunch that day. My cousin Linda was visiting from California, and it was hard to tear myself away. To make up the difference, I hustled on the last stretch of Oak Street, and the sight of a few kids up ahead assured me I wouldn't be late.

Tommy and two guys from our football games—Carney and Sam—are clustered together on the footpath in front of the school's main entrance. Bubblegum is my first thought. Or maybe Tommy has more nudie playing cards. Something forbidden is being shared. I'm about fifteen feet away when my friends break from their huddle and turn to face me. Maybe something is unfamiliar in their overall comportment.

A pain sears through my right eye, fierce as a sudden blow.

I buckle into a defensive crouch, and while I'm down there I hear Tommy say something I won't ever be sure of, something like, "Oop—I think he eyed it." As if to say, "He took one in the eye," but with a spontaneous vernacular spin, perhaps to downplay the situation. Because he had to know how far he had pulled that thing back, and how hard it would still be flying when it reached me.

Projectiles are all the rage at Smith School. Kids remove the tubular ink container from the inside of Bic pens and turn the outer clear-plastic casing into a spitball launcher. A spitball is an annoyance, a bit of wadded-up paper in a saliva bath, the mosquito of the projectile game. But there are hornets and wasps too. A miniature slingshot can easily be fashioned out of a rubber band, while certain innovative fifth-graders have discovered that a slightly unbent paper clip, hooked onto a tautly pulled rubber-band loop, results in greater distance and greater pain. I've just met with the sharp end of that proposition.

The guys lead me inside and into the main office. They can't stay with me because it's past one o'clock and they have to scurry to class. Mrs. Schneider, the school secretary, is not terribly concerned. She has me wait in the nurse's office until she returns from her lunch break.

The tears my eye is making have a pink tinge. Worse, when I cover my good eye, it's all black. Not blurry. Black. After a little while, Mr. Mueller arrives, thankfully not brandishing a handsaw. Even though I'm legitimately injured, he still unnerves me, what with the chair incident and the recent nudie-card debacle.

A few weeks ago, Mueller had called a bunch of us out of our classrooms and into the hallway, and gone all Elliot Ness on us—everybody from lowly card purchasers like me, to card dealers like Tommy, to the supply guy, Jimmy Harris, who lives in an impressive house near the Cotswold with his mother, the Tony Award-nominated actress Inga Swenson. Jimmy had been doing a brisk business selling cards from a deck issued by Playboy Enterprises for a quarter apiece.

Oh, the *salaciousness* of it. Mr. Mueller warned us that if anything like this *ever* happened again, we were all dead meat.

"OK, Mr. Klein," he says. "So what happened? You guys horsin' around again? Like I always say, it's all fun and games until..." he trails off and forces a chuckle. "Tell ya what. Let's close up that good eye and tell me what it says here," he instructs, pointing to a box of, I guess, educational materials.

"It's all black. I can't even see it. I can see just fine out of the other," I say, and still wanting to be cool with him, I start to read the educational jargon on the box, showing how good a reader I'm getting to be.

"Know what? You probably just stung it."

"I did? I mean, just stung it?"

"Yeah, you just stung your eye. It's... you'll be OK. Mrs. James'll be back from lunch any minute now. So meanwhile, you can just go ahead and sit tight."

I wait, but it hurts.

How come I've never heard of stinging your eye before? When you sting your eye, does everything go black for a little while and then your vision returns to normal? I'm not the savviest eleven-year-old, but even to me this sounds highly unlikely. Still, I maintain a shred of trust in his status as an adult.

Who knows. Maybe I *had* just stung the damn thing. In breezes Mrs. James, a robust woman in her mid-fifties with short salt-and-pepper hair and bifocals attached to a thin chain.

"So, David, Mr. Mueller tells me something happened to your eye. Something hit you in the eye, is that right? You were playing outside?"

"Not playing. Well, I wasn't. I was just walking up and my friends were playing, I guess."

"I see. And do you know what it was that hit you?"

"A paperclip, I think."

"A paperclip. Well, I always tell you kids, it's all fun and games until... Let's have a look-see," she says, tilting my chin up with a tap of her fingers. She takes out a little pen light and shines it in my eye, and it spooks me.

"David, if I can't look at it, how can I help you?"

For the first time, I'm about to cry.

"I'll tell you what. Let's give Mother a call."

Dr. Seligman's waiting room is three-quarters full and there's nothing to do but wait. I'm in a loose fetal position on my left side, one hand cupped over my eye, my head on Mom's lap as she strokes my hair. Only the most innocuous pop music plays in Dr. Seligman's office: WPAT, Easy 93, "Nothing but beautiful music." But sometimes the radio is singing your life, and just as the pain in my sad, aqueous eye begins to grow intolerable, the glistening arpeggios that open the Stones' "As Tears Go By" emanate from the embedded ceiling speakers. Each moment is gold and rewards contemplation: "It is the evening of the day"—a seemingly contradictory state—but I know it intimately on this particular day. "I sit and watch the children play"—what an idyllic image, only sometimes children play with projectiles. That heavenly string-quartet middle bit—I have to remember to play it for Dad. The song ends with a bit of humming, the same way "Yesterday" does. Never noticed that before.

For two minutes and forty-three seconds, I'm becalmed, but when the song ends, an ad for beautiful Mount Airy Lodge ("America's premier honeymoon retreat") comes on, and my eye starts throbbing again. Mom tells the woman at the desk that I need to be seen right away. Soon I'm guided into a dim room and steered toward one of those chin-caressing eyeball-examination apparatuses. I detect a hint of movement as Dr. Seligman bends toward me in that weirdly intimate tete-a-tete betwixt patient and ophthalmologist. Then I hear him gasp.

"Joan," he sputters, a little phlegm catching in his throat. "Joan, he needs to be admitted right away."

The eye is a tiny thing, and it can't tolerate a lot of trauma. A flying object has pierced my cornea and caused bleeding within the anterior chamber, which is behind the outer corneal layer and in front of the lens. Any further bleeding could cause irreparable damage, so my eye has to keep still. Both eyes do, because when you look with one eye, you look with the other.

I'm propped up in a hospital bed with gauze patches taped over both eyes, sedated. Mom has wisely tuned the TV in to Channel 11, whose afternoon lineup begins at 4:30 with *The Munsters*, followed by a full hour of *Batman* reruns.

In "Fine Finny Fiends," the Caped Crusaders are lashed to a wall in a room full of candy-colored balloons, and they'll die when the last one pops. ("HOW WILL THEY LIVE? WILL THEY BE VANQUISHED BY A VACUUM?") A tiny crack where one of the patches isn't fully secured admits a trace of light, but I keep my eyes shut like I've been told to do. Besides, I know they'll escape, thanks to the bat-knife and mini-bat-oxygen tanks hidden in Batman's utility belt.

Hours later, I awaken in the double darkness with "Dueling Banjos" running through my head. Mom and Dad saw *Deliverance* last summer, and in true Dad fashion, he couldn't keep from telling me about the horrifying rape scene, although he managed to avoid using the word "rape" by asking if I knew what the word "sodomy" meant. I've scoured *Deliverance* in search of the so-called good parts, but I crave to see all of its unspeakableness unfold on screen, like the scene where badass Burt Reynolds avenges that poor SOB Bobby with a bow and arrow. Thanks to good old Tommy Morgan, I know all about it.

My guitar playing has progressed to the point where I can play the easy parts of "Dueling Banjos"—before it gets all fast. Lying there, drugged and patched on the giant hospital bed, the fingers on my left hand begin to move along an imagined fretboard. A pick materializes between my right thumb and forefinger and the song from the movie starts to play. Now I'm doing the fast parts, and instead of the strange-looking boy on the porch, it's Tommy Morgan on banjo.

Casting Tommy as a banjo player goes sharply against type, for banjo is a character actor's instrument and Tommy is a leading man, but I'm all hopped up on Phenobarbital and not thinking straight. When we play football on the dusty field behind Smith School, Tommy is the quarterback. He just has to be. He's naturally athletic, has a good arm and can scramble, but beyond that he possesses some non-physical quality that makes it seem like he should be the leader. Not because of a particularly strong or dominating personality or an uncanny magnetism, but rather an unwavering belief in his own instincts.

Tommy just seems to know. He'll turn his palm into the football field and show you exactly where to run, and you'll go out for that pass and run the exact pattern he put down—straight for ten strides, then a fake to the left followed by a quick pivot right—and wham. The ball is coming right at you, chest level, like a birthday present. For conceiving and delivering on plays like that, I accord him an almost mythic status.

Blindness has been a longtime fascination. At my grandparents' apartment in Flatbush is an image of Helen Keller in a giant book of photographs, her fingers splayed gently over the face of a cooperative man, her eyes looking rapturously heavenward. I've spent many minutes peering at it, just as I've stared at the cover of Dad's copy of *Ray Charles Greatest Hits,* straining to see something behind Ray's dark glasses. My interest was initially stoked by a Scholastic paperback about Louis Braille that had Braille text on the back cover. In the book, Louis is depicted as a willful boy who causes his own injury by playing with the sharp leather-punching tool that his dad has sensibly left lying around where his kid could find it. Louis is even responsible for spreading the infection from his injured eye to the other one by excessively rubbing at it. You might almost conclude that inventing a way for blind people to read was Louis's way of apologizing for being such a total fuck-up. My blindness fetish peaked with *Longstreet*, an ABC series starring James Franciscus.

Longstreet (first name James, not that it matters with a name like Longstreet) is an insurance investigator blinded by bad guys in an explosion that kills his wife. With a firm jaw and the assistance of his faithful white German shepherd, Pax, our blind detective takes down cutthroat criminals through dogged insurance-industry tactics and the Way of the Intercepting Fist, which he learns from Bruce Lee. For me, Longstreet's most astounding trick is his ability to listen in as suspicious person places a call on a rotary phone and discern the number by the length of the dial's return rotations.

I won't be blind like Longstreet. Tops, I'll lose an eye and be the kid who lost an eye—the ignominious someone who put a stop to all the fun and games. Call it a slight improvement over the kid who got his head stuck in a chair. And now Tommy and I are united in some strange way.

The patch comes off my good eye after a week, when the danger of casual usage is no longer likely to affect the healing eye adversely. From there, I have to remain in situ for another week. One day, the tedium is broken by the arrival of letters from my fifth-grade class. Each one is exactly the same length yet encapsulates the personality of the writer in a way that touches me. Sam's letter is newsy and forward looking:

Hi, David,

Not doing much in school. I'm sleeping at Eric's house Friday. Mabey we can play Saturday. Hope you get out Wednesday. Your Friend, Sam

Margot, sweetly naïve, tries to empathize:

Dear David,

I hope your eye doesn't hurt too much. It must be hard for you to have much fun if you can't see. I'm sure the doctor will help you and you can come back to school soon.

Cynthia's is notable for indicating just how quickly Tommy has circulated the story that my injury was caused by a rubber band:

Dear David,

I was sorry to hear about you getting hit in the eye with a rubber band. I hope you get better and come back to school soon. Class is so quiet without you.

In time, I begin to feel like myself again, which means restless. Something pisses me off, and I throw my head back against the pillow in disgust and am immediately warned not to do it again, because I can still jar something loose—and then I really will lose the eye. So I will myself to chill. Urging on my own blindness like Louis Braille is not going to be my fate.

My eyes are extremely light-sensitive afterward, and I'm given a pair of pretty cool sunglasses with metal frames to compensate. I can't bring myself to wear them to school, but Dad takes me along on an errand, and the teenage kids of his medical colleague snicker at my rad shades. Soon I'll be fitted for a gas-permeable contact lens that has to be cleaned with distilled water in a little machine every night and will never be comfortable. If getting hit in the eye with a paperclip pays any dividends, I sure am not seeing any.

Back at home, despite the omnipresence of the Carpenters'"Sing," the radio offers brief moments of comfort and escape. Songs take on new meanings now. Elton John's "Daniel" is easy to project myself into. *"Your eyes have died, but you see more than I"* is like a mythical version of me—wounded but possessed of a level of insight beyond that of most mortal men. "I Can See Clearly Now" by Johnny Nash is the soundtrack to my good days. "Drift Away" by Dobie Gray (*"Day after day I'm more confused"*) is for the darker ones.

Only two relatively tiny spaces on the human body can be seriously injured by a flying paperclip. The only lesson to be learned is that there's no cure for bad luck. At least scientists are working on an anti-death pill.

Chapter 10

Tull Zeal

Tommy Morgan roots for New York sports teams—the Mets over the Yankees, the Giants over the Jets—with fierce Catholic devotion. One evening, we ride in a crowded bus rented by the Tenafly Recreation Commission to see his beloved Knicks play the Buffalo Braves at Madison Square Garden. Tommy understands hoops way better than I do, and he has on-court skills to match, not to mention a pair of Puma Clydes. I hope the Knicks win, but I don't really care if they do. It's enough just to be with Tommy in the city and watch these outsize heroes in the flesh: Willis Reed, Walt Frazier, Dave D, and Bill B. And Hawthorne Wingo, who has the best name, and whose third-quarter entrance has the crowd ecstatically chanting *"Wingo, Wingo! Wingo!"*

Afterward, as we make our way back to the bus, happily stuffed with popcorn and hotdogs and savoring a Knicks victory, I glimpse a figure familiar to me from the front cover of Jethro Tull's *Aqualung*. Standing with his back to a pretzel cart, the man has a narrow face, a wispy beard, and a crazed tangle of hair. His coat goes past his knees.

"Holy crap, Tommy. Look—it's Ian Anderson. Over there."

"Get out. Who, that guy?"

"Yeah, *that guy*. That's him. Come on. We have to go talk to him."

Tommy assents, but obviously I'll do the talking.

"Excuse me, but... are you Ian Anderson?"

He smiles and, in a voice that is English and plausibly Anderson-esque, says he is. "Would you like a chestnut?" he says, tilting the bag toward me. Tommy, naturally suspicious, tugs my arm—like, don't eat that, it could be poisoned.

"I've never had one before," I say.

"Oh, do try one," he says. "They're awfully good."

Noting my hesitation, he reaches into the steaming bag and plucks one out for me. Tommy's look says, Go ahead—it's your funeral. Chestnuts taste like they smell, which is not bad at all, but they're kind of chalky and require a bit of chewing. Ian doesn't seem anxious to move on, but the minute I get a good swallow in, I make sure to ask for an autograph.

"Oh, yes indeed," he says. "Happily."

I hand him my program and regulation navy blue MSG pencil stub.

"What's your name then?"

As leader of Jethro Tull, the shaggy-headed, codpiece-wearing Ian Anderson was famous for playing the flute while balanced on one leg. Throughout most of the 1970s, his band could sell out Madison Square Garden on consecutive nights. They were so big it wasn't even necessary to say Jethro. Tull was enough. To many of us, Tull was even the preferred terminology.

A junior counselor at Camp Greylock with a big blond frizz and starter beard initiated me into the cult. All it took was the six diabolical opening notes of "Aqualung" to strafe my mental landscape with Tull bullets and scar it forever. For this was no bright, shining Beatles lick. This was pure sinew, kind of ugly almost—but beautiful ugly. The benign weirdos I'd met through the Beatles—Nowhere Man, the Fool on the Hill, the barber showing photographs—had not prepared me for the medieval village of grotesques living within the green-brown covers of my copy of *Aqualung*. There was Cross-Eyed Mary ("She'll do it for a song"), the bearded lady, a chicken fancier, the jackknife barber—and that's just Side 1. The era's Christ fixation was represented too, in "Hymn 43," with its refrain of *"Jesus save me!"* But it all begins with a wizened beggar, improbably named Aqualung, whom we first meet, famously you might say, "sitting on a park bench, eyeing little girls with bad intent." And then, the lyric that sealed the deal: *"Snot is running down his nose!"*

Beatles songs were tidy affairs. Only the implicit cranial spray from Maxwell's silver hammer and yellow-matter custard dripping from a dead dog's eye besmear the Beatles canon with gross liquids. In giving snot pride of place, Tull spoke to us as few others had.[7] Gang-vocaling that line among a chorus

---

7. Anderson doubles down on *Aqualung*'s successor, *Thick as a Brick*, with lyrics mentioning sperm, blackheads, and other adolescent fixations.

of bunk-mates brandishing air-tennis rackets is as close as I've ever come to unison church singing.

In true progressive rock fashion, "Aqualung" is episodic, full of sudden pivots. One minute, you/me/us is scampering along in the "sun-streaking cold" as the grubby protagonist "bends to pick a dog-end." (Why, Aqualung, why? Sure, "dog-end" is British slang for a discarded cigarette butt, but how were we nine-year-old Yanks to know it didn't mean dog turd?) Next, Anderson's got his busker's voice on, lulling us into submission with plaintive "dee dee-dee-dees" and "dah dah-dah-dums." But look out—here it comes again: that behemoth guitar riff. Those monster drums. That damnable park bench.

What's undeniable, by the end of this six-minute mini opus—whether it's your first or five-hundredth hearing—is that you can't help but love the old coot. The leering? The questionable morals? The lack of hygiene? Just Aqualung being Aqualung.

This was the first album I wanted to own really badly. One weekend morning when Dad was about to drive out to Sam Goody on Route 4, I announced my intention to spend my allowance on a particular record. I was cagey about it because the unfamiliar clank of the word "Aqualung" was sure to arouse suspicion. At the cashier, I handed my prize to Dad along with some dollars. He studied the cover painting of the bent-over vagabond, the words "Jethro Tull" and "Aqualung" rendered in white medieval typeface at the top left corner. On the back, a mock Bible verse begins, *"In the beginning Man created God, and in the image of Man created he him."* I imagined Dad might be impressed by such high-minded verbiage, but I detected a trace of disapproval in his narrowing brow.

Listening to the *'lung* through Dad's pillow-soft light-gray headphones, the land of Tull was just as I remembered it from summer camp: mini-epics interspersed with beguiling acoustic reveries, power chords do-si-do-ing with flute soli. Conceptually, *Aqualung* never revealed its secrets to me. That whole "Man made God, and God made man" business went right over my head. Even the album's gatefold painting—scruffy men in a pub, depicted in a sort of Caravaggio lighting—baffled me.

Jonny found my Tull zeal bemusing. He was buying records like Leon Russell's *Carny* and *Spaces*, by jazz-fusion wunderkind Larry Coryell, which *Rolling Stone* called "one of the most beautiful perfectly realized instrumental albums in a long while." To me it sounded like chaos. Jonny's choices sometimes vexed Dad, who was dumbstruck when the kid brought home *Europe '72*—a *three-record set*—by the Grateful Dead. But purchasing critically acclaimed LPs was in accordance with family tradition. Critics knew their stuff, and once *you* knew your stuff, you could be a critic too.

I wanted Jonny to love Tull, but he didn't share my enthusiasm. No doubt he'd read some of the cutting reviews the band began to rack up once its lineup shifted from a blues-based ensemble to an unwavering focus on Anderson and his flute-flavored folk-rock epics. I alone would have to hoist the Tull torch. Not that I took to wearing a dirty trench coat or anything, but when the conversation came around to music, it was always "Are you into Tull?" And woe be unto he or she who responded, "Yeah, he's great."

He???

How delicious it was to convey to these poor deluded souls that Jethro Tull was just the name of the band, *man*, and that the lead singer was not named Jethro but Ian. This stance didn't win me any friends, but I felt entitled to my junior pedantry. The lesson, at least at 5 Sherwood, seemed to be that when you were totally, 100 percent right about something, you were allowed to rub it in a little.

Well, how were we to know that on February 25, 1973, Jethro Tull was somewhere between Finland and Sweden in the midst of the Thick as a Brick Tour? Even if Ian Anderson had a few nights off and managed to jet stateside for some R&R in Gotham, it's hard to imagine he'd spend Saturday night solo at a basketball game—or even that he would have been feeling so convivial. Tull had just churned out two side-length religion-themed concept albums *in a row*, the latest of which, *A Passion Play*, was stoking new forms of rock-journo abuse. Stephen Holden of *Rolling Stone* called it "45 minutes of vapid twittering [that] strangles under the tonnage of its pretensions."

The coming years would bring more self-serious Tull records and Tull concerts at the Garden. My fandom never wavered, even as my patience was tested by Anderson's perplexing sartorial choices—*Songs from the Wood*, for example, where Ian appears as a dandified Renaissance-era archery instructor, or *Heavy Horses*, the cover of which shows him flanked by two of his prized equines. Did this shameless display of wealth make him any less relevant or relatable to a Jersey teen adrift in the soup of high school? Hardly. He was a rock star and he had earned his baubles. It took 1979's *Stormwatch*, with its cover showing Anderson clutching a pair of military-grade binocs and the LP title in bright red alarm clock font, for me to finally let go.

Somewhere in the digital age, when Anderson's crazy hair was almost gone and he was playing solo engagements at classy theaters, I found myself staring at that Knicks program, specifically the full-page ad for Eastern Airlines ("The Wings of Man") on the back cover, with its fading soft-penciled inscription in the lower right corner:

Good luck, David. Ian Anderson

A Google search reveals that Ian Anderson has a distinctive signature. He tops his cursive capital "I" with an oblong loop resembling an upside-down half note. The one on my Knicks program has a similar loop, but on the bottom segment of the letter. Anderson's "A" has a sharp pointed peak, indicating a strong ego, while the one on my program is round as an apple, often an indication of a reserved or cautious personality. Not only was the guy we met not the lead singer of Jethro Tull—he and Ian Anderson were polar opposites. At least if handwriting analysis is any indication.

Still, that meeting became enshrined in our shared childhood. The guy looked like Ian Anderson, sounded like Ian Anderson might have sounded, and said he was Ian Anderson. That was enough for me to eat food from his hand. I suppose he could have been more like Aqualung, an unstable, possibly dangerous street person eyeing little girls (and naive kids from the suburbs) with bad intent. Where were the authorities? We had been instructed to meet back at the bus after the game. How we got there, and who we stopped to nosh with, was up to us.

The question remains as to motivation. Why would anyone go through such a charade? In retrospect, I see it as a minor crime of opportunity. We approached the man and credulously posed a question. Where was the harm in having a little fun at our expense? He didn't do anything to make us feel uncomfortable. Hell, he made our night. Never did we dream we'd been duped. We came away believers: That rock stars walked among us. That we had met an actual one. Even that some residual coolness had rubbed off on us. After all, we were the ones it happened to.

Chapter 11

Spare Ghoul

The transition to junior high is jarring. Suddenly, my familiar one-story school building located right up the street is supplanted by an imposing three-floor brick facility in the town's center, where the pupils of four elementary schools are unceremoniously dumped. It takes me a good half hour to get there on foot, even longer when I have to lug my guitar for band practice. The hallways are wider, the kids are bigger, and no longer are you issued a single teacher to grapple with in a given year. Now there's one for math and science, one for social studies and English, and a half dozen specialists.

I count myself lucky not to have landed with the dreaded team of Davis and Raymond, widely acknowledged as the strictest and most humorless of the bunch. I get Lindeman and Roznofsky, one of the better pairings. Mrs. Lindeman is flinty, short-haired, and sarcastic, but she laughs easily and has a no-nonsense Queens inflection. Mr. Roznofsky, who is paunchy and walks with his feet facing slightly inward, is harder to peg. He's a longtime fixture of the Tenafly public school system, yet he does not appear to be a very learned man, especially when regurgitating his own brand of arcane wisdom. Whenever he sees a kid leaning back in his chair, Roznofsky walks up behind him (it's always a him) and says, "Keep slouching that way and you'll end up round-shouldered"—in this maddeningly mild "just trying to keep you from becoming a cripple" kind of way. If he spots a kid chewing on the eraser of a pencil, he'll sing, "Lotta *bacteria*..." and just let it hang there. The king of all Roznofsky-isms was his lesson on the multiplicative inverse.

"If anybody ever puts a gun to your head and asks you what the *reciprocal* of a given number is—not that it would ever happen, God forbid—but if it did, all you would have to do is put a one on top of the number or flip a fraction over."

Mr. Roznofsky doesn't like me much. One time, as he was reading a word problem having to do with a fictitious town called Vista Villa, I pointed out that in Spanish the "LL" sound is actually pronounced "yuh."

"Oh, is that right, Mr. Klein? It's actually pronounced how?"

"It's pronounced *yuh*, so it would be "vista *vee-ya*."

"Oh, *I* see. Vista *vee*-ya."

"Si, Mr. R. Muy bueno."

"Well, David," he said, lowering his voice in false earnestness, "mucho gracias for the Spanish lesson." He then rolled his eyes for the class to see and got a pretty decent laugh. I was not expecting this. I genuinely thought there was a chance he would be impressed with my studiousness and view it in the proper pedagogical light. If you were right about something, wasn't that the main thing?

Part of my problem is that, as Kleins, we've been primed for a certain level of righteous impudence. Early on, Mom told us that if a teacher refused to let us go to the bathroom, we were allowed to defy them if the need was genuine. I never did this, but from then on I was armed with the knowledge that you don't always have to listen to the teacher and that rules can be broken under certain circumstances. Maybe that kind of thinking led to "It's OK to correct the math teacher on his Spanish pronunciation."

Tommy Morgan hangs with the so-called cool crowd, the rule-breakers, so that becomes my de facto group. Some of these kids are familiar to me from Little League, the ones whose mothers bellowed at them from the stands in coarse Jersey accents, but sharing classroom space with this bunch is something new. In our first Spanish class, a group of them stand in the back and crack wise as the teacher assigns them Spanish names and chuckle as she prompts us through the Spanish alphabet. The Spanish name for the letter Y—*y griega*—strikes them as especially funny. They do scare me a little, but for better or worse, this is my crowd and these are my people.

On a Friday or Saturday night, when no one's parents are gone long enough to allow for a house party, we head to the railroad tracks, to the Rum Bum, so named because the kids who'd first discovered it had gotten shitfaced there on Bacardi rum. No more than a recessed rectangular space hidden from view by shrubs and bushes that run along the fence proper, it barely qualifies as a place.

A big brother, or an older kid whose experiments in facial hair have progressed to the point where he can pass for eighteen, buys us beer, and down the tracks, toting brown-bagged six-packs we go. At the appointed spot, we crouch down and maneuver through the tangle of shrub to sit in a cramped semicircle in our jean jackets and waffle-stompers, beyond the prying eyes of parents and the cops.

The Rum Bum gang ranges from half a dozen to twenty kids in their early teens, with names like Ricky and Ronny and Kenny and Donny. Most are of Irish or Italian descent and live nearby, on the fabled other side of the tracks. They are proudly belligerent kids whose older brothers taught them how to smoke, spit, and swear.

The gang's most distinctive aspect is a self-invented argot marked by a sarcastic intonation at the end of an utterance, followed by "though" or "though-mabe."

"Such a good haircut, though?"

The language thrives on the creative reuse of words like "though," "well," "maybe," and "might," combined with that special intonation. "Hee *well*, though" is the all-purpose "Yeah, *right*."

Like jazz, the lingo is infinitely customizable according to the taste and sensibility of the practitioner. "Pop ove?" is Scotty Moo's way of inviting you to *pop over* and misbehave at his house while Mrs. Moo is at work. "Butt 'n' best?" is Nick "Zombo" Zirinsky's way of saying, "Gee, this cigarette tastes good." Donny Flaves is really into "might." ("I *might* go out with her. Uh, no way, though?") Sometimes, discourse morphs into straight-up caveman talk. I've seen arguments consisting of little more than:

"Yee!"

"Nee!"

"Yee!"

"Nee!"

"Spare" is big because people are constantly bumming cigarettes ("Spare bub, though mabe?") But "spare" has become a sort of all-purpose modifier, pitched somewhere between adjective and adverb, like linguistic umami. The gang's most clever term has to be its designation for nerds, who are known as ghouls. Thus, "Spare ghoul, though mabe?" means "Check out the nerd" in Tenafly lingo.

I am not a natural among a tough crowd, and being friends with Tommy doesn't always save me from getting pushed around or toyed with. Like the night Billy Ratty turned me on to an oregano joint, or when I wouldn't trade

Prune Merrifield a Heineken for a Bud and he chased me all the way into town, past the diner and around the Dairy Queen, twice. On the third revolution he gave up, huffing and puffing. He is called Prune, after all. But thanks to my well documented lack of self-control, hand-to-hand combat eventually finds me.

Soccer is the one thing I do with quantifiable panache, so when we play the game in gym class, I have a little swagger. In the midst of a close two-against-two game, I had given an order to my partner, Nicky Ribenga: Stay back and play defense. In spite of my directive, he had bounded upfield after my free kick, giving the other guys an uncontested view of our goal.

"Ribenga! What'd I just tell you, man? That's where you were supposed to be playing!"

He gave me a disgusted look and walked away, and that seemed to be the end of it. A second later, Mr. Bright blew his whistle to signal the end of the period.

Returning to my locker after lunch, I discovered a neatly folded note stuffed into one of the little vents in the door. I snatched it eagerly. Maybe it was a love letter; evidently people had been getting them. But instead of the giddy girl-penmanship I was hoping for—i's dotted with circles and lots of underlined words—this was typewritten.

Dear David: **11/6/75**
This is to inform you that I am going to kick the living shit out of you. You are a fagit and a doosh and don't think I won't. You will meet me at the monument right after school today, and be ready to get what's coming. And don't think about backing out fagit because everybody's gonna be there.
--HUMAN

Human. That's the clincher. Of all the guys to piss off, I find one with a nom de guerre. News of my imminent slaughter makes the rounds quickly. My ass is grass. They all but announce it over the P.A.

"Look, you started it, and now he's pissed," says Tommy. "You have to go through with it. You have to show up."

"You mean I have to show up and get my head kicked in."

"Listen," Tommy says. "Ribenga acts pretty tough, but hell, I've never seen him fight. He may not be that tough at all."

"Well, if he fights anything like the way he plays soccer, I think I stand a chance. Then again, he's a schizo. What the fuck should I do?"

"Here's what you do. Surprise the shit out of him. Land the first punch and put him on the defensive. Just walk right out there and slug him."

"You mean, just kind of... walk over to him," I say, moving menacingly toward Tommy, "just go right up and... BAM!" I throw a clumsy right at Tommy's surprised face, catching myself just before I make contact. "Like that?" I say, grinning.

"Just like that, he says. "Ha, we might have to start calling you Killer Klein."

"Oh, eat the load," I say, employing a popular Tenafly insult.

"Look, don't sweat it too much, man. Just do like I say. Me and Tony'll be at your locker. All right? We'll walk out with you."

The Monument (officially named for Theodore Roosevelt) is a semi-circular limestone structure located about two hundred yards from the school. Heavily shrouded by trees, it's the perfect place to smoke pot and stage fights and do other things the hero of San Juan Hill would disapprove of. Even though the police station is within sight, you feel safe at the Monument because you can see anyone coming from a long way off.

Flanked by Tommy and Tony, I make my way on wobbly knees, my throat constricting as if my top button is fastened too tightly, as the chorus of a current radio hit taunts me with its indelible hook: "*You, you've blown it all sky-high / Without a reason why / You've blown it all sky-hiiiiigh...*"

It's early autumn, and gold and red predominate in the surrounding oaks. The ground is awash with layers of fallen leaves. Ribenga watches me as I approach, along with about fifty kids who have turned out for today's grudge match. Without breaking stride, even hurrying my pace somewhat, I walk right up to him, thrust out a fist, and land a glancing blow on the side of his head. He topples backward, and I jump on him. We wrestle—me holding him down and fending off punches, hoping someone will break it up while I'm still on top, him flailing around trying to lift his head above leaf level and get in a good swing. The spectators start tossing and kicking piles of leaves on top of us until the sharp squawk of a police radio short-circuits the pandemonium. The whooping subsides and kids begin picking leaves from their hair and clothes as Officer Gerard Fallon appraises the situation. In the lore of the local hoodlums, Fallon isn't as bad as some of the Tenafly cops. Officer Branchini, for example, is known as a real ball-breaker. Ribenga, his orange Quisp T-shirt torn at the collar, is on his feet and panting, his dark eyes glinting crazily. Officer Fallon levels a steely gaze at the two of us and says only this: "Boys, fighting never solved anything, but if you must do it, don't do it here."

He heads back toward the police station, and the crowd disperses. Tommy lumbers up to me and claps me around the shoulder.

"Ey, champ! What'd I tell ya?" he roars.

"I didn't do bad, eh? I mean, I fuckin' nailed his ass. Right?"

The next day, another note is waiting for me at my locker:

Dear Fuck: **11/7/75**
I hope I did not hurt you because that was no fight. On the 19th I will kick the living shit out of you. Thank you for warming me up yesterday for the fight . . .
--HUMAN

PS: DON'T SHOW ANY ONE THIS BECAUSE I MIGHT DO IT IN THE MORNING, LUNCH AT YOUR LOCKER, OR THE SECOND YOU STEP OUT OF THE SHITTEN SCHOOL, OR THE SECOND YOU TOUCH THE BRIGE . . .

Happily, in the two weeks leading up to our planned second bout, cooler heads prevail. The rematch never takes place, Nicky retires the Human moniker, and life returns to relatively normal at the shitten school. But the threat of bodily harm remains. One day at Angela's, the pizza joint on Tenafly's main drag, Tony D and I are at a table in back with slices and sodas. In come two slice-holding toughs, Jerry and Jack, who seat themselves right behind me. At some point Jerry lights a cigarette and jabs the tip into my upper arm. He and Jack share a hearty laugh when I jump. I also have a knack for making life difficult for myself without any assistance.

I'd been hearing a lot about the fabled Jim Dandy, a deluxe banana split that comes with six scoops of ice cream. One night, to assuage a dire case of the munchies, six of us crowd into a booth at Friendly's, ready to do our worst. This is my first Jimmy D, and I haven't anticipated the detailed scoop-selecting process that accompanies ordering one. Bulldog goes first, and then Donny Flaves, and it's all "double chocolate" and "rocky road" and "triple fudge swirl"—rugged, macho flavors.

First out of my mouth is Dutch Apple, that much I remember. Pretty sure blueberry comes next, followed by something else pastel colored. Midway through ordering Tenafly's most effeminate ice cream sundae, my error is pointed out to me.

"Dutch *apple*? What are you, some kinda fuckin' tutti-frutti, Klein?" barks Frank Gianfranco, who smokes pot with his dad and already has a criminal record and never leaves home without his trusty metal pipe packed with resin-coated weed in the middle chamber. The stuff makes you cough like crazy, and naturally gets you extra wasted once you've finished hacking.

"Fuckin' feggit," mutters Bulldog, scowling even harder than usual.

"So fruity, though?" opines Vinny Sebasco.

My next three scoops are all virile as hell—bourbon, pine tar, gravel—but the damage is done.

I spend much of my tenure among these hoods attempting to keep my inner Dutch apple in check—sometimes with success. Before school one day, a group of us are at the Monument, insulting the intelligence of a local Little League ump named Stuey Delaportis, and I catch myself just before I chime in with a classic Mom-ism. I'm about to say, "He's no mental giant," but instead I come out with, "He's no mental genius," which has a convincing dumbness to it. No one blinks an eye. But fortifying a tenuous social foothold can be a fraught endeavor. The night Mom goes out to cover a council meeting for the *North Jersey Suburbanite* and I invite the gang over to smoke some reefer being a case in point.

It was balmy for February, yet nobody was game for sitting on the softly angled section of roof right outside my bedroom window. I had *Yesterdays* playing, a compilation of Yes tracks from the band's first few albums that were not widely available stateside, and everybody was really into it. Tommy convinced me it would be alright if we just took turns sitting on the windowsill, leaning outside and blowing the smoke out into nature and shit. It was an imperfect system.

Suddenly there's some kind of commotion at the other end of the room—I look over and Tommy's leaning against my bedroom door, struggling to keep it shut and fiercely whispering that *my mother* is on the other side and wants in.

Her work at Tenafly Women for Peace has led Mom back into journalism. Now she's covering local politics for the regional weekly newspaper and even winning some awards for her work. But she's never been a great calendar keeper, and she must have missed the cancellation of the local city council meeting in honor of George Washington's birthday. So Mom forces her way inside and is livid at having her entry blocked. Then—haha—she notices the odor. Naively, I imagine she might not know what she's smelling.

Perhaps she merely detects a novel presence in the air, and just can't place it?

"I was, uh, polishing my guitar," I meekly assert over the fading thunder of my pals' work boots.

Let's just say Mom does not buy the cannabis-scented guitar polish gambit.

Out on the streets of Tenafly, the gang runs into Jonny as he's returning home. When they tell him what happened, he laughs and laughs. Jonny, it should be said, is into way worse. But where I am the bumbling accomplice, he's the master criminal who evades capture through stealth and cunning and deep reserves of nerve. I first picked up on this aspect of my brother at the New Englander, a cozy no-frills restaurant in nearby Teaneck, where all five Kleins, plus Grandma and Grandpa, can easily fit into a single booth. There's a little placard at the cash register in front, showing a rotund man in a derby spearing a morsel of food—caption: "I'LL START MY DIET TOMORROW."

Dad hates fish and his parents in almost equal measure. This is one of the few things I know for certain about Dad. He says his parents love money and showing off, they don't read, and they prattle on about inconsequential people and things. He makes sure we all know this as a kind of forewarning not to become the kind of people our grandparents are. As for the seafood antipathy—there is no precipitating incident I know of, no forced feeding of spoiled gefilte fish that set him off, although it should be mentioned that Dad's dad is an avid fisherman. Bottom line: we're a fish-rejecting household until the night at the New Englander when Jonny orders the fried shrimp platter.

What can Dad do? We have no explicit anti-fish policy; it's just understood that you order a burger or something. With this one iconoclastic act, Jonny upsets the established order, and he's just getting warmed up. For it seemed to me that Jonny started taking bass lessons from my guitar teacher in a similar spirit of bold individualism.

I couldn't imagine why anyone would want to do anything besides play guitar, sing, or play drums. But then, my grasp on the function of the bass was as tenuous as my knowledge of shellfish. In my defense, bass was hard to detect on an AM radio or through a cheap stereo, and it was often kept low in the mix under the best of conditions. One day Jonny put on "Baby You're a Rich Man" and had me listen to what Paul McCartney was doing, and I started to see a new dimension. Jonny had already pondered that dimension extensively; he'd listened hard to Paul's ornately structured bass lines and to Bill Wyman's malevolent rumble. He'd discerned that it took timing and fluidity and feel to make it come out right. Even the most damnably simple bass line had to be felt, not just played. Jonny was a better player after three bass lessons than I was after a year on the guitar. Then again, he was always two steps ahead, and since I was determined to keep up with him, we became co-conspirators. It began with milking our glasses.

One morning, Mom asked us if we'd drunk our milk, and we said that we had. Both of us hated milk, except on cereal, but Mom insisted that we drain a glass at breakfast. Noting that our glasses in the sink were untouched by bovine secretions, she gave us a good yelling-at. I would have straightened up and flown right, but Jonny had a workaround. From then on, each of us would simply pour ourselves a glass of milk in the morning and dump the contents down the drain when no one was looking. Voilà: glasses milked, bottle suitably emptied, house rules complied with. Stealth and cunning!

By the time pot entered the scene, my brother and I were already accomplished sneaks. We'd slip off to the woods near the Cotswold to share a joint, or take a late-night dog walk past the Mount Carmel Cemetery, remembering to grab a "breathie" beforehand to keep from smelling herbaceous when we got back. I took my first cigarette puffs with Tommy Morgan, and by junior high, Jonny and I usually kept a pack stashed. My father being a cancer doctor and vocally anti-smoking was something I wrestled with, but for every time I considered what the smoke was doing to my lungs, I would recall a treasured passage from *Circus Magazine*'s interview with Chris Squire of Yes.

"As they say, a man with a cigarette is never alone."

Chapter 12

The Rover

People who lived through the JFK assassination never forget where they were when they heard the news. I'm the same way about the Hindenburg disaster. I was at the Wilsons' house, watching an ad for a Time-Life record compilation on their fancy wall-mounted TV. The spot featured a medley of iconic moments from the early-to-mid-twentieth century, among them FDR's "a date which will live in infamy," Edward VII's abdication speech, and announcer Herb Morrison's feverish, Steve Reich-ian play-by-play of the Hindenburg conflagration, ending with "Oh, the *humanity.*" That incendiary clip became my personal Zapruder film, to ponder, analyze, and confront. The unreal texture of the giant ship's corrugated skin, the tiny people in the foreground, flung and fleeing from the collapsing behemoth—it scared me to death every time, but I couldn't look away.

Zeppelins, dirigibles, and blimps, in their semi-solid, gelatinous appearance and seeming defiance of natural laws, transfixed me. On most classroom shelves you would find bulky sets of musty, barely thumbed-through encyclopedias—World Book, Grolier's New Book of Knowledge, the occasional Funk & Wagnall's. I sought these out, the more out-of-date the better. You learned to always go for the "A" volume rather than "Z," because when you reach "Zeppelin" you're told to "See: Airship."

Visually, the Hindenburg disaster was a bit like 9/11—an enormous fireball exploding against a vast backdrop of sky, with countless angles and perspectives recorded. The most common vantage was the view that graced the cover of *Led Zeppelin I*, with the ship's nose facing diagonally upward at ten o'clock, torrents of flame ascendant on her lower end just seconds away from consuming the rest of her. But sometimes you'd be rewarded with images from a moment or two later, the flames extending from nose to tail, or the craft grounded and crumpled like a cracked sausage. Once I saw Zeppelin's album covers, I knew the band's sound would be as vast and scarifying as the images I'd been obsessing over.

In my major fantasy of this era, I'm trudging up Westervelt Avenue, guitar case in hand. A limo pulls up and out pops Jimmy Page. Seems the band's equipment van has been nicked, and Pagey needs an electric guitar on the quick. In a dream instant, I offer him mine. He takes it out of the case, unfurls the "Ten Years Gone" lick, and reckons it's a pretty damn sweet guitar.

"Take it," I say.

"Yeah?" A sly grin forming around his cigarette. "You sure?"

"Yeah, man. I—I can call you 'man,' right?"

"Sure you can."

"All right. Take it, man. It's yours."

And he does. There's no offer for me to hop in the limo and come hang backstage with the groupies or anything. My dream was merely that Jimmy Page would relieve me of my guitar, doubts and all.

I bought *Physical Graffiti* with bar mitzvah money. Not especially appropriate, given Robert Plant's sixteen or so high-pitched repetitions of "Oh my *JEE-sus!*" in "In My Time of Dying." Yet Led Zeppelin's sixth studio album became an instant article of faith for me, whereas my bar mitzvah, a huge deal at the time, faded quickly from memory.

Except for the bits about leprosy.

Your haftorah portion, which you chant at your bar mitzvah, is a function of the Hebrew calendar and thus a total crapshoot. You might get lucky and nab an epic Good Book yarn, or you could draw the short straw and get Leviticus 13.3, which reads like a page from an ancient dermatology treatise. I used to thumb through Dad's big green *Pediatrics* textbook and gawk at the photos of kids with rickets and scurvy and other awful afflictions, always with that creepy black rectangle over their eyes. My haftorah portion could have passed for the words that appeared alongside those visuals, as written by a diagnostician with a certain biblical zeal:

> "And the priest shall look on the plague in the skin of the flesh: and if hair in the plague be turned white, and the appearance of the plague be deeper than the skin of his flesh, it is the plague of leprosy; and the priest shall look on him, and pronounce him unclean."

Not exactly a Bible classic.

Sure, I had a little money left over, but the true legacy of my bar mitzvah was *Physical Graffiti*. The draw began with the much labored-over album sleeve. Through the windows of an East Village tenement building, you peered at select images from the modern American cultural tapestry: the Charles Atlas ad, a sepia Lee Harvey Oswald, the G-force test pilot with concave cheeks, Dorothy waking up in Kansas. You could change the configuration depending on which of the inner-sleeve sides faced out, so it had an interactive element. Listed in pseudo ransom-note fashion, even the song names (**Kash***mir*) invited contemplation.

Nothing against "Custard Pie"—sort of a Zeppelin-ized Bo Diddley thing about this really hot chick who works in a bakery, or at least reminds one of a baked good if viewed at the right angle, which is a perfectly banging opener—but track 2, "The Rover," took me to the deep and profound place. Jimmy Page's solo was like a speech or a sermon, so stirring as to summon a weirdly intimate, quasi-religious sense of connection to the music and the rest of the world.

I privately termed Jimmy's "Rover" solo "the peace lead," although I would never admit it. Not even to Tommy, certainly not to your average Zeppelin fan. Though Jimmy and Robert were rail-skinny and prettily handsome, the group's fanbase consisted of the most macho and menacing of my peers: guys with big heads, early facial hair, and aggressive testosterone levels. Jonny and I called them "pubers." As far as the crowd that gathered at the Monument to smoke a few bowls and a few 'Boros before school was concerned, Zeppelin was king. Black Sabbath, the other dark British lords of our nights, were their only competition.

In my other major fantasy of the era, Mr. Roznofsky is saying how one year a kid named Kippy Daily slouched so much that he developed an advanced case of scoliosis and had to be committed to an iron lung following a series of painful experimental treatments, when a subatomic rumbling stops him in mid-spiel. The wall holding the blackboard begins to crumble, and through it, on some kind of combination stage/battering ram, comes Led Zeppelin, Marshall amps stacked high, volume deafening—in a revolutionary amalgam of rock 'n' roll and demolition.

Mr. Roznofsky wets his pants and flees. School is canceled. And a massive, wholly inexplicable concert that no one will ever forget, follows.

There was no better feeling than connecting with Mom and Dad on a song. Catching something good on the radio at the right moment, say, Johnny Cash's

"A Boy Named Sue" in the middle of an interminable car trip, could pull us out of our circumstances and unite us like nothing else. Mom would turn the volume up and we would listen as one. If we were close to home and Hurricane Smith's "Oh Babe, What Would You Say" was playing, we'd wait in the driveway until it ended, Mom keeping time on the steering wheel. Listening in Dad's den, she would slap rhythm on her thigh and her foot would get involved. Dad would start nodding along, or better yet, conducting. He'd pronounce it "a good cut," and all of us would be in harmony.

Jonny and I were always on the lookout for songs they would like. The problem was, if the folks didn't like the song you loved, they were blunt about it. Mom and Dad were not of the "It's not my taste, but what do *you* like about it?" school of thought. In fact, they had several unshakeable beliefs about pop music, mostly of the prohibitive sort:

Thou shalt sing lyrics clearly.

Thou shalt not be repetitive.

Thou shalt not sing in a fluty soprano.

Thou shalt not fade out (except "I Am the Walrus").

Bob Dylan has no business singing.

In retrospect, imagining I could persuade Dad to like my favorite band was an act of sheer blind optimism. Oh, I was crafty, starting him off with "Bron Yr Aur," the brief, bewitching, unpronounceable instrumental on Side 3 of *Physical Graffiti*. But having established in Dad a provisional acceptance of Acoustic Jimmy Page, I moved on to Rock God Jimmy Page, which proved a bridge too far.

Tacked up in my bedroom was an extra-large poster I'd scored in town at Good Vibrations—Jimmy with his cherry red Gibson double-neck EDS-1275, aka the coolest man-made object in the universe. With his curtain of hair framing a face in full guitar rictus, Page plays a chord on the twelve-string neck while hoisting the magnificent apparatus heavenward like a double-bladed Excalibur. I found the image captivating, almost Hindenburg-like in its immediacy. When Dad came home from work one day, I brought him up to my room to show him the poster, and his response was as harsh as a one-star review in the *Times*:

Dad: [arms folded, eyes narrowing, brow crease forming]
Long pause
"He looks...androgynous."

I knew this wasn't a compliment. Jonny later explained that "androgynous" meant someone who looked like both sexes and, at no extra charge, advised me that "epicene" meant someone who looked like neither. Well, if Dad didn't like the *look* of Page, he sure wasn't going to respond well to the man's over-powering sound. I should have known. One time in the car I turned up "Doo Doo Doo Doo (Heartbreaker)" by the Stones, and he was so appalled that I felt something close to shame for having distressed him so.

To be fair, Dad didn't discriminate. When a nurse at his medical practice made the mistake of sharing with him the Moody Blues record *Days of Future Passed,* in the belief that a classical music aficionado like Dad would appreci-ate hearing the London Symphony Orchestra in a progressive rock setting, he returned the record to her along with a strongly worded critique. Even as kids, we knew that Mr. Wilson across the street was suspect because he listened to Mantovani. Dad had a name for easy listening: "bird music." It was the lowest of the low, the toilet water of popular culture. He'd lose respect for you if he found out you listened to bird music. Music in the wrong hands, Dad seemed to suggest, could be so terrible that the proper response was revulsion and contempt—or at least a turned-up nose. But I loved some of that terrible music without reservation. Knowing his feelings on the issue, I have to admit, I loved it a little bit more. But as much as I resented Dad's intransigence, I emulated him in my own way. Like the time my sister said her favorite band was the Ozark Mountain Daredevils.

"But you only know one song by them. How could they be your favorite?"

"They just are."

"Name one other Ozark Mountain Daredevils song besides 'Jackie Blue.'"

"They're still my favorite group."

"That's impossible. You have to know more than one song for the band to be your favorite. Your favorite group is probably the Beatles."

These days they call it mansplaining.

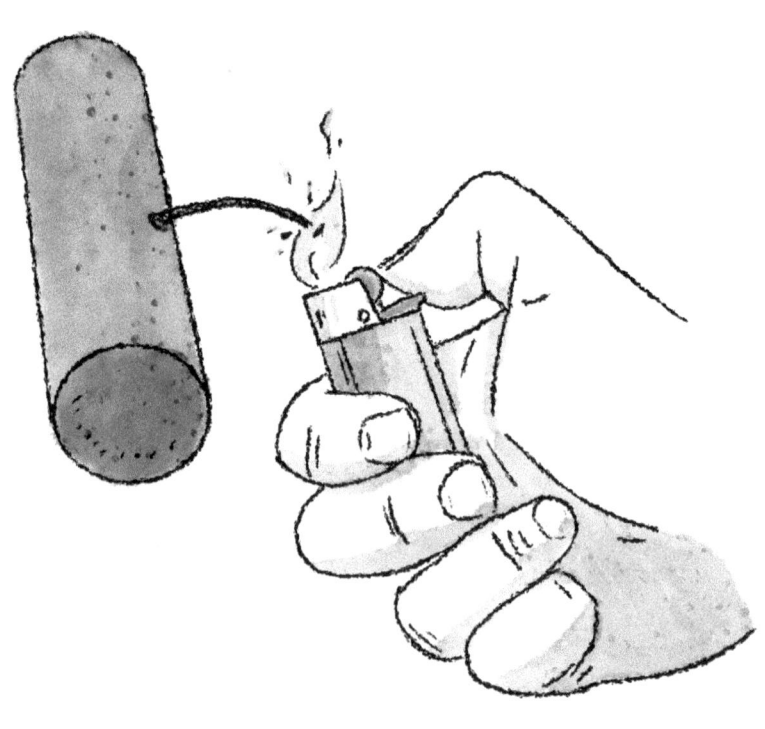

Chapter 13

An Evening with Led Zeppelin

Zeppelin's five nights at the Garden sell out quickly, but Tommy knows a guy. We'll be in the first promenade overlooking stage left—way better than the nosebleed seats we had for Frampton but nothing like Aerosmith-Nugent, where we were in the eighth row. Then again, Zeppelin is a much bigger deal.

In preparation, I score a dimebag from Bulldog and roll up a bunch of joints the night before (in the bathroom with the door locked) and place them in a sandwich bag along with a Bic lighter. I'll shove this contraband down my balls at an appropriate moment before reaching the ticket taker at the Garden. (That's how we say it: *"Ah, just shove it down your balls. They never look there."*)

The occasion demands that I dress defensively. Along with my beloved Zep T-shirt (light blue with an iron-on depicting Page and Plant under stage lights) and tight Levi's with incipient knee holes, I opt for waffle stompers instead of sneakers because they're rugged and make me look a little taller. And despite the warm June temperature I wear a dark blue hoodie because the forecast calls for fireworks. A few had gone off at Aerosmith-Nugent, but the aerial combat will be heavier tonight, and the possibility of a cherry bomb or an ash can, tossed from the cheap seats and landing in my now considerable mop of hair—which refuses to grow down, only out to the side—isn't mere paranoia. Maybe I'm a little sensitive about the possibility of random injury since the Eye Incident, which is how Tommy and I now refer to it.

Mrs. Morgan has the first leg of our nefarious carpool. Tommy rides shot-gun with Darrell, a family friend, in the ample middle of Betty's brown Buick Riviera. Darrell's father will pick us up after the show, which is a good thing. He has a lenient attitude toward delinquency, his older son being a pioneer in that area, and we'll be more than a little dazed and confused.

I'm in the backseat between Tony D and Frank Gianfranco. Frank wears a faded denim jacket that looks like it's been around and seen some shit. He isn't that big, but when he squints at you he looks a little deranged. Frank has played the bully with me a few times, so it's weird being next to him in the car, politely ignoring each other.

On our way up Churchill, the East Hill's main artery, as we're passing the lengthy unfolding of the Hararis' home—rumored to be among the Hill's most opulent—I chance to recall a discussion with my parents on the subject of "conspicuous consumption." And I just can't stop myself.

"The Hararis have *a bowling alley* in their basement," I say, in a derisive tone. "That is so ridiculous. What person needs to have their own bowling alley?"

Frank gives me a look like I've just ordered a double scoop of passionfruit sorbet topped with rainbow sprinkles. The Riviera slows, and the eyes of Mrs. Morgan find mine in the rearview.

"Now, David," she says, "what makes you so sure of that?"

Expecting to hear an assent from up front, having just issued a bona fide grown-up opinion, and figuring that most adults thought along similar lines, I'm fairly shocked at her response.

"How do *you* know the Hararis don't need a bowling alley in their base-ment?"

"Well, I mean—"

"Now, David, *you* don't know that. Mr. Harari is a very important man. Do you think he would live in such a magnificent home if he weren't an important man?"

The old tie-down. "Uh, no…"

"So, when a man like Mr. *Harari* entertains important guests, wouldn't you agree he has to entertain them in the manner they are accustomed to?"

Sigh. "Yes."

"And that means in high style," she says, flashing me a satisfied grin.

At which point I just close my eyes and think of Zeppelin.

Dropped off, our plastic-wrapped contraband properly shoved to balls-ad-jacency, we enter the Garden and join the tribes for "An Evening with Led Zeppelin." Beer is flowing from the concessions, and IDs are not being checked.

Flask-shaped bottles that once held Southern Comfort litter the men's room, which I'm relieved to get in and out of without any hassle from the scary-looking, jean-vest-wearing dudes getting absolutely annihilated in there instead of at their almost entirely unpoliced seats, for reasons I can't quite fathom. The combined smoke of six thousand joints, eight hundred of them canoeing wildly, befogs the packed arena in an oppressive weather-system of acrid dank. As the lights go down, it already feels like a free-for-all.

At the storied Isle of Wight Festival in August 1970, Leonard Cohen addressed the gathered hundreds of thousands, saying, "Could each of you light a match so that you'll sparkle like fireflies each at your different heights? I would love to see those matches flare." In the ensuing years, things have gotten out of hand. Dave Marsh, writing in *Newsday* of the previous night's concert, wrote that Zeppelin's entrance was greeted by "an assault of fireworks that made the Garden seem like Da Nang." Tonight is no different. I pull the strings of my hoodie a little tighter around my head and let the vorpal sword of "The Song Remains the Same" crush through my inhibitions as clouds of commercial weed mix with flash powder and stage pyrotechnics and everybody gets increasingly, improbably high. Good evening, *Vietnam!*

And soon—o bliss! The evil bent-note intro to "The Rover." I'm transported, fully ready for my journey, and the peace lead, and… holy hell. It's all just a horrible tease. Right as Plant's vocal is supposed to come in, the band lurches to an abrupt halt and kicks into "Sick Again," the last song on *Graffiti* and that rarest of Zeppelin songs I don't love so much. This is not the only adjustment I have to make to the live Zep experience. Plant can't hit the high notes too well, which really changes things, and the band is a far messier beast than on record. Being seated above the first loge reduces these objects of fascination to flickering figures. Plant is closest to us and easy to spot in his iridescent pants, while Page—heroin-skinny in white—is tantalizingly out of reach at stage right. Still, they are here, right now, breathing the very same air.

A few songs in, we're treated to the first true fan favorite, "Over the Hills and Far Away," and it's sheer bliss, Zeppelin's knack for conjoining fairy-glade gentleness with ball-kicking oomph shining like a rough diamond. The song swells down like a dove making a gentle landing, and as applause rushes up to meet the fading semitones, I think to myself, We are at a Zeppelin concert, and they are playing for us, and I am so happy.

Right then, something sinister begins to take shape a few seats over. Frank Gianfranco is flicking his Bic, igniting the fuse of the large firework Tommy's holding—an M80 shooter. The shooter is like a Roman candle, except instead of sending a flame ball fifty feet in the air, it propels a lit M80, which explodes somewhere upon its descent. Some shoot out a pyrotechnic star (the technical term for what a Roman candle emits), others a cylindrical tube packed with explosive flash powder. Neither one do you want to land near you.

Tommy holds the thing aloft, away from his body, and the charge shoots off in a high sparkly arc. One second, two… then it explodes somewhere in the second loge. Even from our safe vantage, the noise it makes is huge, way bigger than the pops we've been hearing. A chorus of boos erupts from over the hills and far away, fanning out across the arena—and all for us. And then, in horrible slow motion, Robert Plant approaches the mic, trousers a-glint, to add his voice and moral authority to the Garden's collective condemnation.

Per *Newsday*, on the previous night Plant had genially urged the crowd to "cool the firecrackers—no more of those exploding things." You know, diplomatic. The *Times* confirmed that he "laudably and earnestly attempted to discourage the hurling of firecrackers and cherry bombs." Tonight, though, Percy is in no mood. He employs a far more direct tactic.

"Booooo…" intones Led Zeppelin's golden god. "*Booooooooooooo*," he repeats, a little longer this time, a bit more musically. Was there a third time? Probably. It was hard to tell over the crowd noise.

Being booed by the lead singer of your favorite band and thousands of hostile strangers at the world's most storied sports arena—you're never really prepared for it. I'm in full hate mode under my hoodie, both to drown out the boos and to disassociate myself from my dipshit friends, just in case a member of the Zep faithful is moved to mete out a little mob justice. Which would serve them right.

Our drawn-out moment of public ignominy ends with the grabby blues lick that opens "Since I've Been Loving You." From here, a lot of ground is covered: there's an acoustic set featuring John Paul Jones on *triple-neck* guitar; "Ten Years Gone," possibly the greatest Led Zeppelin song of them all; "Moby Dick," Bonzo's twenty-minute drum solo, and a thunderous "Kashmir" with trippy laser accompaniment. But the high-intensity joint smoking and swigs from Tony D's wineskin have obliterated any further details. I should probably thank Tommy for making the incoming encore impossible to forget.

The band returns to the stage for "Whole Lotta Love" and another level of pandemonium is reached. Besides "Stairway to Heaven," this is the ultimate Zeppelin song for the gathered minions. Everyone in the arena knows every inch of it, and the place is shaking and quaking. We're all on our feet joining in, and it's almost corny, like those moments in synagogue when everyone stands up reflexively and sings the Shema. This is when Tommy and Frank break out the B-game fireworks.

Now, sparklers may lack explosive power, but Tommy's are no tepid, store-bought numbers that Grandma twirls on the Fourth of July. These are super-charged, Carnival-approved Brazilian sparklers that you can read under. Garden security ascends quickly. Hell, Longstreet the blind detective would have spotted these mooks. Tommy and Frank are apprehended and hauled away, while the speedy Tony D, a local soccer legend, takes off with two in pursuit.

Darrell and I don't know each other well, so when the house lights come on after "Rock and Roll," we're mostly silent except to share some Visine, the eye whitener of choice among teenage stoners. We'll reek of smoke and be slow on the uptake, but at least our eyes won't be poached. ("So red, though mabe?")

We reach the appointed spot to meet our ride, and as Darrell starts to make an excuse for Tommy and Frank's lateness, his father waves him off. One of the cops interrogating the lads had ascertained who was responsible for picking them up and come out to the car to explain the delay.

Tony D shows up first, smirking at having evaded capture through sheer athletic prowess. Tommy and Frank arrive with long faces a while later, and we ride home in silence, ears ringing, synapses sputtering.

On the sixth and final night of Led Zeppelin's 1977 Madison Square Garden residency, Jimmy Page sustained minor injuries when an explosive tossed from the crowd exploded near his hand during "Stairway." After leaving the stage in disgust, he eventually returned for the encore and soldiered on through the rest of the tour.

I soldiered on, too, in my way. I never took Tommy aside and called him on his willingness to potentially injure people in the name of fun. He was surely guilty of, in Dave Marsh's apt description, "stupidity bordering on sadism," yet long after the Eye Incident, two eye surgeries, and our families becoming adversaries in a lawsuit,[8] I continued to be weirdly proud that we'd remained the best of friends. Tommy may have learned nothing from it, but somehow that didn't bring him down in my eyes.

---

8. Eventually it was settled out of court with a substantial but not enormous monetary award.

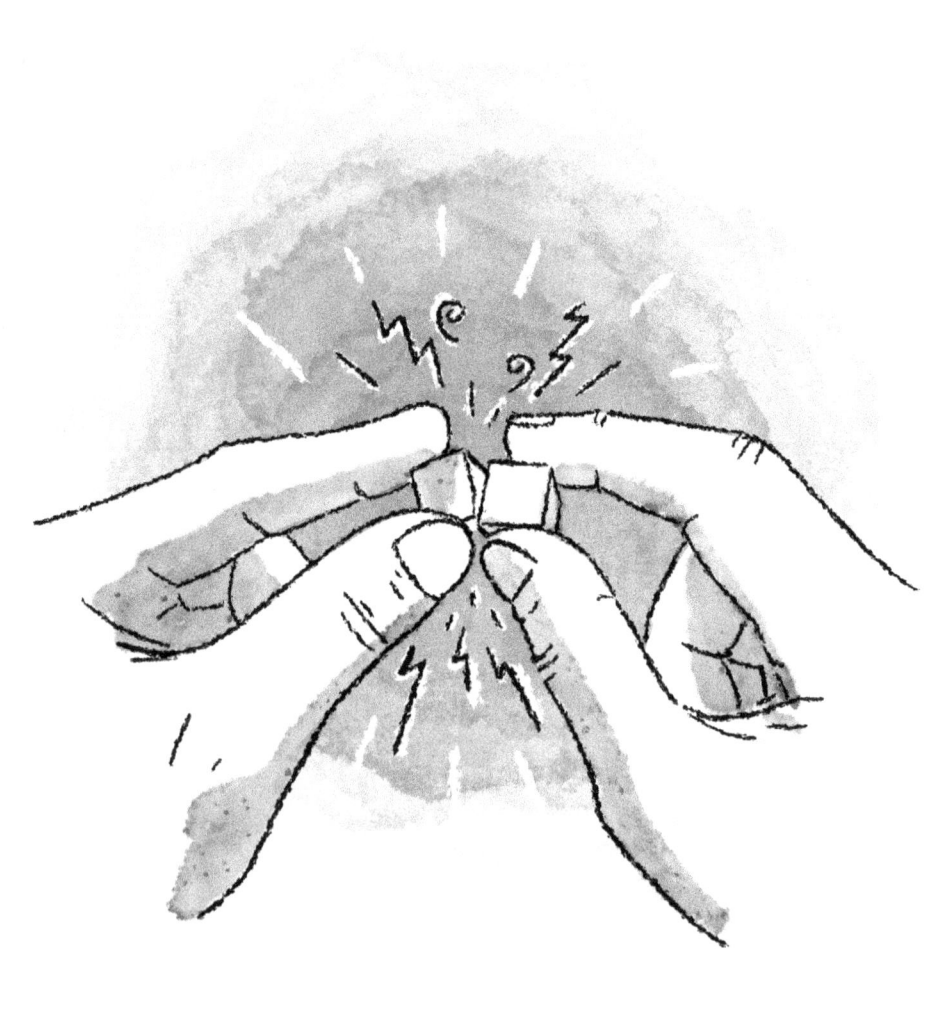

Chapter 14

I Fucked with the Angels

An improvement in David's attitude would be in order during the spring term. David tends to be unnecessarily defensive about receiving grades that do not correspond to what he feels he deserves. I wish David would become more interested in improving the quality of his work rather than just in raising his cumulative average.

—A.H. Black, ninth-grade English teacher,
semester II report card, February 1977

Thanks to the pot bust, my combativeness, and a general slide in school performance, my parents enroll me at Dwight Englewood, the same prep school where they sent my brother two years earlier. The differences are clear at once. Academic standards are higher, and many of my new classmates come from wealth, often old money. Their homes strike me as more impressive and refined than the gaudy offerings on Tenafly's East Hill, and everyone seems to know how to ski.

The wool-and-corduroy duds required by the school's dress code make me feel instantly more accountable. Being a ne'er-do-well is much easier when you're wearing a Zeppelin shirt. But the change in garb, the gothic architecture, and the greater degree of rigor doesn't turn me into a good student. It isn't that I lack an interest in books or learning. If a love of music was Dad's gift to me, my adoration of J.D. Salinger and the knowledge that certain authors are gods among men came to me through Mom, who speaks of Jerome David in the same hushed tones she reserves for Jess Stacy's piano solo at Carnegie Hall, Sinatra's phrasing, and Pauline Kael's movie reviews. One of Mom's few flights of fanciful behavior is ending a sentence with "buddy," a signature turn of phrase from the male half of *Franny and Zooey*. When I reach certain lines in *Nine Stories* that I know to be Mom's favorites—"a stunning and final girl," or "It isn't often we have visitors in our little chapel"—I think of her in a sort of moved way. Mr. Black gives me a B minus for my "report" on *The Catcher in the Rye*, and he's probably being generous. My mind just isn't on my work.

Spring is in the air, and girls are my obsession. So is Pink Floyd's *Animals*, and pot, and getting away with stuff. I've been befriended by some seniors—guys I look up to, who have reputations and sideburns and cars to drive, and don't behave like jerky kids anymore. Jed Resnick, a massive football player, takes me out riding in his 260Z during free periods, drinking Miller ponies, and once obligingly stepped out of the car to put the fear of death into a couple of douches who used to give me grief in Tenafly. I crack wise with lanky, blond-tressed Neil Flamm, famous for totaling his brand-new TR-7 and *allegedly* getting a blowjob while in traction. And not even by his girlfriend; it was just Neil's luck to be a popular, good-looking blond guy in the late 1970s.

I know I'll miss those long-haired, center-parted senior girls. Jean most of all, who makes outstanding charcoal sketches in art class and smokes Parliaments and takes me for rides in her powder blue Pontiac Le Mans. Jean's voice is soft and low, uninflected. If she were a folksinger, she would have no vibrato. One of her core beliefs is that high school is just a game and most of our classmates are game-players, and you just have to know how to play the game.

The last day of school is purely ceremonial. We walk around signing each other's yearbooks, a mutual impatience to just get the fuck *out* of this shithole uniting us spiritually, but I'm harboring a secret feeling that isn't the least bit cool—a sweet sadness that the end of a party has arrived just as things were getting good.

School lets out around noon, and though I know of festivities happening immediately afterward, my mood is subdued and introspective. I'd asked Jean to sign my yearbook, but she was just getting off on a hit of acid and couldn't deal. Letting gravity do the work, I amble in a kind of daze down Palisade Avenue, not fighting the hazy late-spring torpor, Fleetwood Mac's "Dreams" zephyring through my mind and mop of crazy hair. I catch a bus at Grand Avenue and take it home, where I strip off my school clothes and dither for hours until Jonny calls. He tells me a bunch of people are over at Kruger's house, and Chris Clendennon still has a few doses left.

I've been waiting a long time for my first LSD trip. Ever since Uncle Mike sent me the "Snappy Sammy Smoot Visits the Intergalactic World Brain" issue of Zap Comics, in which this naive but natty "bon vivant and man about town" takes acid and sees God. I imagined taking LSD would be like entering a cartoon and having profound insights. But I was seven, so it would have to wait—until high school anyway. Until now.

Jonny got there first, of course, and his vivid descriptions—of iron gray clouds that shape-shifted into enormous gongs that struck themselves in time to Eddie Harris and Les McCann's "Compared to What," of a book of Renaissance paintings that turned into a web of movies within movies—stoked my curiosity even more. The highest I've ever been up to this point was... extremely high. We took a bunch of cheap homegrown pot, heated it in a frying pan per the instructions Jonny found in a book, ground it into a dark powder, tossed it in honey, and gobbled it up—rendering us astoundingly next-dimension wasted for *Kentucky Fried Movie*. If those honey slides were base camp, I am now headed for the summit.

The wild card is Kruger.

One bright Saturday morning during the Nixon administration, I headed over to Tony D's to play soccer. I was there a lot because spending the day, or sometimes the night, at Tony's house was easy. His home was not fussily clean, just nice and lived in. They left the butter dish out on the oil-cloth-covered kitchen table at all times, and an unframed poster scotch-taped to the wall in the kitchen said, HE WHO IS NOT BUSY BEING BORN IS BUSY DYING. Nothing quite so flimsy and slapdash was ever allowed on the walls of 5 Sherwood. Tony's household vibe spoke to the variety of experience in our small town like nothing else. On a Saturday afternoon, when my father might be found at Willow Run, purchasing bags of dehydrated cow manure for his tomato plants, Tony's dad was still in his bathrobe, propped up in bed and watching *Hogan's Heroes*, his booming laugh audible behind the closed door of Tony's bedroom, even as we cranked "Death on Two Legs" by Queen.

Tony, the oldest of three dark-eyed boys with the same brown bowl cut, had an unyielding competitive streak. The two of us could never just shoot hoops; we had to play one-on-one, and he had to win. Usually he did, but when I squeaked out a one-point victory, he'd throw a fit. Tony would argue about anything and refused to concede on even the most idiotic point of contention. He insisted that the chorus of Redbone's "Come and Get Your Love," a wonderful and inescapable single from 1974, was actually *"Comin' gift of love."* Which made no sense—the phrase is clearly enunciated several dozen times—but Tony maintained that I was the one who was wrong, and that it *did* make sense. Redbone was singing about a gift of love that hadn't arrived yet—a coming gift of love. Eventually you just had to let him win. To be fair, there was a lot of this nonsense going around. Like the time Scotty Moo came into class, all excited about Chicago Anthony.

I said who the hell is Chicago Anthony?

Next day, Scotty Moo brings the record in. The cover's all black except for a blue-and-orange square in the middle, where some words are spelled out in lysergic, hard-to-read cursive. "Chicago" is pretty clear, and the word below it could pass for "Anthony," I guess. But there's another word between them that I can't make out. Finally, I snatch the album from him and tilt out the platter. And there, on the circular red Columbia label, is the answer.

"Look! It's not Chicago *Anthony*. It's Chicago... Transit... *Authority*," I say, with an emphasis on the wrong syllable.

"What? Get the hell outta here."

"Look, it says it right here."

"Pffft. No way, Klein, that's just like... the official name. They have to put it on the record or something. It's Chicago *Anthony*..."

Tony's not at home when I get to his place. I find him a few doors down Highwood, where he and a kid I know from Little League as Gary Krug are in the midst of a rough mini-football catch on the slope of Krug's well-tended front lawn.

"Oh yeah?" [chuck]

"*Yeah!*" [chuck]

"You like *that*?" [harder chuck]

"Not bad. How 'bout *this*?" [harder chuck]

At some point Tony prefaces his throw with a new riff: "Oh yeah?" he says. "I'm not a-scared o' you."

Like a shot, Kruger takes off across the lawn. Tony sprints away from him, whooping and doing crazy swerves around hedges, but Kruger is devilishly quick. He gets Tony around the waist, pulls him down hard onto the grass, and pins him under denim-covered knees. Kruger, barely breathing hard, leans his wedge-shaped face in close.

"What was that, Del Greco? Didn't quite catch that."

"I said... I'm not... *a-scared* o' you," Tony says, panting.

I don't want to watch.

"I'm *petrified!*" blurts Tony, quivering wide-eyed like a cartoon character for emphasis.

A moment of lethal silence passes before Kruger emits a short sibilance by way of a laugh. After a beat he moves off Tony, submission having been duly, if belatedly, rendered.

The impression lingers, and when I get to junior high I know to steer clear of him. But Tommy Morgan deals a little weed on the side, junior businessman that he is, and it doesn't escape the notice of Kruger, who's a little like the Mob now. He hears things. Some kid's dealing reefer, good stuff too, and right under his nose? Makes him look bad. He needs his cut.

One day, Tommy's twirling his locker combination and Kruger materializes phantom-like at his side. The hallway is empty. Tommy's praying someone walks by, but there's only that eerie institutional echo.

"I hear you got some good stuff," he says. "That right, Tom?"

Tommy pauses with one number to go.

"Why you stopping? You don't trust me?"

Tommy has no words.

"Tell you what," says Kruger. "You let me hold onto it—real low-key—and I'll make sure nothing happens to it."

This is sheer insanity. Tommy does not want to lose his investment, but neither does he want to fight Kruger, and he'll have to if he defies this intimidation.

"You wanna fuck with me, Morgan? Is that what you wanna do? Fuck with Gary Krug?"

"No man, I'm not trying to—"

"I fucked with the Angels, Tom. Hear what I'm saying?"

And so Tommy hands over the reefer, the deciding factor being Kruger's fantasy threat referencing the notorious Hells Angels motorcycle gang. Who knows, maybe this is God's way of talking him out of dealing drugs, which Tommy knows on some level is a fairly serious sin.

A week or so later, on the way to class, he spots Kruger headed his way in the crowded hallway. Tommy figures he has nothing to lose and plays his hand.

"Hey, man, thanks for holding on to that reef. But uh, I need it back now."

"Sorry, man," says Kruger with a shrug. "Stash got raided. Almost got busted myself. But I *can* get some for you, Tom. Good stuff, too."

Tommy takes him up on it, and Kruger sells him back his pot at an insider price.

When I get to my new high school, it turns out that Kruger has been sent there too. And since there are only so many social circles and parties to go to, he's unavoidable. I have trouble squaring his sociopathic coldness with the fact that his father is a medical man, an eminent surgeon at a major New York hospital, no less. That is, until I discover that having a doctor for a father isn't a stamp of anything in particular. All of my new partners in crime are doctors' sons. Theo—my first best pal, sort of the mayor who showed me around—his dad's a GP. Corey Kessler, who lives in a palatial homestead with a butler, a maid, and a whole extra house on the property, is the son of a prominent thoracic surgeon. Kenny Whitlock and Simon Vent, cranky frenemies from Tenafly, are the spawn of cranky gastroenterologists. Jean's father is a brain surgeon, and Katrina Burch's dad is a nephrology professor. Hell, Lance Lazaar, who got kicked out in the first trimester for pot and will eventually be expelled from the local public high school for taking a swing at the principal, is the son of an internist—a good one, too, according to my dad.

Then again, as doctors' sons with a fixation on the Grateful Dead, Kruger and I aren't so far apart. Both of us accept the mythos of the band's concerts, that the songs they choose to play, the uniqueness of each rendering, and a certain X factor make each concert a potentially blessed event. Both of us yearn to be at Grateful Dead shows with a baroque set list and a heavy, heavy weirdness factor. I'll always be wary of him, but the circle is wide if you want to party with the big boys.

When I show up, a half dozen cars line the circular driveway outside Kruger's house, including Neil Flamm's replacement TR-7, Chris Clendennon's beat-up Opel, with its dancing bear bumper sticker and books piled high in the rear, and Kenny Whitlock's green muscle wagon, a 1970 Buick Estate foolishly equipped with a pair of B.F. Goodrich fifteen-inch-diameter rear tires. What a dope. Having blown all his savings on the mag wheels, which do nothing at all, Kenny's stuck with the crappiest standard-issue AM radio on the market. Still, whenever a not-terrible song comes on over the tiny speakers, Bob Seger or Steve Miller, say, Kenny reaches for the tone dial and makes minute adjustments, as if that makes a damn bit of difference.

After a tentative knock draws no response, I step inside. Chris and Kruger are exchanging words in front of a vast oil painting of Mrs. Krug clad in fox-hunting gear. Chris is into Kerouac and the Beats and Mayan gods, while Kruger despises reading, school, and pussies, roughly in that order, yet he and Chris are on good terms because Chris's supply of clean liquid LSD necessitates a coalescence.

Chris's source is his brother, Joe, who's in his mid-twenties yet part of an extended social circle that emanates outward from Chris's clique of senior-year stoners to include freshman upstarts like me. Joe Clendennon has a strong Jerry Garcia vibe: the charismatic beard, the corona of dark hair, and behind wire-frame glasses, his eyes have the twinkle. In my mind, Joe embodies the best elements of Captain Trips, Sgt. Pepper, and the Cheshire Cat. Recounting a particular rendition of "Stella Blue" at a particular Grateful Dead show or an episode involving heavy intake of psychedelics, his sentences trail off into silence, leaving only his arched, cosmic Groucho Marx eyebrows to communicate what mere words cannot say.

Kruger wears his straight strawberry blond hair in a center-parted pageboy style and carries a plastic styling comb in his back pocket. He wears a tight T-shirt emblazoned DEADHEADS & COWBOYS, showing an image of Ron "Pig-pen" McKernan, the Dead's tragic founding member. It emphasizes Kruger's sinewy build.

"That was some fucked up shit right *there*, pal," Kruger's telling Chris. "The fuckers played 'Sugaree' for *twenty fucking minutes*, man. I shit you not, Chris man. I shit you *not*. Now let me ask you this, have you ever seen the Grateful Dead play 'Sugaree' for 20 minutes?"

"Can't say that I have," says Chris, raising his eyebrows and giving him a flash of the familial cosmic Groucho behind horn-rimmed glasses.

"Jerome John Garcia must've been on some *heavy* LSD-25 that night," Kruger says. "Some of that good, good, *good* stuff. And *while* we're on that subject," he adds, grinning. "*Speaking* of which. In *reference* to . . . "

"Huh?"

"Some more of those cubes, pal."

"Ah, of course! Oh, but what happened to the—"

"That Visine bottle? Gone, man. Gone! *And nothin's gonna bring 'em back!* Yes, sir, got down to the last few drops last night, so I set my alarm for five a.m., squeezed the last of that shit into my eyes, took a Valium, and woke up trippin' my nuts off."

"No shit," says Chris, sounding genuinely taken aback. Then, bowing slightly, he reaches into his front pocket and retrieves a baggie.

"*Grati*," Kruger says.

The previous summer, Kruger's parents sent him to some kind of Outward Bound-style wilderness program for troubled teens, and he'd returned with this faux-Italian shtick and calling everyone "pal."

Chris responds dutifully with *prego*. This is my cue.

"Got one for me, Chris?"

"Well, well, *well*. Little *Klein*," he says, looking amused. "Et tu?" (Bro's friends like to call me Little Klein, which is redundant—Klein meaning "small" in German.)

"Et tu, Brute," I respond, nonsensically.

"Well in that case... " Chris pulls out a cube and hands it to me. "Happy trails, Little Klein. First one's on the house."

"Ooh, Daaavy's gonna take his first trip," says Kruger, followed by his mirthless laugh.

Unlike the time Ian Anderson offered me a chestnut, I do not munch this magical morsel immediately. I wrap the cube in a dollar bill, tuck it in my flannel shirt pocket behind a half-filled soft pack of Merits, and go see if I can sense any acid vibes happening.

Joe Clendennon talks about vibes a lot. He'll tell you about the vibes he got the other day that told him people were tripping somewhere nearby. He's just tooling along in his Austin-Healey and he starts to notice these little pings and phosphorescence emanating from just beyond a hilltop, and he just, like, knows. To hear Joe tell it, the psychedelic mind imbues trippers with the power of remote viewing—the ability to deduce things normally beyond sensory perception. It's almost as if ingesting these rarefied molecules gives you temporary super powers, which sometimes kick in long after the trip is over, like when you're just killing time on Route 17 and smoking a big fat doobie.

People are spread throughout Kruger's house, a few in every room, but I'm not getting any acid vibes, which is odd for a supposed acid party. And where the hell is my brother? Lately a touch of remoteness has crept into our public interactions. Privately, we still have our smoke-friendly dog walks followed by late-night listening sessions in Jonny's basement lair. We lean toward epics, like Pink Floyd's *Ummagumma* and Side 2 of Be Bop Deluxe's *Modern Music*. But he's starting to befriend people he deems heavy personages and no longer tolerates my adolescent goofiness and lack of social savvy when he's out with his *cool* friends.

At the far end of the main hallway is a sign on a door that reads:
NO TRESPASSING — VIOLATORS WILL BE SHOT — SURVIVORS WILL BE SHOT AGAIN.

Behind it is Kruger's cozy, wood-paneled teen crib, where two sets of bunk beds frame a central space dominated by a steamer trunk laden with smoking accoutrements and copies of *Rolling Stone* and *High Times*. Within easy reach is a pricy blue-lit Pioneer amp that powers a set of giant JBL speakers. Even when his folks are around, you imagine Kruger can do whatever the hell he wants in here, short of burning it down.

Kenny Whitlock and Simon Vent, known as Ventricle, are sprawled on the lower bunks with cigarettes and a joint going. Kenny's an odd duck, a would-be hard guy born into a family of starchy academics. His yearbook quote reads, "Only the good, good women get to drink with the boys."

"I left his dead ass *there* by the side of the road," says Ventricle. "My man Bobby Weir says it clearly."

"No fucking way," Kenny snaps. "Just listen. For once, could you just shut up and listen?"

He cues it up—the last line of the final verse of "Me and My Uncle," from the live Grateful Dead LP officially titled *Grateful Dead* but known to devout Deadheads as "Skull Fuck." But at the operative moment, Kenny can't help from emphasizing his point.

"Now how'm I supposed t' fuckin' hear it with you fuckin' *singing* over it?" moans Ventricle. Kruger materializes out of nowhere.

"You two waste-cases at it again, for cryin' out loud?" Breaking out his best Bob Weir, Kruger croons, " 'And he left his dead ass *dead* by the side of the road.' Now how many times do I got ta *tell* you? Next *question*!"

Kenny gives Ventricle a satisfied look—because Kruger agrees, and they always defer to the psycho.

Slightly nasal, mixing Southern drawl with a Valley boy's torqued inflection, his words strung together in peculiar shapes, Kruger's way of speaking is self-invented, like something he came up with one morning after squirting liquid LSD into his eyes the night before.

"Now *Daaaavy*..." he says, fixing those small pale green eyes on me and cracking a grin. "You take your hit yet, *Davy*?"

"Not yet."

"Well what's the *hold-up*?" he says. "Come on, pal. I'll even join ya."

The thing is, Kruger isn't *always* a bully or a psycho. He's actually given me rides to school on the back of his moped, and I've ridden miles with him, my arms clasped around his torso, the two of us leaning into turns together. I'm wary of him, but we're friends of a sort. Combined with my zeal to make this night a special one and my genetic predisposition to shrug and say "what the hell," this strong jolt of peer pressure outweighs my not unreasonable sense of trepidation. Kruger and I tap sugar cubes like in a toast, and he says, "Now that's more like it, *Daaavy*."

The stuff comes on gradually—everybody says that—so I keep my restlessness at bay with one of Kruger's TOMY toys: push-button-operated, water-based amusements encased in clear plastic. This one is based on ring-toss. I'm dying for one of the little wafted lozenges to turn into an asteroid or a fish or maybe even Mickey Mouse, but they keep on being boring little lozenges. As I play, the weight of the day begins to make itself known, and I put down the game, close my eyes, and pass into a low-grade dream state while maintaining an awareness of the room around me, of comings and goings.

Someone puts on Pink Floyd's *Animals* and I'm in heaven. Maybe I feel something. A twinge? Or maybe it's just my favorite album at work. No, it's more than that. As Side 1 unfolds, things around me begin to glisten. Then the major thrill: behind my closed eyes, a new and improved print of *Fantasia* is showing. I'm spellbound as a symphony of dancing pyramids perform pas de deux in accompaniment with David Gilmour's thrilling, throbbing, piercing solo, which builds to a screaming high note as true as a blade, and then all the dancing orbs come together and explode into impossibly intricate rainbow-colored fractals.

Time, or whatever you want to call it, does its thing, and when I rouse myself and assume an upright position, the silence is so thick with the ping-ing and popping of atoms I can almost taste the night. I'm alone, except for Kruger, who is passed out in a lower bunk. At first the dose was like a foreign substance, like a new set of shoes. Now I've walked around in my acid shoes and I'm ablaze with the stuff. Kruger stirs, and goddamn am I relieved for human company, even if it's the guy who forced my buddy Theo to accompany him to a Jefferson Starship show at Nassau Coliseum a few weeks ago, under pain of a major beating, because the Bob Weir Band was the opening act and he had no one else to go with—and still called him a pussy the whole time. I'm ready to talk his ear off. Only he does not look capable of listening. Kruger, I now recall, "woke up trippin." Kruger has to crash.

Which means, What am I to do with myself in this condition?

"You can stay here," he says, our one moment of trippy nonverbal communication. Kruger gets to his feet and sleepwalks out into the hallway, and I follow him to a little guest bedroom just outside his room. He mumbles something, then heads back and closes the door.

A bed, a night table, a bureau, and a stereo. I'm saved. And my rational mind hasn't deserted me. I flick through a box of records on a small desk next to the turntable, clearly belonging to one of Kruger's sisters, in search of anything promising. Pablo Cruise, Bread, the Carpenters, Anne Murray,

America, Grand Funk, Leo Sayer, the Eagles, Hall & Oates, Steve Miller, Chuck Mangione, Styx, Boston, Frampton, Wings, Chicago... But way in the back is salvation: *American Beauty*.

Thanks to Uncle Mike, who gifted us with *Workingman's Dead* in the summer of 1971, the Grateful Dead are as familiar as birdsong around 5 Sherwood. *American Beauty*, released five months after *Workingman's Dead*, is the band's other undisputed classic LP, yet I've never so much as held it in my hands or heard it play from start to finish. What a perfect bit of serendipity. And the lysergic rose on the cover is certain to reward deep contemplation. But first, I need a bathroom.

Kruger's hallway ends in infinity. The walls, low-lit by a nightlight, undulate like pizza dough, and when I peer down the corridor I see delicate, intricate latticework where ordinarily there would be darkness. Halfway to the bathroom, I spot a mirror on the wall. I stop and look and it's heavy. The mirror edges slip away and I'm on a bridge watching myself go by—old me, young me, devilish me, cool me with sideburns, female me, heroic me, pre-Raphaelite me, *post*-Raphaelite me. The frame is there and not there, and what I see in it depends entirely on what I choose to fill it up with. Just as a wave of fear threatens to take hold, a weirdly wise and patient voice speaks up from somewhere within the depths of me.

"Who's minding the store?"

It comes from an anecdote my brother had related to me about Ram Dass, the Harvard professor born Richard Alpert, who once took some LSD that was so powerful that everything around him disappeared. And then *he* started to disappear, limb by limb. He started to freak out. Where was he? Was he about to float away into the void? Just then, this little voice spoke up from somewhere:

"But who's minding the store?"

Think of it as the person in charge of your mind, a behind-the-scenes figure, a less-judgy superego that does not externalize under normal circumstances but is always there. The message from this wise and invisible, ancient spirit is that there is nothing to fear. Even when the walls drop away, your inner self is there, and it won't disappear. It just won't. And I'm not afraid anymore.

As I pee, I imagine an infinite line of cartoon droplets all lined up inside me like paratroopers, each waiting to add its infinitesimal essence to the mighty stream, ready and willing to leap into the void. Because nothing gold can stay.

Back in the little room, *American Beauty* is my spirit guide. The Dead never sound wiser or prettier or more reassuring. Every song (except "Operator," Pig-pen's contribution, which is nonetheless a pleasant excursion) seems to address me, directly or obliquely: "Make yourself easy," "Till the morning comes," "Love will see you through," and yeah, "What a long, strange trip it's been."

Propped up on a pillow, a quilt covering my knees, I rise solely to turn the record over—twice, maybe three times. On the final play, as I'm about to fall into brilliant embers of sleep, the juddering intro to "Truckin'" yanks me back, and I lurch out of bed to make the music stop. In a few hours, weirdly lucid, I steal out of Kruger's house to face the new day.

Chapter 15

What's on a Man's Mind?

At fifteen, I'm too old for sleepaway camp, so it's on to the teen-tour circuit. Hell, the parents have come to appreciate having my brother and me out of their hair for several weeks in a row, and it's not exactly painful. A month or so after astral traveling at Kruger's, I travel by bus with thirty or so teens across America. We visit the Badlands and Mount Rushmore and Disneyland, and I attain some experience with what Dad calls "heavy petting." The following summer, two weeks into a three-week bicycle tour of Massachusetts, I and another kid are late in arriving at the appointed spot in the Boston subway station. Both of us have attitudes and are not well loved, and so the group leader, a woman in her early twenties, puts it to the other kids to decide on whether we should be kicked off the trip.

The next morning I'm homeward bound, only my parents are in Ithaca, at Dad's alma mater, attending some seminars and socializing with fellow liberal thinkers. Apparently, there's stuff for kids to do too. They arrange a flight for me, from Newark to Binghamton; someone will be there to meet me and convey me to campus.

Brief glimpses of leather and denim jackets, long, glossy hair and tinted shades—snatched from over the shoulder of a stocky nun ahead of me—tell me I'm trailing a rock band. And any rock band worth their salt in 1978 is headed where I'm headed: to the smoking section. My habit is still more cheap thrill than chain-smoke on the tarmac at this point, but it's my first solo flight and I'm gonna do it in style. As I approach my seat, I get a good look.

It's T.P. & the H's. That's how I write "Tom Petty & the Heartbreakers" on my cassette tapes. No need to spell it out.

They are the one new American band that has my heart, my soul, and my gut. Most of the music I'm excited about these days is cerebral and English—Elvis Costello, Brian Eno, Peter Gabriel, and especially the Clash, who are not cerebral so much as extremely political. T.P. requires less mental effort. His songs are never shallow or clichéd like the corporate rock of the moment, and you can easily read yourself into them. But Petty isn't trying to make you *think* exactly, or attempting to shake up society.

Stan Lynch, the Heartbreakers drummer, is seated directly across the aisle from me, close enough to touch. He's long and lean, like Prince Valiant's more dangerous cousin from the North. There's an ease in his comportment, in his not freezing out the kid with the too-tight Jeff Beck T-shirt and horizontal mop of hair, reacting to him with rapturous recognition. Stan even gives the kid a quick nod. Next to Stan, in the window seat, is Ron Blair, the bass player who will, after a few more albums, quit the Heartbreakers and open a bikini shop. Mike Campbell, whose majestic leads send me into the same stratosphere as David Gilmour's or Jerry Garcia's, is seated behind them with Benmont Tench, whose cool but never icy keyboard textures provide a crucial component of the Heartbreakers sound. Farther back, in the very last row, is Tom, in a faded jean jacket and mirrored shades, lighting up. They all look like stars.

WNEW-FM ("Where rock lives!") plays "American Girl" and "Breakdown" and "Listen to Her Heart," but thanks to my station of choice, WPIX-FM ("From Elvis to Elvis"), I'm hip to Tom's obscurities, like "I Don't Know What to Say to You," a sprightly B-side mixing Mike Campbell's nimble Travis-picking with Petty's Dylan-ish doggerel. I taped it off the radio and got almost all of it. For my money, PIX is, to borrow a phrase currently associated with the Clash, the only station that matters. On PIX, you'll hear a set that segues from Sam the Sham and the Pharaohs to Magazine to the Stones to Sam and Dave. Tom Petty songs play side by side with the Specials and the Cure instead of Steve Miller and Bob Seger. They sound much better that way.

Meanwhile it's Day 20 of the forty-eight-stop You're Gonna Get It Tour, and Tom Petty has a lot on his mind. According to *Petty: The Biography* by Warren Zanes, halfway through the tour, Petty had begun ruminating on a conversation he'd had with Bruce Springsteen. Bruce told Tom he'd sworn off doing opening slots and decided only to play for audiences who were there to see *him*. Tom and his band have suffered through a comical run of mismatched bills of late, from Meat Loaf to Be Bop Deluxe to Patti Smith; tonight they're paired with Journey. And four days ago, during a performance at Miami's Jai-Alai Fronton, an electrical charge surged from Petty's mic and knocked him unconscious. So Tom is in no mood.

A quick glance over my shoulder at him in his don't-talk-to-me shades, too alone to be proud, convinces me not to go back there for a handshake. A stewardess (not yet a flight attendant—it's still the seventies) appears, and Stan orders a scotch and a coffee.

A scotch and a coffee. Just think of it. The perfect meal. And at noon no less. I've never seen anyone do anything half as cool.

Stan's the kid in a band, "the lone extrovert in a tribe of introverts," in the words of Zanes. He's a galvanizing force, but he's blunt and unapologetic, and he has a knack for getting under people's skin. He and his seatmate have come to blows, and recently, when Tom asked Stan for his opinion on the proposed album cover image for *You're Gonna Get It*, he said he really didn't care. This did not endear him to Tom. (It's not a good cover.)

Once we reach cruising altitude, I turn to Stan and hit him with a Klein-ian rush of hyper verbiage. Essentially: I love you guys, you're one of my favorite bands, and "I Need to Know" is so good as to render me inarticulate. "It's just so...*great,* I mean, that echo effect? That, um...you know? In the chorus?"

I'm talking about how the title phrase is made indelible by the way it's echoed distantly ("I need to know" *I need to know* / "I need to know" *I need to know*). I mistakenly believe some kind of magical effects pedal is responsible, when it's actually a human being, and not just any human being—Stan himself provides those italicized *I need to know*s. But he doesn't flinch or correct me or look bored or put upon. When I pause to take a breath, he says something like, "Yeah, it's a really cool song. One of his best yet. Glad you dig it."

The middle part of his offhand reaction takes me closer to the rock group dynamic than anything I've ever read in *Circus Magazine*. If "I Need to Know" is one of Tom's best, some other songs must have been less great in Stan's eyes. Which means that just because you're in a band, doesn't mean you love every-thing you do equally.

Stan Lynch and I are now pretty much like any other pair of non-hostile people seated near each other on a plane who don't mind having a casual chat. It's a forty-five-minute flight, he's got his scotch and coffee, so why not? He asks me where I'm heading, and I tell him Cornell University, conveniently leaving out the specifics. Maybe he'll think I'm in college. He says they're playing Cobo Hall in Detroit tonight, and from there they go to New York.

"Can you make it down?" he says. "You could come backstage..."

"Oh, man. That would be wild," I say, wondering how it might even be possible. Soon the plane starts to make its descent, and I manage to pose a surprisingly solid, rock-critic-worthy question before this magic moment ends.

"So, I mean, how do you feel about it being, you know, Tom Petty and the Heartbreakers, with him being the star of the show? Do you ever wish it was you?"

"You have to have a focus," he says. "Know what I mean? Can't be five guys in the spotlight. Just doesn't work."

I leave it there. Let's not blow this brag-worthy episode. We touch ground, and Stan tells me to have fun and try to make it to the Palladium show on Friday. We shake hands in the accepted style among white guys with long hair—the hippie handshake, or the soul shake, which is done overhand, like you're both gripping the same subway pole. And we part—Stan for fabled Cobo Hall, where Bob Seger's *Live Bullet* was recorded and which seats 12,000, me for Mary Donlon Hall, a dormitory on Cornell's north campus, capacity 450.

You had to be having sex to be cool. That was the thinking at the end of the decade, a view propagated by older brothers, kids your own age, and Hollywood. Look at Otter in *Animal House*, the biggest movie of 1978. He's a frat boy, slickly handsome and disingenuous, who fucks anything that moves and is presented unironically as the most fulfilled among his cohort of fun-loving drunks. His pal Boon, played by Peter Riegert, is a more complex guy, whose beautiful girlfriend (Karen Allen) gives him headaches. As a seventeen-year-old virgin, I viewed Pinto, the sincere but naive doofus played by Tom Hulce, as the most relatable. I also knew, in my heart and from experience, that the Otters of the world got the girls.

There was a T-shirt advertised in the back of magazines I read, like *National Lampoon*, that showed what looked like a guy's face in profile along with the words WHAT'S ON A MAN'S MIND? You looked closer and saw that his profile traced out the contours of a naked woman. The idea was that the most normal thing you can do as a young male is think about sex all the time.

Dad's recollections of college life pretty much squared with the goings-on depicted in *Animal House* and *National Lampoon*. In his telling, fraternity life at Cornell was nothing short of a nonstop hanky-panky-fest. Remembering an attractive gal with whom he'd once dallied, Dad would lower his voice and confide in an unmistakable tone of adolescent naughtiness, "She was really stacked." Blowjobs, he reported, were considered "fifth base," something only done by *really* serious couples who were already making marriage plans. The term for an unattractive girl among his frat bros was "a face crash." Implicit in his tales of wild times at I Felta Thi was that premarital sex was no big deal and that one would be remiss in not joining a fraternity.

Dad warmed to recalling these moments as much as we did. When employing that conspiratorial whisper or expressing his unabashed fixation on zaftig actresses like Susan Sarandon and Valerie Perrine, he was at his most open and approachable. Remembering his childhood nickname for his brother, Arthur, ("Farturo") or sharing a smutty joke (punch line: "Ivan, *release the suction!*"), Dad was almost like a fellow kid.

My brother, who was having *lots* of sex, insisted that time was a-wastin'. In defiance of my parents' wishes and the implications of a prep school education, Jonny had rebuffed college acceptances at several very good schools that he hadn't bothered to visit. Instead, he took an apartment in the then-seedy town of Edgewater, New Jersey, and got a job at the local Purex soap factory. The boy who'd won national awards for poetry and nearly aced his English SAT opted to pursue his rock dreams instead. The night I rounded up a bunch of high school friends to go see the Method play at CBGB took me to unimagined heights of brother awe. Uncle Mike agreed that amazement was the appropriate response, calling Jonny's appearance at the legendary Bowery birthplace of New York punk "the furthest evolutionary advance anyone has made in our family," while also declaring in a concurrent letter, "Patti Smith and Devo are as good as Dylan and the Beatles in their primes."

I had a girlfriend during my junior year of high school, a gregarious, conscientious girl with lots of extracurricular interests. Jill did not party and wasn't connected with my social circle, so what was I doing with her? She was good company. She had pillowy lips. It felt empowering to make someone's heart go flippity-flop. She wrote me flirty letters on ski lodge stationery from her family vacations. On weekday evenings, we'd get together at her well-appointed home in Englewood, talk about nothing consequential, and make out and drink hot chocolate in her bedroom. Mom was always within earshot.

"You mean you haven't even touched her tits yet? The hell is your *problem*?" was Jonny's frequent harangue.

Thus, in the summer of '79, one year after flying high with Stan Lynch and Tom Petty, I returned to Mary Donlon Hall, this time as a junior camp counselor, *with wheels*, determined to get the whole virginity thing out of the way.

The camel is a horse designed by a committee, so they say, and the selection of my beige VW Rabbit is a committee decision all the way. Dad is adamant that I choose a vehicle that gets exceptional mileage. We're in the midst of another gas crisis, after all. So, not just a Rabbit, which has very respectable numbers, but a diesel model, whose numbers are even better. Never mind the practicality of owning a diesel vehicle in a gasoline world, or diesel engines' vulnerability to the subfreezing temperatures that mark winters in the Northeast—it's the economy, stupid.

The dealership in Englewood only carries the Rabbit Diesel in yellow, white, red, and beige. Yellow is out, because it's yellow, as is red, which reminds me too much of my zits. Mom says never get a white car—they're too hard to keep clean—so beige it is. Complaints aside, I'm stoked. My cassette tapes blare through a pair of Auratone 5C Super Sound Cube speakers, which Big Bro assures me are the preferred mixdown monitors in New York recording studios due to their flat, full-range response. Since they are not designed with cars in mind, I have them installed on the panel behind the backseat when they don't fit inside the doors.

On the day of my departure, I pack my stereo and a crate of records, because three weeks of playing my cassettes on a cheap portable tape player will be intolerable. Actually, calling it a stereo is a misnomer. Mom said lugging the whole system up there was ridiculous.

"Just bring one speaker," she said. "You're in this tiny little room. One'll be plenty."

I comply with this insane request out of the purest naivete. I'm not completely clear on what the difference will be with one speaker, and I only learn that lesson when I get back home, cue up Television's *Marquee Moon*, and discover a whirlwind of snarling guitar that had never been there before. So *that's* stereo...

Wiping noses, putting on Band-Aids, rolling inflatable balls gently for four-year-olds to kick—this is my day, and it's fairly exhausting, truth be told. In the evening, I'm happy enough to walk through a leafy section of the campus and smoke a doob before repairing to my room to spin my current faves, principally Neil Young's *Rust Never Sleeps,* Graham Parker's *Squeezing Out Sparks,* and that Television record. My mini-fridge is stocked with Molson Golden Ale purchased from a small market in an adjacent building that also houses a nondescript bar. Collegetown, a mile or so away, has plenty of real bars, and I can sometimes get served, but I have no fake ID. Mostly what I lack is the swagger to waltz in like I own the place, something wise older brothers and those in the know always emphasize as crucial to your success in "passing."

Saturday is the quiet day; everybody clears out, and new families don't begin arriving until the next day. You practically have the whole big, boring women's dormitory to yourself. On the second Saturday of my three-week stint, I'm ready for the lull—and for a proper grown-up quaff.

Foreigner is on the jukebox inside the little pub with no name. A half dozen or so patrons are spread around the wooden bar, drinking beer in iced mugs and working at little baskets of popcorn. The students are mostly gone, so the clientele seem to be an assortment of locals and people brought in by happenstance. As I'm about to order, a roly-poly middle-aged guy named Harold rolls up and offers to buy me a beer.

Harold looks like John Wayne Gacy, which is to say stocky, balding, paunchy, and innocuous. This is before you automatically figured the seemingly average Joe on the stool next to you, buying you a couple of beers, harbored evil designs. I dig the spontaneity of making conversation with some garrulous square guy from middle America. His type almost counts as exotic in my world. So we drink a few rounds, and then we leave the bar and amble toward a secluded spot because I have a joint with me. He isn't a smoker, but it's cool with him if I spark one up.

As I'm puffing away, he tells me he's a law enforcement agent. I panic, of course, but he says not to worry, he has no intention of busting me. Harold's in Ithaca for an Animal Control conference, because one of the things Harold does is apprehend escaped animals. He seems to do a lot of things.

The following Thursday evening, I'm back at the no-name pub. No Harold, which is kind of good. Remembering me, the bartender serves up a pint of Michelob in a frosted glass tankard just as before. As I take my first contented sip, over the speakers comes "The Logical Song" and I start nodding along reflexively. Not too much though, because it isn't cool to like Supertramp *too* much. But right now—man, with that cold splash of lager and the first Marlboro drag, they sound fantastic. I'm full-on head-bobbing now, unabashedly giving myself over to the 'tramp. Because who gives a shit? I'm in a no-name pub in Ithaca, New York, and nobody knows who I am (*who I am, who I am, WHO I AAAAMMM…*).

When I open my eyes, she's appraising me. She is, hmm, what is she? Not a girl—older than that, and not polished, not a student, not a teacher. Got a "been around the block a few times" look to her. Hmm.

"You really like this song, huh?" Her voice is low Southern honey.

"Yeah, they really sound like the Beatles in a way, the melody and the vocals…I don't love the band that much really, but this is undeniably catchy."

"This the Beatles?"

"No, it's Supertramp."

"Oh, I see. Supertramp, huh?"

"Yeah, they're an English band? Their album's been getting a lot of airplay."

"I like the Beatles," she says. "But I'm not really up on, you know, the latest thing."

This would ordinarily be a major turnoff. A month ago, at an end-of-school party, Stacy Smethurst said she loved David Gilmour's solo albums, and I rather coldly pointed out that David Gilmour only made one solo album—like a dick. This time, I'm more than willing to overlook her lack of worldliness. I like how she listens as I describe my camp counselor job, and I proceed without fear that she'll find me dull or uncool. As for her own circumstances, she's vague.

"Just passing through" is what she says when I ask what she's doing in these parts.

"So where'd you start off then?"

"Where'm I from, you mean? Tennessee."

"Tennessee?"

"Yessir, Johnson City. Tennessee born and bred."

"You may not believe it, but I was actually born in the South myself."

"Get outta town."

"Nope, I was. Fort Campbell, Kentucky. My dad was in the Army." Holding off on telling her my Hendrix story—because if she's never heard of Jimi, we might actually have a problem—I add unnecessarily, "That's where I was born."

"Well, well, well," she says, extending her hand. "A Kentucky boy. It's a pleasure to meet you. I'm Louvenia."

Her hand is warm and strong and lightly calloused. She keeps it there just long enough to make her interest clear. Once we're into our second round, I make my move. "If it's cool with you, we can go up to my room and listen to some music," I say. "I have something to play for you. Something you'll like."

"Something I'll like, huh? Well, are you willing to guarantee it?"

"I am. I guaran-damn-tee it."

"Well, now," she says. "How could a girl refuse such a kindly offer as that?"

As we ride the elevator to my fifth-floor dorm room, I'm relieved not to run into any of my counselor colleagues. The sordidness of the situation—gangly teenage me consorting with a townie a good decade older—must be obvious to anyone with eyes.

A few years ago, during a teen tour, I racked up some pretty extensive fooling-around experience, so I know what it's like to have an assertive girl leverage your eager hand for her own pleasure. But since junior year I've been restricted to Jill and our regimen of athletic French kissing, and now my head is spinning from the beer and the horniness, my heart thumping at the thrill of the moment having finally arrived. Patting the key in my front pocket steadies me.

My beat-up copy of *Flatt & Scruggs with the Foggy Bottom Boys* has Dad's name rubber-stamped on the back cover and a crude masking-tape repair along the spine. Released in 1960 on the Harmony label, the LP features a studio shot of Lester and Earl posing against a background of blue gray, wearing matching white jackets, white cowboy hats, and bright red bolo ties. Lester has a craggy John Wayne visage and a benign grin. Earl's hair is nearly black, and he has some of that corn-fed look about the jaw.

The needle drops, and spangles burble up from the stylus to my one speaker in resplendent mono, just as it was meant to be. Louvenia brightens at the sound of banjo, and I fetch a Molson from the mini fridge. Popping the top off with the bottle opener built into the painted cinderblock wall (an odd perk, to be sure), I take a sip on my way to the bed, where she's slouched against a pillow recliner. We can share this one. I only have two left. We start to kiss, and she starts undoing my belt.

"Hang on," I say. "I don't have any protection."

"Oh, that's OK, sugar," she says, climbing on top of me.

"Whaddya mean? Oh. You're on the pill?"

"Nope," she says. "*Pregnant.*"

This revelation does not dent my ardor even slightly.

"Don't force it, now," she says. "Just, just... that's right, that's right..."

By track 4, we're already in afterglow—I am anyway—and Louvenia's feeling pretty good herself, crooning along with gusto to a song she recognizes from a Charley Pride album: *"I thought I'd been kissed, and I thought I'd been loved, but that was before I met you..."* When I rise to turn the record over,

Louvenia begins flipping through a sketch book filled with my crazy, acid-inspired drawings. She asks for a pen, and I give her a purple felt-tip marker and open another beer. I skip the first track on Side 2, "Let Those Brown Eyes Smile at Me," and go straight for the manic "Earl's Breakdown" before rejoining Louvenia. She nods along to the music as she sketches a landscape of snow-capped mountains and a winding river. In the foreground is a tree with a hole in its trunk.

She signs her name in perfect Palmer-method cursive, with a swooping, almost grandiloquent "B" to begin her last name. Then she starts putting her things on, unhurriedly and without self-consciousness. I'm starting to fade—sockless, pantless, and satisfied—when I hear the doorknob turn.

"Goodnight, darlin'," she whispers in a low and throaty tone. "Maybe I'll see you at the pub."

I never did make it back there, but in December I received an elaborate postcard from Harold. It unfolded into about ten sections, each one depicting a particular aspect of dairy farming. His handwriting was deliberately clear; you could sense he'd borne down hard on the pen as he wrote. The words were almost a parody of banality, but he ended by saying he'd be in the tri-state area around the holidays and hoped we could get together. "MABEY WE CAN HAVE SOME GOOD TIMES LIKE THE ONES AT CORNELL."

Sure enough, on a frigid night in late December, Harold called and said he was in town. I must have given him my phone number somewhere along the line, which I realize sounds a little crazy. Still, I couldn't see the harm in meeting up for drinks in a public place, not exactly anyway, but just as a precaution I enlisted my brother to come with me.

We met him at Siggy's, a vaguely German-themed bar just across the George Washington Bridge, in Fort Lee, where they didn't check ID, and Harold proceeded to get us unrelentingly drunk on Jägermeister and schooners of Weise beer. He even brought a joint for us to smoke, apprehended from a suspect of some kind. We drank until last call, and then we walked him out to his station wagon and he went to the back and opened the hatch. Aha, I thought. This is where he shows us the corpse of the suspect whose joint we just smoked. Instead, Harold's got a bounty of ornately wrapped presents back there, filling the trunk almost to overflowing. I finally get it. Santa Claus is making his Christmas rounds.

The following morning, once we could think again, Jonny and I retrieved the gifts from the car. Under the bows and ribbons and shiny wrapping were shot glass sets and liquor decanters in the shape of vintage automobiles, one for each member of the family. I got a 1914 Stutz Bearcat that played "Beautiful Dreamer" when you turned the spare tire. Those were different times.

Chapter 16

Alphabet City

My first real home away from home is a fourth-floor walkup apartment in Alphabet City that I share with Dave Schlachet, my former college housemate. My room fits a loft bed and little else, but I can afford it on my restaurant salary. Plus, Dave provides me with an instant social life.

We grew up a mere twenty-three geographical miles from each other, but as a Brooklyn boy, Dave's misspent teen years had a markedly cosmopolitan flavor. While my high school friends and I were gobbling mushrooms in one of Englewood, New Jersey's numerous wooded tracts, Dave was arms aloft at Studio 54, decked out in Fiorucci jeans and naked from the well-toned waist on up—save for a poppy-red neck bandana and a liberal dousing of Halston Z-14 cologne.

Dave is an inherently social being, handsome, genial—a charmer—with buff biceps and a blinding smile. Dave's girlfriend is an actress named Marisa Tomei, who gives him fits with her vexing actress-y ways. I confess to being somewhat smitten with my roommate's girlfriend, but this is not difficult. I hold a purple belt in forming crushes, and Marisa is a first-day-of-class kind of deal.

Like Marisa, Alphabet City is up-and-coming in 1986, but the area is still damn sketchy, with homeless encampments in Tompkins Square Park that will lead to full-scale riots in a couple of years and rampant graffiti proclaiming, DIE YUPPIE SCUM! Mere yards from the tenement pictured on the front cover of Led Zeppelin's *Physical Graffiti,* cocaine is easily purchasable behind suspect-looking storefronts whose display windows feature a few ceremonial cans of Goya beans and a haphazard arrangement of dusty laundry detergent jugs, fooling nobody. A block or so north, on First Avenue, is a corner so reliably rife with prostitution and crack sales, it's like a downtown version of the Ramones' "53rd and 3rd."

Dave and I consider ourselves lucky that on our block, East Sixth between A and B, you can almost always count on *some kind* of regular, non-C.H.U.D. activity taking place, encouraged by a gigantic twenty-four-hour green market on Avenue A that enlivens and illuminates the surrounding blocks. Yet it all remains slightly untamed. Up the street from our place is the hole-in-the-wall Gladiator Gym, where chiseled, mainly Latino lifters sweat at all hours under the weight of primitive equipment, much of it hand-built by the owner-manager. Directly across from us, scowling from behind security fencing and flanked by a hulking German shepherd, a burly white-haired man rumored to be an ex-Nazi is perpetually parked. You have to keep your eyes open—just not too wide. I've learned to avoid making direct visual contact after a few too many unsolicited conversations with men responding to my searching brown eyes.

Our building looks like nothing from the outside—just a stain-resistant steel door planted amid a concrete expanse. The interior is raw and harshly lit by industrial-strength fluorescent tubes, the walls pocked and painted in lurid shades of yellow and red, like a hamburglary in McDonaldland gone unspeakably wrong. Still, the unfinishedness of the neighborhood has its charms. Visible from our east-facing bathroom, etched on the third-floor window of a building across Avenue B, is a faded ad for a long-gone dentist, DR. PUGLIO, whose name appears in white letters above a floating molar.

It's tempting to describe our living arrangement as low-rent, but affordable rent is the better term, and it's what makes our cool situation possible. I can't imagine why anyone would want to live anywhere else, and I've started to envy people who have apartments of their own. Like RJ, who graduated a year ahead of us and has a studio on St. Mark's Place.

Six months ago, RJ purchased a half ton of shower curtain rings in Chinatown for next to nothing and with minimal modifications converted them into earrings. Applying roughly the same principle, he transformed anodized aluminum dowel pins into bracelets and other accessories, the kind that pass for cool in these chic-cheap-loving eighties. RJ is a true hustler, and he has the pep to drive all over the city hawking his wares, no venue too large or too small. He'll start local, making rounds at stands around Canal Street and then head uptown to the Bloomingdale's jewelry counter. When stuck in traffic, he maintains his battleship-mimicking flat-top with sustained mistings of Final Net and a battery-powered hair clipper he keeps stashed in his sample case.

But who am I to poke fun? Through sheer moxie, RJ has nabbed a place of his own. How sweet it would be to have a pad like his, to traipse down the front steps, un-hatch the security gate, and have Sounds—the best secondhand record store in town—fifty paces up the street, and the whole of New York just beyond. A mere crack vial's toss to the west, you have St. Mark's Pizza, *the* place to go for a huge slab of Sicilian at the end of the night, just to tamp everything down good and right. And how sweet to live so close to work as to enable a leisurely late breakfast at Veselka or B&H Dairy before strolling three measly blocks to Iso on 11th and Second.

Despite my complete lack of service-industry experience, I wait tables at a very hot sushi restaurant. How hot is Iso? It was until recently a favorite of Madonna's, who would meet up there with Jean-Michel Basquiat and Keith Haring, the Most Beloved of all Iso Regulars, who drew the fish mandala logo that adorns the popular Iso T-shirts. After her concert at Radio City Music Hall last year, Madonna showed up at Iso in a chauffeur-driven truck, and per Andy Warhol's diary, started drawing cocks all over her friend Futura 2000's pants. The waiters were on the floor.

I may have missed Madonna's cocks, but Iso's reputation for quality sushi and a certain hip factor continues to bring in an array of notable regulars, everyone from neighborhood guys like Joey Ramone—a true sushi devotee—to former Studio 54 co-owner Ian Schrager, who's five years removed from serving a prison sentence for tax evasion and back in the nightlife again with Palladium. One night I flirted with Indiana Jones's main squeeze, Karen Allen. Mark Linn-Baker, co-star of TV's new hit comedy series *Perfect Strangers*, comes in once or twice a week, dining for one and not being ridiculous in the tip department. Last month, I arrived for my shift to find the place rearranged to accommodate a long central table that was reserved for a band I'd never heard of, who were in town to open for Ozzy at Nassau Coliseum. I can still hear their drummer, Lars, calling across the table, "Hey! Try some of this fuckin' yellowtail!!"

Recently I retrieved a black scarf, soft as angel wings, left behind by Elizabeth Saltzman after her late-night nosh with Ian Schrager. Elizabeth, a New York City socialite and fashion arbiter, is electrically beautiful and dating Jellybean Benitez, the top-of the-world record producer and former main squeeze of Madonna. When Schrager returned a few nights later, I brought him the scarf, and he immediately held it to his face and sighed, "Smells like her…" to his dinner guest, Robert Isabell, florist to the stars. And Robert Isabell knows a thing or two about scents. In July, he'll secure ten thousand white lilies for Caroline Kennedy's wedding.

The non-famous Iso regulars are also an interesting lot. A garrulous, blond-dreaded guy who works sound on *Pee-Wee's Playhouse* came in one night, placed his headphones over my ears, and cued up *Dark Side of the Moon*—on a portable CD player. I had physically held a compact disc once before—Steve Winwood's *Back in the High Life*, which Dave owned despite his lack of a CD player. Listening to Pink Floyd via compact disc on a device that fits in a very large pocket? Cutting-edge!

Iso takes its name from the owner and head chef, Shoji Iso, who smokes whenever he can. When things are slow, he'll squat behind the sushi bar and grab a few quick puffs. At the end of a shift, he enjoys a single can of Budweiser with his congratulatory lung dart. Iso is a man of few words, inscrutable, you might even say, but in his unstated concern that my lack of table-waiting panache will one day lead to disaster, he's entirely justified.

As a waiter, I earn A's for effort, but I struggle when it comes to the myriad of small details to keep straight, like the unruly dishes of steaming tempura, each with their separate monkey dishes of tonka sauce and white rice. I've begun hating people based on how complicated their sushi order is. The other night, in the midst of a hectic shift, a guy who's just ordered a salmon skin handroll with shiso leaf on the inside gazes up at me and declares, "Wow, do you ever look *warm*." For my general haplessness, I earn a less than equal share of the pooled tips at the end of the shift and am viewed as sincere but ineffectual by the other wait staff. When Takao returns from a week in Tokyo, he brings me a T-shirt that basically says "I am a stupid foreigner" in Japanese.

Dave and Marisa are either super-hot for each other—making noisy love in Dave's room over loud thumpa-thumpa music—or they're in crisis. Dave is possessive, preoccupied with the state of their relationship, and maybe not unduly concerned with Marisa's many charismatic, leading-man-type actor friends. Just about anything can set him off. He charged into my darkened sleep nook one night as I was engaged in some awkward reunion sex with a girl from Vassar, assailing me at high volume because Marisa happened to mention that we'd run into each other earlier that day, on St. Mark's Place, in front of her apartment, and talked and smoked a little roach together. How dare I neglect to report this incident to him?

If that's Dave at his most needy and irrational, Marisa is every bit his equal in angst creation. The usual last-minute flakings, the bouts of crankiness, and occasional diva behavior are one thing—she's an actress, after all, and a damn good one—but things have grown complicated in ways that Dave, a serial juggler of relationships for years now, has never had to put up with.

During a chilly New York spring, shortly after I'd moved in, Marisa had come down with a bug of some kind and taken refuge in Dave's room for an extended encampment. Dave worked double-time to keep her comfortable and turned out to be an exemplary private nurse, serving as the liaison between Mar*iss* (she was often just Mar*iss*) and her very concerned mom—supplying frequent health updates and eventually coordinating the doctor visit Mariss clearly needed—way uptown on Park Avenue.

Dave has a car waiting downstairs. He escorts Marisa to the doctor and back, guides her gently up the four flights, tucks her into his bed, kisses her lightly upon the brow, then heads to Mrs. Tomei's preferred pharmacy (not local). It's pouring rain, but he's out there doing the good. Returning home with antibiotics, a medley of juices, pain relievers, and magazines, plus a roll of wild cherry Lifesavers (just because), he mounts the staircase with arms full and heart bursting with goodwill. But when he reaches our floor, he detects a funky odor, and as he's digging for his keys, he notes with alarm that the smell seems to be coming from inside. Feeling a bit panicky, Dave jams in the key, turns it, and gives the door a hard shove—but it catches. The security chain is attached.

"Hey!" he bellows through the gap. "What the fuck?" He yells again. And again. At last, a portion of an unfamiliar woman's face appears behind the chain.

"You can't come in."

"What the fuck do you mean I—*Marisa! Tell her to let me in! What the fuck is going on in there??*"

At length, the door is unlatched and the source of the smell becomes clear. Pots of bubbling liquids roil on the stove, painting the adjacent surfaces with a noxious steam coating. Two large ladies in kaftans glare as Dave pushes past them into his bedroom, where he finds Marisa on top of the covers, sans clothing, carefully balancing a half dozen strategically placed crystals upon her slender torso.

"They're healers," she says with closed eyes. "They're healing me."

"Healers? Are you shitting me? Healers?? Look at the size of them—who needs healing? Marisa. I have your antibiotics."

"I'm not taking it," she says, eyes clamped, crystals quaking.

"Marisa, please. It's what the doctor prescribed."

"The doctor doesn't love me."

"The doctor doesn't love you?"

"*They* love me."

"The doctor took the Hippocratic oath. He doesn't have to love you. Just take the fuckin' medicine!"

Eventually, once the healers have been banished and one of Dave's cooking pots is tossed out the window for good measure, Marisa comes back around to Western medicine and ingests the antibiotics. Soon she recuperates and things return to relatively normal.

Who's to say which remedy really sealed the deal?

Weirdly enough, RJ, who seems to have his shower-curtain-ring-bedecked finger on the pulse of things, is our Ecstasy connection. I say weirdly because he seems utterly impervious to the drug's empathy-enhancing effects and always retains a used-car-salesman-ish aura no matter what he's ingested. RJ's source is a guy called Norman, a taciturn Englishman who has a fabulous apartment on the roof *and turret* of the Chelsea Hotel. Norman is fond of plaid jumpers, always wears a hat, and came up with the perfect description of what happens when you smoke pot on Ecstasy. "It throws a spanner in the works."

The obtainability of the Norman stuff has brought about a radical, if temporary, rewiring of the senses. Ecstasy has a way of bringing you closer to people—those you're already drawn to, and even those you just met. Along with the interpersonal, barrier-reducing quality, there's a tactile component, which is akin to discovering heretofore unknown pleasures of the body, of simply having limbs, skin, sweat glands… *a pulse.* At times, the feeling of it flowing through you like warm syrup can even pass for a kind of transcendence.

Picture this: I'm motoring northbound on the FDR Drive in my beat-up Datsun Honeybee, heading out for Memorial Day at 5 Sherwood, just as the sun is coming up, and the radio gods serve up gold: "Alive and Kicking" by Simple Minds. And when the gospel vocals come in, I'm weeping tears of Ecstasy gratitude as it plays over my beyond-terrible AM radio, because everything's just so goddamn beautiful.

On a Friday afternoon in August, Dave and I catch *She's Gotta Have It,* the day it comes out. The funny parts are funny as hell, and we do "Please baby, please baby, baby baby *please*" all the way back home, but I'm not sure what to make of a woman bold enough to keep three dudes hanging on, and I sure don't know what to make of the rape scene, which is kind of played for laughs.

Around dusk, the all-stars from our Ecstasy Summer begin to arrive.

Though cramped by any objective measure, 543 East Sixth Street, apartment 4R, is fairly cozy now. Dave has installed shiny black-and-white tiles over our brief hint of kitchen floor, one of several small but noticeable improvements that he's cannily exchanged for portions of the rent. Adding weight to the proceedings, Steve, our old college housemate and Dave's future business partner, is here. His presence, not just his physical presence, which is formidable, but his actual presence, is always a special event in itself. Even in college, on the biggest nights to party, when you fuckin' *had* to show up in your best pair of parachute pants and tucked-in blousy shirt, Steve would be chilling in his off-campus apartment with his lady, Lisa White, who was a few years ahead of us and about to graduate. That was Steve: not participating. Not even conflicted about it. Beyond it.

Vassar was one of the original Seven Sisters and had only been coed for about a decade, yet even at Vassar, Steve was known as someone you wouldn't want to cross in a street fight. He also has an introspective, mystical side; he believes in angels and once pressed Dorothy Bryant's *The Kin of Ata Are Waiting for You* on me, saying it would change my life. I myself have witnessed the dark side of Steve only once—I was cranking "To Hell with Poverty" by Gang of Four in the middle of the day, not realizing Steve was trying to catch up on Z's in his downstairs bedroom. He really looked like he was about to lay me out. (That bass line is pretty unrelenting.) But he's a pal, and on E he's like a giant lion lolling in a dusty veldt. Steve's major contribution to the night is when he kills the lights and fetches a handful of votives from the kitchen cupboard, having left them behind when he moved out a few months ago and made way for me.

Accompanying Steve is Tim White, the brother of Molly White, the sister of Lisa White, Steve's girlfriend at Vassar. The previous year, I'd spent a week with Steve at his place in Seattle, where he'd migrated after college, and fallen swiftly in love with Molly White. And she with me, in a way. Smitten letters and heartbreak followed. Somehow her brother Tim, a gentle-eyed stage actor who's landed in our orbit, is a lovely presence. If I can't have Molly, at least Tim seems to bring some of her alluring spirit around.

Mike Hart, whom I've only recently met while bagging earrings at RJ's apartment for ten bucks an hour, is a high school friend of Dave's. He'd been scuffling around, crashing on couches, and avoiding scrapes just barely until one night out on the town. Dave introduces him to Hayne Suthon, a striking, outrageous New Orleans-born lawyer cum friend of the fabulous, and based on nothing more than Mike Hart's charm and leprechaun twinkle, Hayne lets him stay in small quarters at the top of a building she'd just bought, at 24 First Avenue—in exchange for a minimal amount of rent and walking her twin Dobermans. File it under good luck, or good teeth, but the real miracle of Mike Hart occurred a few weeks later.

Mike's taking a smoke break during an earring-bagging session at RJ's place, now the primary business hub for RJ International LLC. Dave's there too, just to hang out I guess, and Mike's leaning out the window because RJ won't let anyone smoke inside. (We even have to take off our shoes, and at this point it's only Buddhists who do that.) So Mike's leaning out and then suddenly...

No Mike.

A fraction of a moment passes before Dave and I scramble to the window and peer downward. To our crazy relief, he's on his feet—and he's waving. Somehow his body had made one sweet, perfect revolution on the way down and he'd landed feet first in the pit between two buildings. Even the strictest East German judge would have been impressed by how he stuck that landing. So Mike Hart is having a charmed summer.

Marisa arrives. She's in a sort of Madonna phase: bangles, white T-shirt with rolled-up sleeves, cut-off overall shorts. The scene is now complete, because Marisa is something of an Ecstasy muse for me by now. At certain moments she is so right there with you, in that delicious stillness of no words exchanged, reciprocating my dreamy gazes, and with that throaty laugh.

We don't *not* drink with E, but not much anyway. It isn't needed. Nothing is, except music. Even pot can mess up the perfection, per Norman's law. Better to wait till you're on the way down, when you just want to extend the feeling a little bit and keep any jangles at bay. We down ours with a beer and soon we're sprawled in the living room, smoking cigs and getting off, the conversational cadence downshifting to a purr.

Be Yourself Tonight by the Eurythmics is a favorite. It's super soulful, a far cry from their spiky synth-pop, with rich, sumptuous eighties production. Even the album title has an E vibe to it. We all swoon to the rousing Stax-style horn section that opens "It's Alright (Baby's Coming Back)," which seems to impart the message that so many great songs do: It's all right. It's gonna be all right. Someday *everything* will be all right.

Right now it's all so much better than all right. I'm sitting back to back with Tim White, our dorsal regions melding against each other in perfect support. I've never made out with a guy or anything, and it's not like I want to kiss Tim White, but I dearly want to pet his shoulder. And I do, and it's fine, for the syrup has hit us, one and all, and nothing can possibly be wrong.

Whereas a pot conversation is discursive and laugh-infused, and a coke conversation is verbose and taken with itself and ultimately useless, the talk on E is less hyper because the mere act of speaking becomes a physical pleasure.

"It's like a mouthful of stars," I say, co-opting the famous declaration of Dom Pérignon on discovering bubbly ("Come quickly, I'm drinking stars!"). And so we sprawl together on the rug, relishing prostrate-ness and corporeality and the company of warm others who are digging the very same things at the very same time.

The only thing about *Be Yourself Tonight* is it ends on a downish note—so does Peter Gabriel's *So*, another popular E favorite that you can't quite let play through. Maybe it's an eighties thing. I don't want to get up, or even to move, but I rise to fade the tape player.

"Oh, play that song! You know the one."

I do know the one Marisa's calling for: "Calling Your Name in My Sleep," a split 45 on the Techniques label, credited to Ernis Wilson. Months ago, Dave returned from a trip to Jamaica with a passel of seven-inch singles of popular reggae hits. They were in plain paper sleeves, and that lack of adornment gave them an extra element of authenticity. They were a different kind of reggae than what I thought of as reggae—lighter and more playful than Bob Marley's songs of freedom and more in line with the earthy fun of Toots & the Maytals. Ernis Wilson sings in a lilting soul voice on top of a springy two-chord vamp, and it's irresistible—like an Otis Redding song. When it ends, we hit up Dave's reggae trove for a few more boppers based on that same springy little pattern—"Girly Girly" by Sister George and Audrey Hall's "One Dance Won't Do"—and then Marisa takes over DJ duties.

"Rock the Bells" by LL Cool J is a little jarring, truth be told. Steve and Tim don't seem to be digging it at all, but Dave and Marisa are shaking it on down on the parquet. Then it's "Rock Me Amadeus" (the extended 12-inch remix, because Dave is a 12-inch remix kind of guy), and now we're all up and swaying as one, even Steve and Tim. Dave and Marisa lean in close for their favorite bit, when the soul diva vocals come in at about the five-and-a-half-minute point:

Baby, baby, do it to me rock me / Baby, baby, do it to me rock me /
Baby, baby, do it to me rock me / yah yah yaaa-aa-ah...

That seals it. We're going dancing.

In a city teeming with nightlife, Area is the place to be, the nexus of the downtown art, music, and fashion scenes, full of beautiful people, club kids, weirdoes, and wannabes, and suffused with an undeniable buzz of excitement and transgressiveness. Steve and Tim can't see the point and stay behind.

We hail a cab on Avenue A, me up front, Dave, Marisa, and Mike Hart in back, and head down Sixth across B, C, and D to the East Side Drive, which is the fastest way to Hudson Street. South of Houston is still a no-man's-land. You only cross that frontier to go to a gigantic club, or if you're from out of town, perhaps to check out Odeon, the spot celebrated in *Bright Lights, Big City*. Not long ago, feeling young and spry in my black jeans, Chuck Taylors, and newly purchased vintage paisley shirt, I made my way through the hundred-fold Area crowd, approached one of the door guys, and talked my way in—"steamrolled" in Steve's words. This did great things for my ego, and after that, whenever Sean was on, there was no waiting. Sean is on tonight, and so is George, whose blazer jacket pocket fills up all evening with bindle upon cocaine bindle.

We breeze through the velvet ropes and make our way down a long and cavernous stone hallway, passing a series of display windows reminiscent of museum dioramas. Every six weeks or so, it all changes. This constant reinvention makes Area the envy of every other club in the city. The elaborate installations—created around themes like suburbia, the word "gnarly," and the color red—incorporate everything from live lizards to live humans, taxidermy, enemas, and what have you. The nights when a new theme debuts are absolute madhouse events. Even JFK Jr. has to wait outside, for a little while anyway.

We enter the club, moving toward the music with Dave leading the way, and it's the song of the moment: "Life's What You Make It" by Talk Talk. I first heard it here a few weeks ago and it just knocked me out. We pause so a pair of drag queens can lay gently appreciative fingers on Dave's deltoids. "Have a well evening and be gay," one of them trills. Then we snake our way into the delicious darkness of the dancefloor. The Talk Talk song—so full of oomph, yet spacious sounding over the big club system—registers with a visceral kick. It even echoes the refrain from our tenement party: *"Everything's all right…"*

When you live in New York you get used to seeing certain well-known people as a matter of course. They just happen to be out-and-about people, and you live in their neighborhood, so you see them. Thus catching a glimpse of Philip Glass or Allen Ginsberg or Luis Guzmán is as common for me as spotting the possible Nazi with the German shepherd across the street. So it goes on the club scene—and on the dance floor. Sighting the designer Stephen Sprouse with his trademark bandana, or *Village Voice* downtown columnist Michael Musto with his disco whistle, is like seeing Norm at the Cheers bar. "Musto!"

Dave and I make our way to the most centrally located of the club's famed multi-use lavatories. A previous generation had a penchant for stuffing themselves into phonebooths; at Area something similar happens in the bathrooms, but with coke-snorting and sex. A few yards from where we pee, a miniature bacchanal takes place in two adjacent stalls, replete with giggles, grunts, and an ensemble of sniffing. We banter with the two middle-aged Rumanian women who preside in front as attendants. They tell us we're looking good tonight, so we avail ourselves of the adjacent photo booth. Our eyes blaze and our foreheads glow with the sheen of E.

On our way back to Mike and Marisa, I cross paths with David Spada, a regular at Iso who, like RJ, is making anodized aluminum jewelry, only on a much more accomplished artistic level. Spada is close with Keith Haring, and Iso and his wife, Masako, always treat him like a Picasso in the making. He's young, our age, and always a sweet guy to wait on. Apparently, he's poised to break out nationally. His latest project is a Josephine Baker-inspired banana skirt held together with his signature anodized aluminum.[9] Of course, seeing him now, under these conditions, I'm just delighted—a bit overly so.

"Well, you sure seem like you're in a good mood," he says. And I respond, no filter at all, that I am indeed in a good mood because I've ingested "the love drug." I don't call it Ecstasy; I call it the love drug. And he... recoils.

And this is awkward.

See you at the restaurant? Appetizers on me?

As I continue toward the bar, relishing the deliciousness of physical movement, I'm thinking, wow... Not everyone thinks drugs are good.

Mike Hart and I have our backs to the bar and we're enjoying the cold wet brilliance of a bottle of Rolling Rock when the sinister electro funk of "Set it Off" by Strafe creeps up, and we both start chin-nodding in sync. This song is just stone-cold cool, with a bass line you can feel in your viscera, and there's this wonderful spaciousness in the production that invites your head to do infinity circles in the cool, cloud-free zone above your shoulders, a place where distortion pedals are not welcome.

"Mike..."

"Klein?"

"What do you think this song is about?"

"Set it off I suggest, y'all / Set it off I suggest y'all / Set it off! / Come on let's set it off!"

---

9. The dress, a collaboration with the artist Patrick Kelly, is now part of the collection at the Philadelphia Museum of Art. Kelly died in 1990, Spada in 1996, both of AIDS.

A long pause.

"Sex."

And it's just so succinct and deadpan and totally Mike Hart, I have to hug him. He's got another half hit, and we take it with a slug of beer and go back inside. Just in time for, seriously, the song of the moment. Like the Strafe song, there's something gorgeous and unsettling about the way Malcolm McLaren's "Madame Butterfly" creeps in.

You can see her from miles away—Marisa, spot-lit, like the flickering image of the tragic Cio-Cio-San. We reach her just as the soprano part comes in, the aria from the Puccini opera, and we all sink into the song's tremulous flow. And then?

No Mike. Just like out the window that time.

Now it's just us two, and it keeps on being too perfect. "Madame Butterfly" melts away, and now I'm doing slow arm circles to the beat of Janet Jackson's "When I Think of You," and it's so supremely pleasurable that I don't even care that I look like I'm trying to keep from falling backwards down a flight of stairs. Plus, Marisa's doing them too. This is the peak.

At some point later, we can't find Dave or Mike. This isn't unusual. Friendship clusters often lose each other in the crowd this way and end up meeting up at a different venue later on in the night. It's easy enough to leave a message on someone's answering machine. But Marisa has an audition the next day, so we take a cab back to the East Village and get out at St. Mark's and Third, around the corner from her place, in order to grab that perfect end-of-the-night slice—just to tamp it all down good and right. She says she has a joint, so we go up to her place.

Nothing happens. We smoke a teeny joint and maybe a cigarette. We're both pretty wiped out, and she says I can crash on her futon. A few hours later, I steal away while she's still sleeping. Obviously nothing will be said. I have an excuse ready if Dave asks where I've been, but he's not even home yet. He's probably still over at Save the Robots, a basement-level after-hours club located a few blocks south on Avenue B, which has a sand-covered floor to mimic the beach and is dark as a dungeon, like a dirty Vegas.

There was actually one other time I never told Dave about.

Marisa and I took my Datsun Honeybee to some park she knew of, where her parents used to take her when she was a kid, and we spent the afternoon there. On the way back, driving fast with no cars around us and the sun blazing, Marisa fell asleep, and I remember placing a very small blossom I'd taken from the park in her open palm as I drove, and it miraculously staying there, even with the wind blowing through the car like mad. That was the kind of summer it was.

In a year or so, Marisa will become a fixture on *A Different World,* forcing Dave to compete for attention with her new bestie, Lisa Bonet. At this point, though, her brief turn as "Mandy the Waitress" in *The Flamingo Kid* is the stand-out on Marisa's cinematic résumé. Meanwhile, my brief turn as "David the Waiter," as eye-opening as it's been, cannot sustain me. In September, I start my first teaching job and begin grad school, our Ecstasy summer released into the past like an airborne blossom slipping free of a gentle hand.

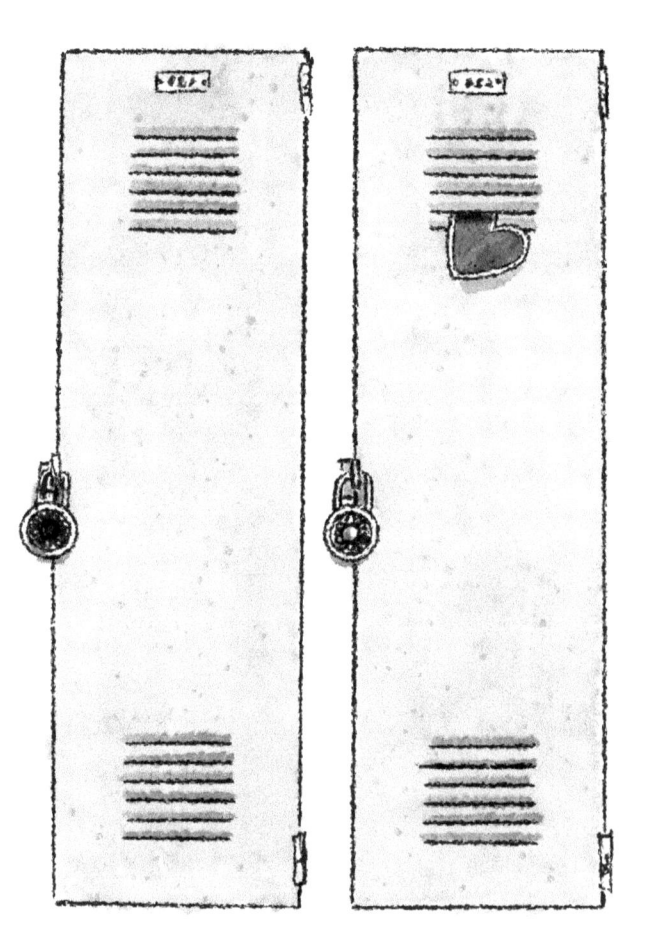

Chapter 17

Clenches and Clover

It's Summer 1987, and the era of AIDS is in full swing. The title track of Prince's *Sign o' the Times,* referencing "the big disease with a little name," is the song of the moment, and the BBC has just banned George Michael's "I Want Your Sex." Two years ago, the death of Rock Hudson propagated the idea that AIDS was a gay disease; and I've surely rationalized the relative okay-ness of meeting and hooking up with women I've just met, in light of my status as a straight non- IV-drug-using man. But AIDS is a worldwide epidemic, and no one is exempt from the risks. I know this now because the *New York Times* just told me so.

According to the assorted scientists, pundits, prelates, and politicians quoted in the paper's science section, the only safe way to have sex is *not* to have it. Condoms, it says, are never *completely* effective in preventing pregnancy or disease transmission. Therefore the upbeat campaign for condom use is sending the wrong message. Casual sex, even with protection, is like playing Russian roulette.

"Unless you're married and you're with a sexual partner who has had *no other sexual experience with someone else,*" adds New York's odious mayor, Ed Koch, just in case anyone was scheming for loopholes.

24 First Avenue previously housed a men-only sex club called Club Baths, which the city shuttered, along with others like it, amid the spiraling AIDS crisis. Dave's fabulous friend Hayne Suthon has just purchased the space, with plans to reopen it as an Ancient Rome-themed restaurant called Cave Canem ("beware of dog"), and Hayne has enlisted Dave and his burgeoning construction company to do the interior demolition work. One afternoon he takes me along when he goes to check on how work is progressing.

Club Baths was actually part of a business chain, one of forty or so venues operating around the country. Opening in 1970, the New York franchise was the city's first openly gay bathhouse, and dozens more followed. Keith Haring lived across the street and was a regular there, especially on "buddy nights," when people lined up in pairs to take advantage of the two-for-one deal that entailed no obligation to remain with whomever they happened to come in with.

The club's entrance intimates nothing of what lies behind it. The company office is nondescript and all but empty save for a wall covered with scores of Polaroid photos and drivers' licenses tacked up in haphazard, overflowing rows. Dave says they belonged to people who got banned from the premises. I wonder what one would have to do to get banned from a place where anything goes. Dave leads the way down a flight of stairs and into a room that opens up into a vast space. Its most notable remnant is a length of thick chain that descends from the apex of a vaulted tiled ceiling and ends in a kind of playground swing, only the seat part has some daylight showing through. (Really puts the chain in business chain.)

We pass in silence by rows and rows of half-smashed wooden bunks resembling army barracks and down a corridor lined with cubicles, each big enough to hold a single cot. In the sub-basement is a neoclassical pool defiled by construction debris, which one day, at Hayne's direction, will be populated with koi.

Just by riding the subways, living in Alphabet City, and going to clubs, I'm aware of a vast range of humanity. But now, standing on a floor strewn with thousands of popped poppers, amid the ruins of a dying culture, I'm at a loss as to what to feel. Dave, however, surmises that a three-man crew will be able to gut the rest of the place in a single day, a satisfying result. Before we go, each of us takes hold of an industrial-strength Hefty bag full of construction detritus and drags it to the company dumpster parked at the curb.

Despite the New York Times, Ed Koch, and the infallible nature of rubbers, I continue my pursuits, albeit with a newfound sense of caution and dread. One example will suffice. Maribeth is the ex-wife of Dietrich, a well-connected friend of Dave's via the club scene who's mostly interested in men at this point. One night, at some club or another, Maribeth is after Dave again, but Dave is not one for repeat entanglements. So, with him unresponsive and me an eager substitute, also named Dave, Maribeth settles for me. (P.S. I'm shrooming.)

Briefly, we go to her place, I join her in the tub, and, while we try to avoid any actual penetration, we're not completely successful. At which point we both get totally freaked out. Because who knows?

Who she's been with...

Who her husband's been with...

Who Dave's been with...

The night haunts me, as do similar encounters in subsequent months. For this is the new math, and you have to factor it into every potential sexual encounter. Given their inherent tawdriness, one-night stands suddenly count double. Beyond the risk factor, there is little joy in waking up in a strange bed with someone you barely know, whose walkup is covered in cat hair and who wants to go get brunch when all you want to do is go home and take a shower. In the end, the authentic danger posed by sex with strangers and the abject awkwardness of such encounters makes the necessity of finding a dedicated girlfriend all the more urgent. A year later, I have one.

We'll get back to this.

Armed with a master's degree, I'm a preschool teacher at a private school in the West Village, located in a stately old church. Don't get me wrong. The place is not stuffy. It's an extremely progressive, liberal, learn-by-doing kind of place. The kids call us by our first names, we're closed for Yom Kippur, and Susan Sarandon's daughter is in the classroom down the hall. As teachers, we're not there to hasten the growth of our young ones, or even to teach them things per se; our role is to facilitate the children's own discoveries and intellectual growth via a variety of classroom materials, including water, sand, paint, wooden unit blocks, and variously textured, interlocking molded plastic doodads known in educational jargon as "manipulatives." The approach we take is extremely specific. We deliberately don't say, "I love your painting,

JoJo," Instead, it's, "Ah, I see you've put a big blue blob next to a small yellow blob." You know—leaving things open-ended and not just offering a rote display of approval. The cardinal sin is to ask a kid, "What is it?" because the question implies that a painting has to be of something.

In April, my assistant, who despite her best efforts never quite gets the reasoning behind the whole paint blob thing, has to bow out due to complications of a pregnancy I'm pretty sure she wasn't planning on. My employer, the church, looks within its ranks and finds a willing congregant to serve as a replacement for the final six weeks of the term.

Amanda.

She's a natural with the kids and skilled in all sorts of ways. She creates beautiful signs for the classroom, leads miniature apple sauce-making symposiums, becomes a magnet for some of the quieter girls, and bonus, she's easy on the eyes. I find her regally pretty, but there's nothing reserved about her. She's not shy about her big laugh or making a goofy face to augment an anecdote.

When our hands aren't busy with books and mittens and paintbrushes, we stand back and watch our brood acting out their dramas, or we goof on something a snooty parent said that morning at drop-off. And we talk about ourselves. Her husband is a remote stoner who runs a small but lucrative family business manufacturing buttons and trimmings. They married long ago, when she was still in college, and whatever warmth ever existed between them has all but ceased to exist. He doesn't ask about her day, won't hold her hand when they're out on the street together. Family dinners take place on their king-size bed, in front of the TV. Hearing about Amanda's wreck of a marriage, I reciprocate with tales about Clover, my girlfriend of a year or so and co-tenant of a few months.

Cracks in our happy-couple facade had been showing even before Clover and I moved into a bright little Chelsea apartment together, a decision motivated as much by real estate as by a desire to cohabitate. Fresh out of grad school and searching for suitable employment, Clover is stressed out and feeling insecure about our relationship. Worse, her foibles have stirred up a sense of peevish dissatisfaction in me.

Clover smokes clove cigarettes, and her favorite color is crimson. She assures me this has nothing to do with the chart-topping hit by Tommy James & the Shondells or even the remake by Joan Jett & the Blackhearts; she just genuinely prefers the taste of clove cigarettes and a certain shade of red. I've never quite believed it, and over time I've started to wonder how many of her other quirks are self-concocted. Why else does she surround herself exclusively with obscurely named people? Is it a complete fluke that every last person in the social orbit of Clover Lynnette Gribetz has a name like Sinjin or Minard or Beata? The mere existence of a casual friend named Nancy or Mike or Chuck would blow the whole theory out of the water.

Whenever a familiar song comes on the radio, Clover has to harmonize. Has to. It could be a song meant to be sung in unison—a Gregorian chant, Martin Luther's hymn "Ein feste Burg ist unser Gott," "Celebration" by Kool & the Gang—and she'll still supply a harmonic counterpoint. The butterfly tattoo on her ankle, I recently decided, is corny, as is Sugar Bear, her latest romantic nickname for me. And then there's Clover's dad, who insisted on meeting my folks for dinner very early on in the relationship and, over hangar steak and sweet potato fries, recounted a lengthy anecdote about jerking off an Irish Setter with priapism. Angus, if memory serves. Amanda finds it all very amusing.

The school year ends on a sticky day in early June. Teachers have to return the following week, mostly to clean our classrooms from top to bottom. We scrub the variously shaped wooden blocks known as unit blocks with Murphy Oil Soap; set the brightly hued "bristle blocks" in warm soapy bins to remove a year's worth of accreted gunk, funnel tempera paint in primary colors from jelly jars into plastic jugs, and since everything in a progressive early classroom is labeled, from where the kids stand when they line up to the shelves that house the manipulatives, there's much tape to be removed. And I don't mind a bit. I've got Amanda in my midst and my tapes are playing on the classroom boombox. This means the Smiths, the Chills, the Go-Betweens, the Feelies, Julian Cope—and all of it new to her.

On the eve of our last day of classroom cleanup, I dismiss all sense of professional reserve and fall back on my collegiate training, setting out to make an irresistible, no-holds-barred mix for her to ponder over the summer and beyond (code name: "Amanda Seduction Tape"). Well, what do I have to lose? She's in a different league, age-wise and echelon-wise. She's married—unhappily married but married—with two kids and a raging church habit. And when will I even see her again now that she's no longer my assistant? Remember, this is before you could depend on the casual exchange of email addresses or a low-stakes social media follow. Unless we run into each other on the street, that's it. Our time is up. So I don't hold back.

Songs for Amanda

DEEP FASCINATION – THE FEELIES

LOVE GOES ON – THE GO-BETWEENS

SIDE OF THE ROAD – LUCINDA WILLIAMS

YOU MAKE ME FEEL – THE WOODENTOPS

ASK – THE SMITHS

OH YEAH – ROXY MUSIC

LOVE AND AFFECTION – JOAN ARMATRADING

NEVER SAY GOODBYE – BOB DYLAN & THE BAND

THE MEETING PLACE – XTC

THE INDIA SONG – BIG STAR

THERE IS A LIGHT THAT NEVER GOES OUT – THE SMITHS

WHY WON'T YOU STAY? – AMERICAN MUSIC CLUB

TUPELO HONEY – VAN MORRISON

THE GREATNESS AND PERFECTION OF LOVE – JULIAN COPE

DON'T DREAM IT'S OVER – CROWDED HOUSE

SEE A LITTLE LIGHT – BOB MOULD

EVERY DAY I WRITE THE BOOK – ELVIS COSTELLO

YOU'RE THE WISH YOU ARE I HAD – XTC

GOLDEN BROWN – THE STRANGLERS

THROW YOUR ARMS AROUND ME – HUNTERS & COLLECTORS

ANDALUCIA – JOHN CALE

LITTLE WING – JIMI HENDRIX

WET BLANKET – THE CHILLS

Sometimes love is just the theme of a tape. Not every lyric is meant literally. In the Go-Betweens' "Love Goes On," when Grant McLennan sings, *"There's a cat in the alleyway / Dreaming of birds that are blue / Sometimes girl when I'm lonely / This is how I think about you,"* I do not mean to suggest to Amanda that he speaks for me directly, but for love unrequited in general. Hell, the opening couplet of "Throw Your Arms Around Me" by Hunters & Collectors (*"I will come for you at night time / I will wake you from your sleep"*) could get me arrested if she were to take it at face value. But there are times when you choose a song because the singer expresses exactly how you feel, literally and poetically. The tape's final song, despite its seemingly vibe-killing title of "Wet Blanket," is the most unambiguously about us: *"Well I'm not in love with anyone, but I could fall in love with you / Because you're so, so, so beautiful, why aren't you mine?"*

I spend the summer working as a burrito roller at Kitchen in Chelsea and fighting with Clover in the evenings. In mid-August the director of the school calls to let me know that Amanda will be returning as my assistant. I feel a weird tingle in my stomach. At the first staff meeting, we have a moment together and she tells me that she and her husband are living apart as of a few weeks ago. And she's been listening to my tape all summer.

Tingle tingle…

During the first few weeks of school, when my mind should be focused on gaining an understanding of my students—the kids who fall apart at rest time, those who need their shoes retied with double knots, the apple juice spillers, the P.B. & J. stashers—I'm full-on obsessed with my assistant. At home with Clover, I concoct fictitious errands just so I can go out and *think* about Amanda, completely unfettered, as I pace up and down Eighth Avenue.

Throughout much of the workday, the two of us engage in an ongoing conversation, verbal and otherwise. Some of our interactions suggest to me that *something* is going on here. Did our hands stay touching for an extra moment accidentally on-purpose as we shook out that newly donated rug for the reading nook? Did we just hold eye contact for way longer than was strictly necessary during the fire drill? Because it sure felt that way. We're not flirtatious, exactly, but when you know, you know.

There's a small room off the classroom where we stow our personal stuff in old-fashioned school lockers. One morning, after escorting the kids down the hall for music instruction, we're there at the same time and I pull her to me and kiss her quickly, because it isn't at all safe to linger. Like Adrienne in *Rocky*, she doesn't have to kiss me back, but she does. A few mornings later, she mentions that her kids will be picked up by an aunt that afternoon and will be spending the rest of the day with her. When class lets out, we clean up and chatter as usual, but when we finish, instead of going our separate directions, we amble together on an eastward course. Without a word being uttered, we queue up at the Art Greenwich Theater on West 12th Street and buy tickets for a critically acclaimed film that's already in progress.

And finally, we're alone together in the glorious, unsupervised dark.

It's all so forbidden—so "not OK," as we tell our young charges when a serious infraction occurs—like one kid biting another kid. The feeling is more intense than anything I've ever experienced. I could almost explode. And it's mutual. Amanda says she gets overcome with a feeling in her chest when we're close together. She calls them "clenches."

As Amanda and I start operating on the ultra-top-secret down-low, Clover and I begin to unravel. We meet with a relationship counselor—at her insistence and on her parents' dime—who listens to us and asks questions and then speaks with us one-on-one, where we can be more candid. I have to assume it's after hearing my version of things that the therapist is convinced we should break up. But Clover and I are married to the lease we signed, and the landlord insists on being paid until he, or we, can find a new tenant.

I put an ad in *The Village Voice* and squeeze in showings during my lunch break. A couple shows some mild enthusiasm, but they didn't dig having to step over a pile of vomit on the way in, and also expressed concerns about the towering Covenant House rehab facility just up the block. (The two may or may not be related.) When I can barely stand to look at the place, much less enter it, I begin staying at my sister's mercifully vacant apartment on the Upper West Side.

During our estrangement, Clover shows up at my school one day after dismissal, in a state. She tells me she can no longer tolerate having to look at my personal items anymore and is about to put them in the hallway, starting with my Sony Trinitron. She leaves in a huff, and I chase her up East Ninth Street for half a block until I'm able to catch hold of her jacket sleeve—my jacket sleeve, actually.

"Clover, my grandmother gave me that TV. Do not put it in the hallway where someone will steal it."

"Well why the hell did you move out and leave it if it's so important to you?"

"OK then. That's my jacket."

Irked at having to first unsnap and then unzip my leather bomber jacket (thank you, Brooks Brothers design department), Clover shrugs it off in a perverse shimmy, panting from the accumulated effort and emitting fog clouds.

"And, um… " I say, casually gesturing.

Maintaining unbroken eye contact until the yanked sweater briefly conceals her fierce glare, Clover slams my crewneck to the concrete and takes off westward toward the slanting sun, protected from the winter air by nothing more than a tank top and one of her flesh-colored, antique-looking camisoles. I take off after her, and once she promises to lay off Grandma's TV, she gets the warm clothes back.

It's springtime and balmy by the time the landlord consents to let us out of the lease—for the low, low price of an additional one-month's rent. Clover and I meet at the building owner's office in Tribeca to sign the final paperwork, and in minutes we're done.

Time slows to a crawl as the Gilded Age-era elevator clanks its way to the sixth floor. At one point Clover's father had threatened to sue me, for breach of contract or something. This was, after all, a guy who saw things through to the bitter end—just ask Angus. And Clover has finked out on various mutual associated costs along the way, out of her intense aggrievement, so there is no love lost here. The elevator arrives, the doors lurch open, and we descend to street level in a black cloud of hostile silence. Liberated, we start walking in opposite directions, and it dawns on me that our long national nightmare is finally over.

Suddenly I start to sashay like Groucho. Then I'm leaping for all I'm worth, my fist raised in triumph like the protesting Olympic athletes in 1968; then I'm streetwalking Travolta in the opening credits of *Saturday Night Fever*. As I'm about to launch into a potentially injurious jeté, I feel, rather than hear, the ominous crescendo of rapidly approaching footsteps.

"I saw that!" she shrieks. "I saw that! You're *celebrating*? This makes you *happy*?? Fuck *yooooou!*" she howls. "You think you're so great? You're twenty-eight years old and you make eighteen thousand dollars a year! That's how great you are!"

As bemused New Yorkers veer nonchalantly out of our way—they've seen this kind of shit before—she has a few more choice words for me and my station in life, before turning on her heel and burning up Broadway, never to be seen again.[10]

Well, she hit me where it hurt. I'll say that much for Clover. But I'm out of her financial yoke, and Amanda and I are free to carry on—as morally questionable as it may be. And we do carry on, for a good while after we stop teaching together and into the new decade. On nights when her kids are with their father or aunt, she makes me shrimp and couscous, because it's my favorite. No one has ever done this for me: taken the time to know what my favorite is, much less make it for me. We take the subway to Long Beach, stopping to buy a bottle of Veuve Clicquot before we hit the sand, and we sip Champagne in the sun and do crosswords and play backgammon on a blanket. On Sunday nights we meet for dinner at Manhattan Chili and go back to her place in time for *Twin Peaks*. Once we sneak out to her friend's unoccupied second home, where we luxuriate in a completely forbidden weekend together. We also grow close in ways that don't involve stealth and cunning.

The effect of that initial tape had been seismic. She says that "Side of the Road" by Lucinda Williams (*"If only for a minute or two / I want to see what it*

---

10. Until Facebook

feels like to be without you") played into her decision to leave her husband. The tape also revives her love of music. She starts exploring the record shops she'd walked past for years without ever entering, chatting up the taciturn clerks at Kim's on St. Mark's Place to see what's new and interesting. One day she plays me one of her discoveries, *Seizure* by Chris Knox, one of the founding fathers of the New Zealand indie scene. I know nothing of him, and it floors me. *She* floors me.

Those heart clenches she spoke about? I start getting them too.

Chapter 18

Klein Living

The word 'man' comes easy to MTV Europe head of on-air presentation Jonathan Klein. Almost as easy as words like bullshit, masturbatory, fuck, Dadaism, and visual hype.

An American in London, Klein describes himself as a volatile exile, a one-time ABC News tea-boy cum writer/producer who has made good in the land of dreamy dreams, or, in his case, Music Television.

"Where else," he asks pointedly, "could a guy of 27 get to be head of on-air presentation for a TV station that's seen all over Europe?

In the summer of 1988, my brother is the subject of a profile in a glossy arts-and-culture magazine called *Invision*. Title: "KLEIN LIVING."

Accompanied by a full-page, low-angle photo of Jonny gazing coldly out the window of a London black cab, the feature presents him as a motor-mouthed media sage with an unwavering vision for MTV Europe. Jonny says the station needs to move beyond music videos and showcase visual innovation more broadly. He says MTV Europe should reflect all of Europe, not just England, and that VJs should speak as little as possible. Immediately, dutifully even, I run off a few copies of the article on the Xerox machine at school, where I still have key access during summer months.

My brother is on a tear. In a few years, he's vaulted from doing overnight fill-in work at an ABC News affiliate to MTV's Times Square newsroom to a position of power and influence across the Atlantic. By providence, luck, or miracle, he's found his way into an industry where his kind of manic creativity is prized. Jonny's mind operates at Warp Factor 1, generating ten ideas in the space of five minutes, seven of which might be feasible. And since the corporate creative process entails a lot of spit-balling, eyeballs tend to rivet his way when he starts emitting ideas. The smartest guy in the room? It's a fair description. Me? I'm just the tallest guy in the room.

I wipe noses, zip jackets, comfort the crying; I refill disposable juice cups, distribute pretzel rods, and maneuver rain boots onto rubbery feet. At rest time I read from a well-thumbed hardcover volume called *Told Under the Blue Umbrella*, a collection of stories published in the 1950s. "The Poppy-Seed Cakes," in which a greedy goose stuffs itself with baked goods until it explodes, is a classroom favorite. When school ends, I oversee the extended-day program, where kids horse around and play games until a parent or caregiver, usually toting a small sibling or two, arrives to pick them up. More apple juice, more pretzels.

I haven't got a single male friend who's doing anything similar. The other teachers are mostly married women in their thirties and forties with kids of their own, Upper West Side liberals who get their tortellini at Fairway and love Paul Simon's *Graceland* and are very earnest about progressive education. Sometimes I wonder what's really driving me to pursue a path where money, power, and prestige will never be found. I truly get a kick out of being around young people, listening to them, reading to them, seeing things from their perspective. But the singularly sincere nature of this kind of work occasionally has me feeling like a fraud. Part of me is still a hothead from Jersey who wouldn't mind a life that rocked a little more.

In March '88, a few months before "KLEIN LIVING" comes out, I cobble together the cash to fly to London over spring break and stay with my brother at his flat in hip Primrose Hill. I pack a journal, because the last travel journal I'd kept—during a solo trek to St. Maarten where I ran out of money—had yielded my first honest-to-goodness story, one that Uncle Mike had praised in a recent letter:

Dear David,

I finally had a chance to read your short story on the plane to LA last week. Rob Lowe, nominated for best supporting actor (Square Dance) invited Noni to be his date at the Golden Globe awards. Cindy and I went to catch it on TV and do a few other things.

You're a born writer, Davy. You have a nice easy flowing style far more suited to the novel form than the short story. You take your time, like to build up to things. It really reads like Chapters 1 through 4 of a novel. Continue writing it. Chapter 5 should be a giant 3-way sex scene with Alexandra, Ellen and the narrator, and then go on with it from there. Maybe a novel of the intricacies of triad relationships, or the narrator goes on to something (or someone) else. I was <u>really</u> getting interested just when you stopped writing. So: don't stop (unless you're bored with it)...

Love, Uncle Mike

I arrive at my brother's spacious, gloriously record-strewn digs, and the first order of business is to purchase a futon. His not anticipating my eventual need for a bed does not feel like a welcoming gesture, and characteristically he offers no apology or explanation. It's just, oh, right—you'll need to sleep somewhere, won't you? So off to the high street we go, Bro with a bike messenger bag slung over his shoulder, stuffed with promotional LPs scored from MTV's offices. We stop in at a half dozen music shops where he trades in LPs for cash, and we return with a futon, the cost offset by vinyl. When evening settles, we head to Mr. Kong in Chinatown for Peking duck, the best in London, I'm assured.

Inside knowledge of fine eateries is a Jonny specialty. He used to take me to this fantastic hole-in-the-wall Thai place in Queens where they seemed happy to accept his cooking suggestions as part of his continued patronage. Like this special shrimp dish that involved a bit of flattening before the shrimp were quick-fried, and which Jonny could never order without a flourish of culinary pantomime. He was an early sushi adopter, when the concept of consuming raw fish still frightened the average American. At Japanese restaurants, he orders a maki roll with shiso leaf *on the inside*—at least in part, it seems to me, to establish simpatico relations with the waiter. He overtips in the same performative way, so the server will be blown away by his generosity—and also to show me *how it's done*. At Mr. Kong, an exchange of knowing banter takes place about the duck broth. But as promised, it's out of this fucking world.

Back at his flat, we smoke up a giant hash joint—the British way, mixed with tobacco, which makes me hack my brains out—and start a new tape. He already has a title: "NO WEAK SHIT."

Of most major urgency is Sort Sol, a Danish band whose name means "black sun" and whose lead singer has an arm stunted by Thalidomide. Jonny says he partied with the band in epic fashion over a recent weekend in Copenhagen. "Boy/Girl," Sort Sol's duet with Lydia Lunch, is track 1, followed by their seething cover of Roky Ericson's "The Interpreter," which completely blows my socks off. Up next, the Stomach Mouths, Stockholm garage punks named after an item culled from a tragically imprecise Swedish translation of *A Confederacy of Dunces*; "My Life Is Like a Stanley Knife" by Golden Strings—Buzzcocks worshipers from Maastricht, Netherlands; and a Boston band called the Pixies, who sound nothing like what their name suggests.

I'm at the banquet of my dreams now, at liberty to gorge upon these rare and exhilarating sonic morsels. When Jonny's with you—really with you, fully participatory as he is now, cueing you to the next song and the next and the next, "Oh, you fucking *need* this one"-style, there's nowhere else in the world I'd rather be. It's why I'm here.

With Side 1 complete, yawns and goodnights are finally exchanged. He pads off to his room, and I flop onto the futon in a state of happy exhaustion, the memory of its awkward purchase blurring into inconsequentiality.

No Weak Shit

BOY/GIRL - SORT SOL W. LYDIA LUNCH

THE INTERPRETER - SORT SOL

DON'T PUT ME DOWN - THE STOMACH MOUTHS

MY LIFE IS LIKE A STANLEY KNIFE (CUT CUT CUT) - GOLDEN STRINGS

VAMOS - PIXIES

CRASH - THE PRIMITIVES

WALKAWAY - SURF DRUMS

LOLLIPOP - THE LEATHER NUN

SWEET WATER POOLS - SCREAMING BLUE MESSIAHS

BEAT DIS - BOMB THE BASS

MOTORCRASH - THE SUGARCUBES

DON'T IT MAKE YOU FEEL - THE BAMBI SLAM

In the morning, we take a cab to an audio session on Denmark Street, an iconic address in British popular music that I know from the Kinks song of the same name. Founded in 1954 by a bandleader/session violinist named Ralph Elman, who played on "I Am the Walrus" and "Within You and Without You," Tin Pan Alley Studios is located in the sub-basement of No. 22. Jonny's here in this high-tech cave to direct a thirty-second promo for an MTV contest. The clip combines narration and footage of an island getaway over a Cabaret Voltaire loop. Jonny dictates directives to an engineer who executes the commands. At Jonny's suggestion, one of the technicians—a long-haired Englishman with a hyphenated surname—picks up an electric bass and comes up with a sparse funk pattern. Savory Indian takeout food is brought in, cigarettes are smoked. It takes all morning. We then head to a different studio to do a promo for an "Australia Rocks" competition, scored to—what else—Midnight Oil.

The novelty wears off pretty quickly, and I decide to fly solo. The next day, I check out the Tate Gallery and the National Gallery, and take in *Withnail and I*, the most English of movies, relishing the simple pleasure of consuming a pint of beer in a darkened theater. And I spend hours knocking around Camden Town, listening to my freshly made mixes on a crudely repaired Sports Walkman. One day when it's pissing down rain, I stay at the flat making tapes and waiting to hear from Bro. Eventually he calls, and I get lost and drenched making my way to a raw industrial rehearsal space, where he and his bandmates in Mona Lisa Overdrive are jamming.

Jonny is the human lodestar for a crew of talented co-workers at MTV Europe, all of whom will go on to make formative pieces of nineties alt-rock culture. Over the course of the week, at pubs and over dinner, I meet them all. Henryk Schyffert, the guitarist in Jonny's band (naturally named for a William Gibson novel), is a garrulous, completely self-assured twenty-year-old from Stockholm who will, in five years, achieve indie rock glory with "Hobo Humpin' Slobo Babe." I spend an afternoon listening to the Sundays over and over with Mark Pellington, an imposing Baltimorean director-producer who will, in five years, win the MTV Video of the Year Award for Pearl Jam's "Jeremy." Then there's John Dunton-Downer. Svelte and vaguely Kennedy-esque, he's a familiar kind of wunderkind, an amazing high-energy talker in the Jonny tradition and passionately knowledgeable about Ballard, Burroughs, Salinger, and Sanskrit. In five years, he'll be a producer of MTV's *120 Minutes*. Double D has a deep, abiding love of the sick/puerile humor found in English comics like *Viz*, home of "Johnny Fartpants" and "The Bottom Inspectors," and I love him immediately.

Everyone I meet through Bro, even this very posh woman we cross paths with on Primrose Hill High Street—who turns out to be a former lover with a fanciful British name like Pippa Coppersmith-Heaven—strikes me as in Jonny's thrall to one degree or another. Witnessing London's widespread acknowledgement of my brother's special brilliance fans the flames of my lifelong worship.

The weekend rolls into view, and we drive out to Winchester, about ninety minutes from London, with Double D and a guy named Alan, whose parents are away on holiday. Also along is a pale English girl who just needs a lift, who drinks from a carton of Ribena and upon whom I form a crush as we motor out to the countryside. At Alan's parents' house, I spring my surprise: four hits of

Uncle Mike's purple windowpane. I had been praying we'd have the right time and place for it and am thrilled the moment has arrived.

We take it in Alan's parents' kitchen with Ruddles Best Country Ale (not nearly the best and actually quite horrible) and head out to this wide open, I want to call it a heath—and we have a mad old time. Something ancient in this cathedral city, inhabited since the Iron Age, calls to us, leading to unhinged capering and crazed speeches aimed at the starlit sky. I distinctly recall telling off the moon that night: *"Ooh, err! Look at me, I'm the Moooooon! Oh, don't give me any of that 'I'm the Moon' shit. You're just the big round shiny thing in the sky. Why don't you call yourself that, you fancy fucker?"*

I only get down to serious journal writing on the flight home. Thus far I've managed to jot down cursory notes on people, places, and meals, but now that I have the time and inclination to sort through the last ten days, I'm most moved to ruminate on the horrible fight we just had.

It was my final night and I figured we could take in from the great Vietnamese place he'd been raving about and finish Side 2 of "NO WEAK SHIT." But he had arranged to meet up with a young woman at a pub. I played the brother card, and he threw it back at me double, basically saying my entire visit had taxed him unreasonably, starting with the forced futon purchase.

Still, when the dust settles, what lingers of my London trip is the knowledge that Jonny has the coolest life in the world. Jealousy is not what I feel—more like a trace of disappointment in myself for not walking the world with his kind of swagger. A month later, Jonny's in New York on business, and with a little pressure I get him to visit me at the school where I teach. I want him to see what I do, maybe even recognize that some of my nobler characteristics have come to fruition. He shows up, takes in an hour of preschool activity, and has very little to say afterward, which is rare for him. We grab a sandwich and find a bench in Central Park. Taking note of a braided loop of colorful yarn threaded through a buttonhole of my jean jacket, he says, "So, what's up with the hippie look?" Kinda snidely.

"This? Oh, one of the kids in my extended-day group made it for me. I'm not trying to look fashionable or anything, so it doesn't matter if I'm in step with the times or not."

"Yeah, yeah," he says. "I know all about semiotics."

See, I don't know a thing about semiotics—the science of symbols and signs—but he does. That's why he's in such high demand.

MTV Europe is still in its infancy in late 1989. Its parent company is not yet a truly global presence, and the Berlin Wall has just fallen. So my brother's timing is perfect when he pitches *Buzz*, a news show with an international focus that will leverage MTV's worldwide affiliates. This way, Guess Jeans and Nike can sell their wares in Brussels or Bangkok or Berlin. It seems obvious now, but this is a gargantuan leap for a station that had trumpeted its commercial-free status at the beginning of the decade. Meanwhile, Jonny's pal Mark Pellington has just made an eight-minute pilot for a show called "Sign of the Times," consisting of video imagery and music connected by a particular theme, and all of it "put it through a little blender." The bigwigs decide to mix the chocolate with the peanut butter, and Jonny and Mark are commissioned to "come up with something."

What the suits have in mind is something basic and inoffensive: say, a George Michael video plus a piece on a local band and a couple of news packages, all tied together by the dulcet tones of Kurt Loder. Jonny and Mark, on the other hand, seek to reflect the world in all its confusing, contradictory messiness—think televised acid.

It's all very post-*Max Headroom*, a mind-melting mix of video, news footage, interviews, super-8, avant-garde film techniques, and projections, loosely secured to the chassis of a news show, with the voice of William Burroughs woven throughout as a sort of ghost narrator. The show operates at two speeds: cocaine and heroin. It begins at full throttle, with a confrontational title sequence that's like being pummeled by a jackhammer. In smack mode, words and images flicker, morph, and dissolve in sync with an otherworldly soundtrack. Undergirding the mind-blowing visuals is a genuine zeal to hip the young people of Earth to those on the artistic and technological vanguard: word artist Jenny Holzer, the virtual reality pioneer Jaron Lanier, the radical environmentalists of EarthFirst, Sid Mead, the visual designer of *Blade Runner*, and, of course, a pair of foundational Williams—Burroughs and Gibson.

Jonny and Mark proudly advocate for cultural appropriation, and they gleefully plunder MTV's holdings. Any video that the station has ever aired is considered fair game. MTV will still be clearing rights to *Buzz*'s use of images six months after the show is canceled.

As Pellington later explained, "They stuck us in a building and didn't know what we were up to till it was too late. We never even thought about it until they said, 'You gotta stop.' They said, 'You're weird, you're depressing, and you're expensive. And you can't be all three.'"

MTV markets the show as best it can, but *Buzz* is too much, too soon—too fast. Each of the thirteen episodes of *Buzz* Season 1 airs exactly once, in the spring of 1990. I own VHS copies of the whole series and have viewed it multiple times, but I'm adamant that Amanda and I watch the show when it airs—in the purgatorial time slot of 10 P.M. on Sundays. Coming on after the Top 20 video countdown and followed by yet more music videos, *Buzz* reveals those videos for the slick advertisements that they are. I'm so familiar with it by now that it no longer leaves me gobsmacked, but I do savor the micro-bits of inspiration that raced past my synapses on the first, second, and third viewings. Amanda, knowing how much I care, murmurs her approval, but I sense she finds it all a little befuddling. Hey, who wouldn't?

Then the show just disappears—not only from the airwaves but seemingly from collective memory. Even as some shushed part of my mind wishes it was a little more approachable, maybe, it never really clicks that the point of creating a show like this is for it to actually catch on, and like, make money. I figure thirteen episodes is a whopping lode of *Buzz* that will stand for eternity. Jonny never mentions that by Episode 10, he and Mark already knew the show would not be renewed. When we do get around to discussing the show's demise, Jonny says they just didn't get it. *Buzz* was ahead of its time. Fuck 'em. He has bigger fish to fry.

To the MTV moguls, the show might have looked like a colossal waste of 1.3 million pounds at the time, but ultimately the investment is well recouped. For one thing, they get a bead on the power of the word "buzz," which predated the show in the form of Buzz Clips but would soon be slapped on all things new and cool, like the MTV Buzz Bin, where you can catch avant-garde videos made for "buzz-worthy" acts (Fiona Apple, Radiohead, Bjork) by a new New Wave of soon-to-be Hollywood directors (Spike Jonze, David Fincher, Jonathan Glazer), and even *MTV Buzzkill*, a hidden-camera prank show precursor to the much more popular *Punked*. Beyond that, MTV's look—its promos and bumpers and increasingly caffeinated pace—takes on an increasingly *Buzz*-like character as the decade wears on.

On the one hand, it's criminal that *Buzz* isn't held in the same high, nostalgic esteem as stuff like *The Real World* and *Beavis and Butthead*, less radical programming that predicted whole genres of the cable TV ecosystem on the rise. But the timing was off, and the kinder, gentler version of *Buzz* that survived its first season still probably wouldn't have limped on for a half-decade to be a generational touchstone, the brain-melting lead-in to *Aeon Flux* cartoons that it was destined to be.

You can see the future and still misread the bus schedule.

Chapter 19

The Talented Mr. Stench

I've just been Tased by Johnny Depp's Taser. Not by Johnny Depp, though, which would be a lot cooler. Sadly, I consort with the kind of people who would Tase me with Johnny Depp's Taser at a moment's notice, simply because I let them hold Johnny Depp's Taser. And that's not cool at all.

My first cousin, Winona Ryder, Noni to me, is engaged to the Depper, and this has afforded me a weird kind of occasional close access to Johnny, a rising star who's on the cusp of epic hugeness. We first met in the spring of 1990, at a sparsely attended daytime showing of *Cry-Baby* at the Paramount Theatre on Columbus Circle. At this point, he had already been a victim of Freddy Kreuger, a certified TV star, and a bona fide teen idol, but this was his first starring role in a movie. I'm a huge John Waters fan, given to reciting lengthy stretches of dialogue from *Female Trouble* and *Desperate Living*, and proud of my Bal'more inflections. ("Mr. *Weinberger*, Dawn Davenport is eating a meatball sandwich *right out in class*. And she's been *passing notes*.") I sincerely wanted to love *Cry-Baby*, but as a sendup of teen exploitation movies it struck me as pure pastiche and not nearly outrageous enough. I kept this to myself. Anyway, Johnny wasn't interested in doing a postmortem. After the screening, in the cab with Noni and Amanda, he turns to me and initiates a game of Would You Rather.

"So, Skysby," he says, employing the nickname Noni calls me and I call her, "would you rather be tossed into a swimming pool full of greased naked epileptics on Ecstasy, or snort a line of Larry King's ear hair?"

"Hmm… am I clothed or unclothed?"

"You wear a small neoprene loin cloth."

"Ah. The pool then."

Eventually, he brings up a recent tape I'd made for Noni, which they've been listening to on repeat. Two songs especially.

"The one that goes, *'This is a love song / for John and Lesia's mother,'*" he whisper-sings.

"Oh yeah. 'Not Given Lightly' by Chris Knox."

I should give credit to Amanda here. I really should. She's the one who hipped me to Chris Knox. But she and Noni are having their own conversation, and since Depp is so impressed with my musical taste, I see no point in dispelling the notion. The other song he mentions is Julian Cope's "China Doll." This I talk about.

Julian Cope led the British neo-psychedelic post-punk outfit the Teardrop Explodes and earned a reputation for copious LSD intake. The band had hits in the UK but was not well known stateside. Julian cleaned up his act a bit during the latter part of the decade, and *My Nation Underground,* his 1988 LP, contained several odes to smitten-ness, delivered in a courtly baritone not far from Scott Walker, which were just the thing to express the yearnings of my unfulfilled heart. Every romantic mix I've put together in the past few years has had some Julian on it. What girl could resist? I love Julian all the more because my brother actually knows him. They would spend afternoons at Bro's flat, skinning up joints of cheap commercial pot, "settling in for the slow stoning" in the words of Copey. During these sessions, Julian's encyclopedic knowledge of Druidic history, German motorik music of the 1970s, and a host of other disparate subjects leaves my brother dumbstruck.

Depp is hip to many things, but not to Cope, and he falls hard. I can see why. "China Doll" is like a four-minute musical miniature starring Johnny as the brooding romantic (*"Cause I'm an earthbound boy, and so I worship you, China Doll"*) and Noni as the ingenue (*"Little black-haired girl, pale and unsure"*). For a while, it's their song.[11]

Crafting the soundtrack of a famous couple's romance strikes me as a kind of validation, as if my lifelong fascination with pop music has finally paid off

---

11. And in a way, it never stopped being their song. Two decades later, Johnny left a message of himself singing "China Doll" on Noni's answering machine.

and imbued me with a sort of expertise. I put a great deal of care into the follow-up mix, which I mail to them in Florida, where they're filming *Edward Scissorhands*. It includes the Lemonheads, the Clean, Robyn Hitchcock, and the confoundingly catchy "I Gonna Be (500 Miles)" by the Proclaimers.

The next time I see them, at a backyard party thrown by my parents for my newly married brother and his wife, I have a fresh tape in hand. I'm in the driveway with Mom, moving patio furniture out of the garage, when their limo pulls up.

"Can I help?" asks Johnny, after greeting me with a warm hug and Mom with a courtly handshake.

"Sure," says Mom. "Well how do you like that. You just got here, and already we're putting you to work."

"Oh, that's OK," he says. "We're family."

Dressed conservatively in a crisp white shirt and black trousers, Johnny talks jazz with Dad, Salinger with Mom, and Old Hollywood with my grandmother. He charms the pants off everybody. I ride back into the city with them, and we spin Tape 3, which is heavy on London's darkly jangling The House of Love.

Johnny and Noni have just moved into a prewar loft on Duane Street in Tribeca; coincidentally, I've recently sorted out my own living arrangements. After three consecutive apartment situations went south for a cornucopia of reasons, the New Testament God has graced me with a place on West 10th Street that Amanda's church friend is not occupying. I can actually afford it on my meager savings, and no security deposit is required. I'm lucky as hell to have an apartment of my own in the West Village for $350 a month. That's what I keep telling myself.

Located on the fifth floor of a narrow walk-up, 5RW is 150 square feet max. The front door is secured with what's called a police lock, a steel pole that runs diagonally from the lock fixture to a groove in the slanted, pitted floor. Ninety years ago, when the building was constructed, people lived in fear of losing their possessions and were willing to barricade themselves behind heavy-duty locks of all stripes—whatever worked. And these ones, produced by the Fox Police Lock Company on West 21st Street, worked very well indeed, a fact confirmed by firefighters who testified that it took considerable effort to bash through them in emergency situations.

The basic human necessities greet you as you enter: a claw-footed bathtub topped by a plank of wood supporting a dish rack, a squat fifties-era fridge, and a functional gas stove that might have served up dinner on the night Warren

G. Harding was elected. In a space adjoining the eating/bathing zone, there's room for my futon to unfold, beyond which south-facing windows, obstructed by thick security gating, admit a diffuse light. On the northern end, wedged in a crevice-like space, is a commode that's operated by a pull-chain mechanism attached to the ceiling. Beyond that, a dusty bead curtain demarcates a darkened no-go zone cluttered with items you'd find on a neglected highway shoulder. But it's the steel pole, more than anything else, that constantly reminds me I'm occupying someone else's space and I'm not where I'm supposed to be.

After four years as a teacher, the last two spent earning a master's degree in education, I'm done with it. Another year of co-teaching with Amanda is not an option—that would be pushing our luck—and the prospect of returning to the classroom in September with anyone else fills me with dread. Frankly, so does the thought of another year of pretzels and apple juice, rain boots, routines, and rest time. I can no longer sustain the belief that teaching is so righteous a vocation that there's no need to explore other, potentially more lucrative paths. Seeing my brother's young, vibrant friends doing all kinds of cool media-centric work in London got me thinking, why not me? So when the school offers me a contract for the following fall, I decline. Not that I have anything set up, but I'll land on my feet.

Months later, an article in the *Times* informs me that Noni and Johnny have flown the coop. I haven't seen them since the backyard party in August but figured they were just busy doing movie star stuff. Speaking from a newly bought unfurnished bungalow in LA, Noni explains the failure of the New York stint to the paper of record:

"I couldn't deal with the fact that if I got hungry at night, I couldn't go anywhere because of the crime factor. Why live that way by choice? And I was too far away from my parents."

I'm blindsided by the news, and a little miffed to have to learn about it just like the rest of the plebes.

"So you're gone, huh?" I say, when I get Noni on the phone some weeks later.

"Yeah, it just didn't work out. Sorry, Skysby. I should have said something. We were never really there. I mean, we never even really unpacked."

"Hmm. So what'd you do about the apartment?"

"Oh…do you want it?"

"Well…I mean, if you're not using it."

"No, that's fine."

"Seriously?"

A Fed-Ex package arrives a few weeks later, with a note.

DEAR DAVID =
AS PROMISED HERE ARE
THE KEYS TO THE APT. #3-N [134 DUANE ST.] FRONT DOOR,
ELEVATOR, AND FIRE ESKAPE. (WHY?)
CAN'T FIND THE MAILBOX KEY
OR THE BACK DOOR. SORRY.
USE THE PLACE ANY WAY YOU
LIKE. HOWEVER THERE ARE CERTAIN RESTRICTIONS:
    NO CROWING AT SUNRISE
    NO PEEING ON THE FLOORS
    NO FARM ANIMALS OF ANY SORT
    (UNLESS MARRIAGE IS ON THE HORIZON)
    NO FARTING (NO EXCEPTIONS)
    NO SCUD MISSILE LAUNCHING
    NO READING OF PORNOGRAPHY (PICTURES ONLY)
    NO KUATI DISCO PARTIES
AND THAT'S ALL. ANY WAY HAVE
A GOOD. THINK OF US OFTEN, ESPECIALLY
WHEN STEAMING OR TAKING A DUMP.
THANKS FOR THE TAPE. SEE YOU THEN.
ALL OUR LOVE —
JOHNNY & NONI

It's a weird kind of luxury. Everyone I know and love is somewhere between Houston and 14th Street, so having the keys to a massive loft in TriBeCa is a thrill, but not easy to put to good use. Especially since I've finally landed a job at Disney, in the children's publishing arm, which is a stone's throw from my West 10th Street matchbox. And I find the whole thing slightly intimidating. I have no legal right to have access to this pricey residence, but then again, I'd be a fool not to check it out. To Noni and Johnny it's no big deal—why should it be for me? Still, weeks go by before I make it down to Duane Street.

Located on the third floor of a five-story building, accessible by private elevator, the loft is vast, with twelve-and-a-half foot ceilings, wall-size windows, elegant Corinthian columns, and gorgeously weathered floors. It's mostly devoid of furniture, save for a king-size bed, a bureau, and a vintage salon-chair hair dryer. There's some fossilized laundry in the washer and a balled-up trench coat on top of the dryer. I pace around as dusk comes on, but there's nothing to do here; it's just big, beautiful, and empty. I don't stay long, but I come away with the realization that the only way to take full advantage of the Duane Street loft is to throw a party. Adhering to house rules, it is not a Kuati disco party and peeing on the floors is kept to a minimum. My one regret is I never manage to try out the steam-shower, because soon after the shindig, the landlord figures out that his incandescent tenants have jumped coasts and wants the keys back, pronto.

The job at Disney turns out to be Dullsville, but, urged on by my cool connections, I make a few moves. I wangle a lunch meeting at Coffee Shop, the hip eatery on Union Square West, with the head of the whole publishing operation, Michael Lynton, who now heads up Snap. Michael really likes my prototype for an advice column called "Ask Goofy" and sends an email to Disney head honcho Michael Eisner touting it for a syndicated national column. I figure I've finally found my niche. At some point I mention to Lynton that my cousin is Winona Ryder, and he comes up with a project based on an extremely witty and clever YA title called *The Diary of Adrian Mole, Aged 1 3 3/4*. I bring it up with her, and she doesn't exactly say no, but eventually she balks when Lynton says she would have to contribute some writing to the project. Hey, she's an actor, not a writer. She sure doesn't need a book deal after *Heathers*.

Not only is the diary project a bust, so is "Ask Goofy." The Magic Kingdom kingpins give it a pass, saying they don't want to risk diluting the monetary value of the beloved anthropomorphic dog by spreading him too thin. Meanwhile, my boss, who keeps a framed picture of Minnie Mouse on her desk, resents my hobnobbing with Michael Lynton, her boss.

On the upside, Disney has recently branched out into the grown-up publishing business, and the company's new imprint, Hyperion, is keen to break into non-Disney realms. Just as Touchstone Pictures brought Disney a share of the R-rated movie market, Hyperion will do the same for Disney as a book publisher. And what better way to signal that this isn't your old man's Disney than to sign Lou Reed? Which is how I've managed to wangle a pair of tickets to hear Lou read—from *Between Thought and Expression: Selected Lyrics of Lou Reed*, a handsome hardcover edition published by Hyperion in the fall of 1991.

Discussing his work in a concurrent interview, Lou likened certain kinds of pop songs— where the lyrics can't bear scrutiny without the music—to novelties, whereas, he said, his aim was to write lyrics that could be appreciated on their own. Thus, to promote the book, Lou has agreed to do a small author's tour, exclusively in non-rock settings. He'll simply stand at a lectern and read his song lyrics out loud. No guitar. No bass. No laughing.

Johnny Depp is a big fan of Lou Reed and the New York school of rock—the Velvets and Patti Smith and the Ramones. I pass him an invite through Noni and he's into it. The event takes place in the theater of the New York Society of Ethical Culture on Central Park West. We agree to meet on the steps, and he shows up right on time.

The room erupts when Lou appears and makes his way to a spot-lit podium at center stage. With reading glasses in place, he delivers the opening benediction: "I'll be your mirror, reflect what you are, in case you don't know." Spoken in that dour, deadpan New York-by-way-of-Long Island accent, his words are a balm to the soul of the assembled. Some of the rapture begins to wear off as we enter the darker places and make our way toward a closing series of death songs from Lou's latest, *Magic and Loss*—all without the release of rock 'n' roll. When it's done, despite all the computations, I'm actually glad to be back in the crisp November night with Johnny.

"So, where to, Skysby?" he says, lighting up.

"Maybe we should toast Lou with a drink or three."

He nods, exhaling smoke. "Yeah," he says, in that quiet purr of his. "We should do that."

We amble at an easy pace, turning east onto 59th and proceeding lackadaisically toward our destination, the Mark Hotel on 77th and Madison, where Johnny is staying under the name "Mr. Stench."

His hair is cut short and nondescript for *The Arrowtooth Waltz*, his current oddball movie project, which is kind of in traction while the director sorts out some psychological issues. It puzzles me that Johnny's involved in something so outside the mainstream when he's such a blazing hot commodity. Since he plays a regular Joe in it, he looks pretty nondescript for Johnny Depp—handsome as hell, to be sure, but not obviously a movie star. Having learned in *Premiere* magazine that Johnny had become friends with Iggy Pop while filming *Cry-Baby*, I bring up how much I dig *Brick by Brick*, Iggy's most recent release.

"You know the song 'Butt Town?'" Johnny asks.

"The cops are well groomed... with muscled physiques... in Butt Town," I recite, doing my best Iggy.

"Iggy wrote that song about my butt."

Seriously?

He assures me it's true, that somewhere in the course of hanging out in Texas with Iggy and some friends, during a debauched weekend of Hunter S.

Thompson-grade shenanigans, Iggy had written "Butt Town," or been inspired to write it, in homage to the butt of Depp. He tells me not as a brag, but because he knows I'll appreciate this piece of info. (I resolve to steal a look at Johnny's butt at the next opportune moment, just in a research kind of way.)

"Do you know the song 'I'm a Conservative?'" he asks. "One of my favorite songs by Iggy. Can't remember what record it's on. But it's like, 'Hey, look me over… lend me an ear… I'm a conservative.' Eyes closed, remembering, he continues: 'I like the small black marks on my hands… I'm a conservative… I like the crazy girls that I screw…' You need to track that one down, Skysby."

I bum a cigarette and Johnny lights me up with a gassy old-school Zippo. Walking and talking and smoking with Johnny Depp is fun. In the final scene of *The Arrowtooth Waltz*, Johnny and Jerry Lewis improvise dialogue using their own made-up Inuit-sounding gibberish. Johnny's about to favor me with a few choice words when we reach the Mark, an ultra-luxury hotel on New York's Upper East Side. He leads the way into the bar-lounge, which is slightly sunken from lobby level—a soft-edged, red-lit pleasure grotto where each step we take is cushioned by high-value textiles. Johnny is right at home in five-star hotels. In a few years, he'll be wrecking them. We take a banquette away from the bar, and a hotel employee makes a gentle approach.

"Mister Stench, sir, if you don't mind," he says, holding out a portable phone. "Someone in the lounge dearly wishes to speak with you."

Johnny nods, takes the phone, raises it to his ear. He listens patiently, offering a murmur of assent here and there. "Well, that would all depend," he says finally. "On what? On how much your mother would enjoy being tied up and having me take a shit on her," he says, in that quiet purr of his. Then, placing a hand over the mouthpiece: "Champagne?"

The phone is retrieved, Johnny orders a bottle of the good stuff, and we watch in amusement as an older couple sways into view. They're obviously from out of town, and hammered, as if after a day of imbibing free drinks at a casino. Sprawled over a C-shaped leather-and-animal-print banquette, she's in a boxy iridescent dress and matching high-heels; he's in a light-colored sports jacket, tie loosened, slightly disheveled behind Vegas shades. A passing server takes their drink order and they start to make out.

This bit of theater of the absurd comes as a welcome flipside to Lou Reed's noir recitations. And it gives me the chance to reprise a riff I'd tossed out on the way over. "Waist deep in the Big Muddy," I say, referring to a protest song made famous by Pete Seeger that some say helped end the war in Vietnam, but which I am leveraging solely for its vague, puerile sexual innuendo. Repeating the line in a mirthful whisper, Depp sees some humor in it, and we laugh and drink some more. When we look up again, the couple has passed out—him, knees akimbo and jaw agape, her with one leg crossed at the knee, a dangling high-heel refracting the beam from a sleek overhead spotlight.

Emboldened by Champagne and my guide's magnetic pull, I rise with the men's room in mind and an idea forms. As I pass the passed-out woman, I swipe the giant Christmas ornament that is her shoe without disturbing the lady's slumber or calling attention to myself. Johnny looks up when I say his name. I toss him the shoe, and off I bop to the men's room, relishing the liberating effects of mischief.

Depp's penchant for pranks will one day be documented in think-pieces commemorating the twenty-year anniversary of *What's Eating Gilbert Grape*, during the filming of which he coerced young Leonardo DiCaprio into sniffing a rancid pickled egg. But Johnny's delight in antics at the expense of others is not yet an established part of his persona. He has, however, shared a few stories of his childhood with me, of growing up dodging ashtrays and shoes thrown in anger, and as I pee on a urinal wrought from Carrara marble, I'm confident he'll know what to do. Re-entering the lounge, I spot the shoe immediately, suspended by the heel from a minimalist chandelier.

Later on, we hang out up in his suite with a Florida buddy from Johnny's pre-fame days, passing around an acoustic guitar. I play a few feeble runs, then hand it over to Johnny. Shirtless, wasp-waisted, cigarette dangling, arm emblazoned "Winona Forever," he takes a turn, and the bastard lays down some ace-sounding blues licks. It's a moment that many would give their eye teeth to witness.

Before I go, I give Johnny the tape I promised him: ninety notorious minutes of surreptitious recordings, including Orson Welles's fish-stick ad, famed jazz drummer Buddy Rich abusing his band members, the Troggs profanely fretting over the follow-up to "Wild Thing," Jerry Lewis savagely toying with an elderly fan, and the profanity-rich "Red's Bar" series of prank calls immortalized obliquely on *The Simpsons*. Then, a tad reluctantly, resisting the urge to ask if he's up for stealing another shoe, I say goodnight.

In the cab on the way back downtown, my head lolls and a goofy grin takes over as I replay the past few hours—I don't want any of this conversational gold to lose its luster. Then I'm on to Champagne fantasies: me and Johnny catching Tin Machine next month at the Marquee…us knocking around the village, talking Kerouac and playing Would You Rather…playing guitars together and him saying, "Actually Skysby, you're not bad at all. Show me the lick you just did…"

That weekend, I come across a Spanish import copy of Iggy Pop's *Soldier*, the one with "I'm a Conservative," in a long-gone East Village record store. It costs more than I like to shell out for an album, but I want to be familiar with *Soldier* the next time I see Johnny.

Which turns out to be never again.

This takes a while to become apparent, of course. When *Benny and Joon* comes out in early 1993 and makes stars out of the Proclaimers and "500 Miles," I immediately think of Tape 2, and I'm convinced that these Scottish gits owe their now huge career to me. By then it's clear that Noni and Jonny are through, so I can't reach Johnny and confirm whether he passed the song on to Mary Stewart Masterson (the reason it ended up in the movie).

At least I have his trench coat, which is Army green, belted at the waist, and made of dense, weather-averse material. There's this amazing weight to it, which I attribute to the military-grade fabric—until I stumble on the Taser wedged deep in an inside pocket.

Crackle crackle...

The batteries even work.

As I head over to the Telephone Bar wearing Johnny's trench coat, I imagine the Depper being accosted by the Baseball Furies gang from *The Warriors* and unleashing the power of Edison on their uncomprehending jawlines. My cool new coat garners some praise from my drinking buddies, and after a few pints, I break out the Taser and show it to Pete, one of the regulars. And, as alluded to earlier, set myself up for the world's most naive Tase. Once the shock wears off, though, I can't suppress a rueful smile at the memory of the talented Mr. Stench.

Chapter 20

VIP Riser

In 1989, Jon Bon Jovi wondered to an interviewer why everybody in the know—from critics to the band's most famous fan, my cousin Noni—was in love with the Replacements, when he had never heard of them. Three years later, the Replacements are toast, and everybody, including Jon Bon Jovi, has heard of Noni's new favorite band. For U2 has found a place inside my cousin's heart, and so has the lead singer, in some mysterious way.

I am not a rabid fan, but the prospect of seeing U2 play at Yankee Stadium is pretty enticing. They're indisputably the biggest band in the world, and the current *Achtung Baby*/Zoo TV era is their most interesting phase yet, a satisfying pivot from the earnest, chiming anthems of old to something altogether crunchier and more experimental. And I can think of worse ways to spend the last Saturday in August, when all the shrinks are in the Hamptons and anyone who's anyone has somewhere better to be, than at a storied sports arena in the company of rock stars.

Ever since that snowy weekend at my parents' house when I played ten-year-old Noni cassettes of my favorite new wave and indie rock tunes, I've mailed her mixes crammed with my latest discoveries and obsessions, from Paisley Underground bands like Game Theory to New Zealand bands like the Chills to perennial favorites like XTC. Three years ago, I took a teenage Noni and her closest friend (actually named, no shit, Heather) to see South African supergroup Mahlathini and the Mahotella Queens perform in Central Park. Noni's sixth movie had just come out (*Great Balls of Fire*), and while admittedly a bomb, its premiere at the Ziegfeld Theatre enabled me to shake hands with

Jerry Lee Lewis and make small talk with John Cale. But even while the girl had already done two bona fide classics (of a sort) in *Beetlejuice* and *Heathers*, and been celebrity tabloid fodder since the romance with Johnny, we made no advance preparations for hanging out in a large, sprawling New York City crowd. She wore an oversize white T-shirt, sleeves rolled up, and a red baseball cap showing a pair of dice—a low-key look, to be sure—but we weren't concerned about anyone recognizing her, and no one did.

Fast-forward to 1992. This time she's taking *me* to a show. Partially, at least a smidge, just to have someone with her, a strong arm to hold onto in the event of a throng. She's small, and I do feel protective of her.

I'm starting to get used to high-priced digs. Not long ago I met up with Noni and other members of the clan at an apartment on Central Park South belonging to Luciano Pavarotti, who was happy to let Noni crash there for a few weeks while she was in town doing publicity. Peeing in Pavarotti's potty—now that's some operatic shit. Today we're meeting at her suite at the St. Regis, a venerable five-star hotel on Fifth Avenue. She's trying on looks when I arrive.

"Is this too slutty or wannabe groupie?" she asks.

I tell her she looks great. But of course she does. How can the cover girl of *Rolling Stone*'s "Hot" issue not dazzle in a black T-shirt and leather pants? As for me, it takes a little more work. I've brought along a prized item for the occasion, but when I slip away and return wearing it, Noni scrutinizes my shirt with a quizzical expression.

"I don't think so, Skys," she says finally. "You don't want to upstage anyone."

I'm a little stung. More than a little. This is, after all, the cool vintage tab collar shirt that my brother gave me—a royal blue number. Do I really accord my little cousin veto power over the way I dress? I guess this is part of the bargain. Maybe she just doesn't want me to look like a dope when I meet Bono.

The two of them have become pals, mutual admirers, backstage hangout buds. He's a married rock star and she's still technically engaged to the Depper, but clearly some kind of mutual infatuation is afoot. As a testament to this connection, our ride out to the stadium is none other than Paul McGuinness, U2's manager, which is the nineties version of the Beatles sending Brian Epstein to come fetch us in his town car.

Like Epstein, McGuinness has ushered his four lads from humble beginnings to worldwide dominance through tenacity, business acumen, and unwavering belief. Impeccably bearded and wearing a suave summer suit open at the collar, Paul charms effortlessly. The afternoon is gorgeous, perfect for baseball in fact. As the stadium comes into view, he shares a lovely historical anecdote about the House that Ruth Built. I've climbed highest mountains and run through the fields, but I still can't remember what he said.

We drive up to the venue—I mean right up into it. A chain-link fence parts for us and our vehicle creeps a little closer. We step out into bright sunlight at the players' entrance and follow Paul through darkened passages into the bowels of the stadium. Gradually, a low throb becomes detectable, then some chiming arpeggios, and we just keep following the sound until we emerge into blinding daylight.

Blinking out sunspots in the Yankees dugout, my head spins with thoughts of the legendary baseball men who have stood in this very spot and cussed and spat tobacco juice. The first glimpse of ballfield green always stirs me, but this view is another thing entirely: the world's biggest band is playing full throttle and we are the only audience.

The stage is in left field, and we make our way toward it diagonally to the strains of "Until the End of the World." I'm actually surprised that U2 sounds so much like a U2 record. As polished as they are in studio recordings, the sound they make is truly theirs, not a contrivance or a feat of engineering. A woman approaches us with a camera, and because it's loud and I don't realize she's taking a picture of each of us for an all-access laminated pass, I put my arm around Noni's shoulder, thinking we're being snapped together for posterity.

We reach the rows of seats in front of the stage, and I sit and marvel at my good luck. Noni, a few rows ahead of me, waves to the guys and they all wave back, clearly delighted. She looks back at me over her shoulder and smiles, and I take her picture. I use up almost half my roll of film documenting the band doing their soundcheck in the empty stadium. How else will anyone else believe it?

When the music stops, I trail Noni as she approaches the stage. A strong arm reaches down and helps her up. I climb on without assistance. Rising from a crouch, I'm close to the Edge, who greets us with a warm smile framed by a neat goatee. He gives us a short tour of some of his favorite pedals and gadgets; I take a picture of him and Noni, and then he leads the way to some sort of deluxe VIP backstage quarters, where the rest of the band is cooling its expensive heels. The lead singer spots Noni. He comes over and they hold a warm and meaningful embrace, like a sort of homecoming. She introduces me as Skysby.

"It's a mutual nickname," I say. "Most people call me David."

The name came about years ago, at Iso restaurant in the East Village. I was showing Noni some photos from a recent trip to Europe, and I said, "So these are these guys we met."

"Huh? Skysby and Matt?"

"No, these *guys* we met. Skysby and Matt? What kind of a name is Skysby?" Immediately we both became Skysby. We rarely call each other anything else.

Bono takes my hand and leans in, leading with the shoulder. He's not tall, but he projects largeness, as if his atoms are packed extra tight and straining to get out.

"You actually know my brother, Jon Klein," I say, feeling slightly empowered by this. Besides my connection to Noni, U2's great friend and fan, I'm also the brother of Jon, who directed "The Fly" video for them. Released as the first single from *Achtung Baby*, "The Fly" did not make much of an impact in the U.S., as a single or a video. "Mysterious Ways" and its stunning video was the one that established *Achtung* stateside. Still, as the first single, "The Fly" announced a radical revamping of the band's sound, and the Fly persona is a crucial part of Bono's act for the Zoo TV tour. Bro having directed the video, or co-directed it, anyway, feels like a significant connection.

"Jon *Klein*," says Bono, nodding with emphatic recognition. "Very talented guy, Jon Klein. Truly—the only person I've ever met who could actually interrupt himself."

I wince a little at the thought of Jonny being remembered for this dubious talent, but I know exactly what he means. Jonny's mind works so fast it sometimes overflows. And Bono is a pretty garrulous talker himself. He's curious about all kinds of things, and peppers me with questions about the Bronx Bombers, the Yankees-Mets rivalry, the neighborhood surrounding the stadium, and the sound of the local Bronx accent.

"Oh, do a Bronx accent, Skysby," Noni says.

Regional accents are nuanced. I don't know how the Bronx version differs from basic New York-ese, but obviously Bono doesn't either. I opt for the seduction scene from *Rocky*. Balboa was supposed to be from Philly, but Sly Stallone employed a big, dumb New Yawk accent reflective of his youth in Manhattan's Hell's Kitchen neighborhood. That's fifteen miles from the Bronx, but hey—close enough for rock 'n' roll.

I place my hands on Bono's robust shoulders. "*Adrienne*,' I say. "Adrienne. I'm gonna kiss ya. Ya don't have ta kiss me back. But I'm gonna kiss ya."

He places his hands on my shoulders and says it back to me: dramatically, Irishly— badly.

"*Might* need a little work," I say.

"Ah, Dave," he says, with a weary smile. And with that, he places the flat of his hand, which is dry and slightly calloused, against my forehead and gives a playful shove.

Backstage is a vast warren of activity, with technical crews, U2 personnel, and stadium staff all scurrying around, pursuing critical missions. Morleigh Steinberg, the dancer in the "Mysterious Ways" video, glides into view, and she and Noni embrace. She'll do her tantalizing swirling thing—familiar to anyone with MTV—when the song is performed later. Much later, years I mean, she and the Edge will marry. I watch as a large video crew gathers to work out logistics, and the leader turns out to be someone I recognize: Mark Neale, a lovely Englishman I'd met two years ago at my brother's wedding.

It was a two-day affair, the second day of which took place in Barnet, outside of London, at a stately home known as Wrotham Park. The setting was regal, from the John Singer Sargent paintings on the walls to the presence of Kylie Minogue and Michael Hutchence among the uniformly posh-looking invitees. As my parents and sister and I made our entrance, a beefeater proclaimed our arrival in a plangent tenor voice like a silver cornet muffled in silk: "*Richard* and *Joan*... Klein. *David* and *Elizabeth*... Klein... Of *Tenafly*."

And now here's Mark Neale, who got his foot in the door editing segments on Jonny's MTV series, leading a film crew on U2's plush pound note. Bro's former co-director, another Mark—Pellington—is here too. In spirit anyway, via the fast-moving *Buzz*-style video collages that feature in U2's current stage show. And it occurs to me that besides "The Fly," Jonny hasn't done much else of late. Taking stock of the graduating class of *Buzz*, coupled with Bono's genial goof at my brother's expense, dampens my all-access laminated giddiness for a long moment.

After a small meal that I'm too hopped up to eat, Noni and I wander about taking in the scene. We stop for a bottle of water in a brightly lit kitchenette where Tony Visconti and his wife of three years, May Pang, are finishing dinner. May Pang is famous as John Lennon's girlfriend during his notorious "lost weekend" period in the early 1970s. Tony, the studio mastermind behind *Ziggy Stardust* and T. Rex's *Electric Warrior*, and May are extremely tickled to meet Noni, whose effect is instantaneous. It's not so much a matter of her lighting up a room, more that others light up in her presence.

Noni and May go for a walk, and it's just me and Tony. Thumps from the opening act, Disposable Heroes of Hiphoprisy, are audible, yet he appears content to sit and chat. He says he met the guys in U2 while doing some remixes for them during the *Unforgettable Fire* LP, but that was the extent of their connection. I share that Noni and Bono have become good friends, and that I'm her lucky escort for the evening. He asks what I do, and I give him the upbeat version of my job in publishing and throw in that I'm also a writer. As we're talking, it occurs to me that I'm at liberty to ask legendary producer Tony Visconti anything I want.

"Can I just—how'd you get that crazy metallic voice on the chorus of 'Scary Monsters'"?

"That's called a gate, David. Do you know how a gate works?"

In a soft voice combining the Brooklyn of his youth and decades spent in music studios with Brits, Tony explains that a gate is a device that limits the length of a signal, and when you take a gated signal and bounce it back through another gate on a different machine and then send the signal back and forth and back and forth and back and forth, something indescribable happens. He talks about other instances where he's gotten a particular effect by means of the gate technique, most notably on Bowie's unforgettable "Heroes" vocal, and our conversation snakes in all sorts of fascinating directions. At some point, kind of out of nowhere, he hits me with, "So why haven't you written a book yet?"

It stops me cold. Here's a guy who by thirty had produced *Ziggy Stardust*, talking to a thirty-year-old who hasn't produced much of anything. I have no answer for Tony. Short stories are my thing. Short stories are of a manageable length. Hell, one weird night in the East Village and you have a short story. But a whole book? A whole book that isn't a bunch of short stories? What would it even be about? Still, I guess being taken for someone who *should* have written a book by now, by someone at his level, is kind of good.

Noni and May come to fetch Tony and me. The headliners are about to go on. At May's suggestion, we exchange contact info, and then someone from U2 HQ appears and guides us to the VIP riser, an island of exclusivity reserved for the very special and their fortunate guests. Scoping for the first time the tens of thousands of people who have paid good money for this event, I can't resist a smirk.

Lenny Kravitz is hard to miss. Noni gives him a quick hello and we move on. Hey, look, it's John McEnroe and Tatum O'Neal. You cannot be serious! This kind of stargazing is diverting, not nervous-making, at least not until I spot Peter Gabriel. Peter's long been an object of fascination for me, going back to high school when he split from Genesis and put out a series of really curious, immaculately produced solo albums, each with an eye-assaulting cover by Hipgnosis. Noni is also a huge Peter Gabriel fan. I've never seen her starstruck before.

"We have to talk to him."

"I know," she says, "but I don't know what to say. You have to do it."

"Me? Come on, you're... one of them. I know you can come up with something adorable."

"I can't. You start it. You can do it, Skysby."

I take her hand and we approach Peter, who is well over six feet tall, has the bearing of a statue and still plenty of hair. Noni hangs back a bit as I stammer an introduction.

"I've been a fan of yours for the longest time," I say, recalling the night I tried to kiss Doreen Alvarez while *Peter Gabriel* I was playing, and my kiss landed squarely on the air. "Since that first solo record, with the mirrored contact lenses," I add, referring to the unsettling eye accouterments he wears in the inner sleeve photograph. He gives no nod of acknowledgement, no obligatory "thanks." Instead, Peter shifts his gaze toward Yankee Stadium's famously short right-field porch for a theatrical moment, as if reimagining that first solo effort—sessions with the London Symphony Orchestra, shooting the album cover in the rain, the time producer Bob Ezrin gaffer-taped him to a pole in order to get a more heartfelt vocal take...

"That was," Gabes says finally, "a long, long time *ago*."

Just in time, the industrialized lurch of "Zoo Station" kicks in and we slink away. As the band falls into its groove, I feel a rush of excitement at the enveloping fullness of the sound, coupled with the same feeling you get at any performance by someone you know personally. Only this is no mercy gig on Bleecker Street with a few office colleagues; the guy I was just shooting the shit with is now onstage in front of thirty thousand people. But as far as I'm concerned, it's just me and Skysby taking it in together among thousands of distant though receptive souls. I'm feeling so agreeable that I even partake in the corny call-and-response segment of "Angel of Harlem," a song I've never been keen on until this very second.

The performance is punctuated by a rush of video art flashing across giant display screens behind the stage, a distorted blur of sensory overload meant to mirror life in the digital age. The set climaxes with "Where the Streets Have No Name" and "Pride (In the Name of Love)," and the band leaves for the first, but by no means last time. When they return, Bono is Mirrorball Man, a sleazy televangelist alter ego in a mirror-studded suit and twenty-gallon hat. They kick into "Desire," a Bo Diddley rave-up, as Bono preens into a full-length mirror under caustic Vegas lighting. At the operative moment, he steps to the mic, mirror still in hand, and intones to his reflection: "I'm a-gonna kiss ya! Ya may not kiss me back, but I'm a gonna *KISS YA!!*" On the VIP riser, our high-five reverberates across the zeitgeist as the crowd goes wild.

Later, backstage, we wait along with a dozen others for our moment of communion. Lisa Robinson and Phil Spector are here. She was once a very big name in rock journalism and a close friend of Led Zeppelin. Phil Spector, formerly the most famous record producer on earth, is known these days primarily as a paranoid, gun-toting grotesque. He's a jangly presence in the not-huge green room, and it doesn't take long for him to make his way over to Noni and me. Phil's aviator shades are violet tinted, and the hairpiece he's selected for tonight suggests a mid-eighties country-star—middle-parted with a fringe of bangs and feathered mullet sides. He doesn't wait for an acknowledgement from Noni, just walks right up, speaking rapid-fire like a crazed DJ.

"Winona Ryder, Winona Ryder, hello, hello Winona Ryder. Y'know what? I got ta tell ya. I got ta tell ya your name has got this thing, this thing that really reminds me of that classic song originally recorded by Ma Rainey in 1924," he says, cracking a grin. Suddenly he has one palm upturned and the other is clapping out a beat in fierce downward strokes:

"Oh I said see, see rider / Won't you tell me / What you've done…"

He's in the studio now, giving instructions to the Wrecking Crew in his mind. Noni might even be on the verge of responding, but Phil's muzzle suddenly points toward Tatum O'Neal. Turns out her name has a thing that really reminds him of that classic song "Beale Street Blues" by the great W.C. Handy.

"If Beale Street could talk / If Beale Street could talk / Married men would have to take their beds and walk…"

Bono emerges, dressed casually for Bono, shades unmirrored, crucifix earring sans sparkly gemstones. He works the room, stopping to greet Spector first and then spending a little time with everyone else. In Lisa Robinson's subsequent account of the evening, she describes Noni as "gazing adoringly at Bono," and that description feels true enough. We have a brief moment with him, and then Skysby signals that we're going. I know not where, but I will follow.

A Team U2 guy leads us through a passage or two and then we're outside, where a long black limo is languishing in idle. The door is opened; I climb in and take the rearward passenger-side seat. Noni and Bono come around the other side and take seats across from me by about eight feet. The chief tech guy takes the seat to my left and we take off, bound for the Rihga Royal on West 54th Street. In the interior's dim light, we sprawl in our soft seats, sipping plush luxury bubbles. The streets have no name.

"You sounded so great," Noni says, sounding fanlike.

Bono emits a soft grunt.

"You don't think so?"

"There were some good points," he says. "It's just, sometimes you're up there, and there's a moment where you're just positive that ten thousand people have all gone off and taken a piss at the same time."

So here's how it really feels to be a rock star in 1992. Quite a far cry from the prime of Robert Plant, who memorably told Lisa Robinson of times onstage when he wanted "to fuck the whole front row." The future sure ain't what it used to be.

"Well, you totally nailed that bit from *Rocky*," I say.

"Ah, Dave," he says. "You're such a wag."

"What exactly is a wag? It's not a word you hear all that often, I mean, as a noun."

Bono tells me a wag is someone who sees humor in things not everyone would find funny.

In the hotel suite, we sprawl on even softer leather and listen to Van Morrison through sweet speakers—none of that chintzy hotel equipment up in here. Bono says certain songs, like "Tupelo Honey," are ancient things, and Van was sort of a conduit for something that existed already. I have no trouble with this kind of mysticism. What is music if not my religion anyway?

Edge and Daniel Lanois stop by. Ten years ago, Daniel was producing acts like Nash the Slash, a Canadian new wave violinist who performs with his face wrapped in surgical bandages, and his sister's band, Martha & the Muffins. Now he's about the hottest producer around. Daniel picks up an acoustic guitar and plays us a few songs from a solo LP he's been working on. Maybe he finds his title tonight. The record comes out the following year under the name *For the Beauty of Wynona*.

Sometimes there's a moment when you just know that ten thousand people have all gone off and taken a piss at the same time, just like there's a moment when you know that you've nodded out in the company of rock stars, some of whom have also nodded out. I count to ten in my head, then get to my feet. Because it would definitely be too slutty or wannabe groupie to ask if I can crash here.

Chapter 21

High-Grade Chutzpah

After things crap out at Disney, landing at ICM looks like a modest step in the right direction. ICM is one of the three major talent agencies, and the literary department is the crown jewel of the company's New York office. Amanda "Binky" Urban is perhaps the best known literary agent in the country, famous for making dazzlingly lucrative deals for her clients—established stars like John Irving, ascendant ones like Donna Tartt, and more than a few objects of outright reverence, like Raymond Effing Carver and Cormac Bloody McCarthy. Esther Newberg, on the same power hallway, is just as heavy a hitter, presiding over the likes of Pulitzer Prize winners like Seymour Hersh and flagrantly commercial entities like Don Imus, who likes to have Esther on his nationally syndicated radio show where they goof genially. Plenty of other authors I love, most notably Spalding Gray,[12] whose *Impossible Vacation* I just read, are attached to agents along this tastefully lit stretch. Too bad my services are required just around the corner, in a fluorescent zone that accommodates a pair of exposed cubicles, the occupants of which serve at the pleasure of ICM's primary theatrical agents.

---

12. Gray was an occasional patron of the Telephone Bar & Grill, and one night he got to talking with me and my friend Steve Hall, a charming Scottish painter. Eventually, he asked how the food was, and we said it was really quite excellent. He said that was good to hear, because he was getting hungry, and would we care to join him in a meal. Because his greatest skill was as a conversationalist, our discussion was so easygoing as to be almost unremarkable. We talked about movies, just like anyone would. He had just seen *When We Were Kings*, the documentary about the so-called Thrilla in Manila, which he liked very much and said we should see.

Where the literary department attracts the savviest, most charming yet ballsy dealmakers, the theatrical department consists of febrile eccentrics who lord over fiefdoms of theatrical properties with a zeal that reaches to the cheap seats. If the literary agents fail to project a strictly literary vibe, the theatrical agents make up for it by being theatrical as hell.

My boss, Mitch Douglas, a Georgia native who once represented Tennessee Williams, looks and sounds like he was born to do that very thing. When I interviewed for the job, he spoke with pride of having brow-beaten more than a dozen male assistants into quitting, but he was hopeful I could flourish in an admittedly gloves-off environment. Mitch is witty, bitchy, shrewd, and, at least once a day, completely inappropriate. "*Day-vid*," he drawls, stretching my name out beyond the two-second mark. "Should I spend the weekend at my country house, or should I just stay in the city and get *laaaiiid?*"

Toiling in the cubicle next to mine is the assistant for Bridget Aschenberg, the other major power in the theatrical department. Rotund, imperious, somewhere between fifty and seventy, Bridget issues directives in a florid, formal, vaguely British voice shaped in strict European boarding schools. The representative for dozens of outsize playwrights and theatrical figures, people like Arthur Miller, Edward Albee, and Wendy Wasserstein, she seems to have no life outside her work. Bridget operates strictly with *Mad Men*-era technology—a telephone, an anvil-sized manual typewriter, and a black metal Rolodex. Beginning with Kobo Abe, author of *Woman in the Dunes*, it's crammed with contact information going back decades, from marquee names to hapless functionaries at music licensing firms. "*Look on your wheel!*" she shrills, exhorting her assistant to plumb her most prized piece of equipment.

For sustenance, Bridget relies on the Chinese place located right downstairs, known internally as Stinky Noodle, to deliver her preferred lunch of "chicken parts." If you've ever seen this item listed on a menu, you probably shuddered and moved on. For her it's an everyday thing.

"Christopher, where are my chicken parts?"

"I ordered them, Bridget."

"Well, where *are* they?"

Bridget types everything out herself before it's typed out on letterhead by her long-suffering amanuensis. In a nod to modernity, she uses yellow Post-it notes for this task, even employing Wite-Out when necessary so that Christopher suffers no confusion as to her meaning. Because she has such a vast and wide-ranging clientele, her office is constantly besieged by those seeking permission to mount new productions of plays and musicals she represents.

A Hungarian production of *Grease*? Two performances of Claire Booth Luce's *The Women* in La Jolla? Simultaneous Swedish and English versions of Ingmar Bergman's production of Yukio Mishima's *Madame de Sade*? They all have to go through Bridget, who is fiercely protective, dispatching lethal memoranda on behalf of those she's sworn a blood oath to protect.

To one of the guys who wrote *Grease*:

> I forbid you categorically to sign this. You are being taken for a "chump," my friend, & I won't have it.

To Catherine Sheehy, *American Theatre Magazine*:

> Dear Ms. Sheehy:
>
> I have tried twice (yesterday & today) to reach you by phone but it was hopeless. You have remarkably stupid people answering the phones. You had called Arthur Miller to ask for his social security number. It is…

To a longtime contact at the Mexican Writers Guild:

> Tell Lorenzo Becker that I will grant him one final extension, for which he must pay an additional $1000. I will not put up with these ridiculous delays. You know the old American saying, Luis: Shit or get off the pot. You may quote me. As ever.

At least Bridget wields her high-grade chutzpah on behalf of icons. Mitch has a list only a mother could love. His bread and butter is *Nunsense*, the schticky off-Broadway musical and mega-franchise in the making. The other biggie is a different franchise, Callanetics, a rival to the Jane Fonda workout tape. True, he's pushing some quality works by talented authors and playwrights. William Poundstone, for example, a multi-genre writer whose *Biggest Secrets* features a fascinating dive into the U.S. Navy's bizarre, homoerotic equator-crossing rituals. One of my biggest coups at ICM is querying *Spy* magazine on behalf of Poundstone, getting a yes from the snarkiest of all magazines, and making the cover—with a doctored image of John F. Kennedy wearing lipstick and the headline WAS JFK A DRAG QUEEN? But the market demands hot commodities, and Mitch is short on explosive new talent. He's currently hyping a square-jawed dog trainer, Judy Carne, aka the Sock-it-to-Me Girl from *Laugh-In*, and the supremely untalented playwright Stanley Michael Hunthausen. With Murderer's Row just around the corner, hitching my star to the Broadway Danny Rose of the ICM lit department feels like a slap.

It soon becomes clear that regardless of where I had landed within the agency, I'm never going to become an agent, or even parlay my experience into a tangentially related career. Mitch sees that I have an eye for good writing, but the business is all about contracts and structuring deals, and I lack the wit, desire, and discipline to force myself to learn such a complex science. I'm no Gordon Kato, the department's newest member, who became an agent after barely leaving the office for a few years, so fierce was his desire to internalize the ins and outs of publishing contracts and agency work. I had a meeting with him once, in his dark den of an office. We talked about Liz Phair and the guitar sound on Eleventh Dream Day's *Beet* while he smoked a hand-rolled cigarette. An author called, and as I listened to him discussing a certain section that had been rewritten per his suggestions, I thought, what a great job he has. But in order to enjoy that end of it, you have to be a businessman too.

I stick around at ICM because it's a place from which bright, talented people are poised to spring, and as someone whose talents haven't risen to the surface quite yet, it makes sense—at least on paper—for me to work here. It pays the bills and sounds fairly interesting when people ask what I do, as long as I de-emphasize the menial tasks and talk up the agent-y stuff. And having a decent story to tell in New York City, one that doesn't elicit a conciliatory wince from whoever you're telling it to, is essential. Everyone I know is up to something cool.

My brother is *en fuego* in London. Noni has survived her first major debacle (backing out of *Godfather III*) and come back strong with her first $100 million-grossing movie, *Bram Stoker's Dracula*, and she has a new one coming out, directed by Scorsese. Tommy Morgan is in Brazil, living in neo-colonial splendor. My former roommate Dave Schlachet—having rebounded from the loss of Marisa Tomei (who's in her full *My Cousin Vinny* glory by now)—has gotten into construction management with Steve, and their company is putting up clubs all over New York, including the ultra-hot 10th Street Lounge. Hell, Dave's *younger brother* has a movie coming out—an art-house queer-centric take on the notorious Leopold and Loeb thrill-kill murder, no less—and it's receiving plaudits in the *New York Times*. ICM enables me to at least *allege* that I'm on some kind of career path, and it's not without its pleasures.

My fellow assistants, most of them a year or two out of college, are up on everything and going places. Some are accomplished writers, already on a literary path and working on novels. Everyone's a reader and conversations are lively. A dog-eared paperback copy of *A Confederacy of Dunces* made the rounds recently, and all of us sat around in the common room, bandying lines from its unhinged protagonist, Ignatius P. Riley, over Styrofoam containers of Stinky Noodle. One up-and-comer, who's somewhere between assistant and agent, plays bass in a band called the Spelvins. They have a deal with Zoo Entertainment, the label that issued Matthew Sweet's *Girlfriend* and a few other CDs I play incessantly. I quiz Bondy about the details of recording for a major label, and he talks about laying down rhythm tracks with their drum- mer—who's *really, really* good. Bondy says Joey Santiago, the Pixies drummer, can't keep time worth a damn. The Spelvins guy can play circles around him.

My response to this assertion is to question whether I know anything at all about music. I love the Pixies, but maybe Joey Santiago *is* a bad drummer and I just can't hear it. The idea that a good band requires a drummer who keeps rigorous time, and that technique is crucial to a band being taken seriously, still counts as gospel. People who understand music on a technical level still pitch themselves as arbiters of whether bands are good or not—and we continue to listen. Even a band as ferocious as the Pixies can be brought to heel in this sad calculus.

Meanwhile, proximity to fame, fortune, and ego, as I already know, is often surrealistically entertaining. The stream of self-important interoffice communication, for example, serves up gold on a daily basis ("It is VERY IMPORTANT that we come up with some motion picture activity for MC Hammer"). More profound is the faint whiff of power I derive from oversee- ing the mail—a zone where manuscripts, both solicited and otherwise, mingle with contracts, invitations to readings, concerts, and premieres, and fan mail of all stripes, making me privy to the infinite variety of human experience that will one day be provided by the Internet. In one morning I might encounter an egregiously apologetic Japanese play producer ("I am very sorry for the trouble caused by this unsuitable happening. I apologize most profusely for the inconvenience you have sustained"); a high school student requesting a piece of Eartha Kitt's garbage for a dubious "trashology" social studies project ("All you have to do is dip into your wastebasket and send something that is representative of yourself"); or an inquiry from a man in Jakarta directed to (deceased) writer Gordon Merrick, volunteering to act as his manservant. (You'll have to imagine that one for yourself.)

I get to know Edwin Newman, the NBC News veteran and foremost authority on proper English usage, through a few weeks' worth of phone calls regarding the reissue of two of his books. Newman, a celebrated lamenter of the dying art of precise language, devoted an entire chapter in *Strictly Speaking* to his deep loathing for the phrase "It is incumbent upon me." He's a curmudgeon, to be sure, but also a gentle man of learning and deeply held convictions. By the end of our dealings, I'm getting pretty relaxed about picking up the phone and bantering with this beacon of formal, tasteful discourse. One morning Ed calls:

"Is this David Klein?" he asks, in that resonant baritone of his.

"Yes, it's me," I say. "Er, I mean… it is I?"

He chuckles warmly. "Either one is fine in this context."

Like any seasoned newsman, Ed has a follow-up question or two, and we talk through some final bits of business, and then we're done. Ten minutes later, the phone rings.

[Throat clearing] "Mr. Klein?"

"Yes?"

"Ed Newman."

"Ah. Hello again."

Long pause

" 'It is I' is correct."

I recall one other moment of surpassing sublimity. The Pulitzer Prize-winning playwright Arthur Miller is awaiting the completion of some contractual paperwork, and just to kill time he starts to walk the floor. This is long before all that open-office stuff. ICM's layout is a simple rectangle, with two long corridors reserved for the powerful and two ignominious short ends for the worker bees. A few times every hour, I push back from my crevice and coast on desk-chair wheels into the hallway, using just enough force to ensure I'll miss the file cabinets on the other side of the aisle. With a rightward glance, I have a direct view through Mitch's doorway, where Arthur Miller is just about to pass. But something causes the great man of letters to pause and do a theater-worthy double-take. I know what stopped him.

Propped in Mitch's picture window is a life-size black-and-white cardboard cutout of Miller's former wife. Now, it's not like seeing images of Marilyn Monroe is an uncommon occurrence for Arthur Miller. But this time, the sight of this promotional souvenir for a coffee table compendium by the photographer Bernard of Hollywood hits him with the poignancy of one of his plays. He stops dead, has to collect himself. Coming off flat feet, he summons his gait, which gives me time to power-scoot back into my nook before I'm spotted.

Mitch and I reach our breaking point after a night out in the city. It begins with a cocktail party at the Museum of Modern Art, in honor of noted conceptual artist Burt Reynolds. Mitch is always getting invited to these things, but he's never asked me along before, and I admit to feeling a trace of excitement.

Despite the smirking, the lame comedies, and the paparazzi punch-outs, to me he'll always be Bow-and-Arrow Burt, kicking redneck ass in *Deliverance.*

"So, Mitch, why the big bash for Burt? And why at MoMA?"

"The man's desperate," he says. "No one takes him seriously."

We arrive at the party, and I get a couple of Manhattans for Mitch and me. A leathery woman comes over, finds out who we are, chats us up, and gives us the business card of Burt's new production company: BURT/REYNOLDS/PRO-DUCTIONS, INC. She makes a little parlor trick of remembering our names, then leads us over to...the Burt. Mitch knows just what to do.

"Why, Burt Reynolds," he says. "I haven't seen you since we did *Mass Appeal* in Jupiter, Florida, and that was a good ten years ago. How're *you?*"

Ten years is an eternity in Hollywood, but for Burt or, one imagines, a guy in Burt's league, being tangentially involved in the same dinner theater production greases the conversational wheels to a more than ample degree. He may not necessarily *want* to talk with us, but now, at least, it's easy.

"Sure, I remember," he says. "Charlie Durning brought down the house nightly." He arches an eyebrow. *"Nightly."*

"Remember that thing he improvised?" asks Mitch.

Oh, Burt remembers the touch, all right. He fixes his gaze on me. I'm in the zone. I can almost hear the opening notes of "Dueling Banjos."

"One night, Charlie enters stage right, and he's tossing a jellybean in the air—fifteen, twenty feet in the air—and he catches it in his mouth every time."

"The man never missed," says Mitch. "One night he used Chocolate Babies."

After briefly working the room, Burt makes his way toward a banquette, which he mounts with grace. The noise dies down as the legend looks out over the industry heavyweights he's taken pains to gather. He starts with an old story about him and Eastwood. Years ago, Burt and Clint were struggling actors in danger of going nowhere. According to the Tinseltown powers that were, Clint's Adam's apple was way too prominent. And Burt—who can be strangely alluring when self-deprecating—deadpans, "Me? I just couldn't act." Big laugh here; the timing is still brilliant. He gets back to Eastwood, recalling a recent conversation in which the squinty one had rasped at him, "Why don't ya just act the age ya are?" Things grow unexpectedly poignant for a moment. As Mitch deduced, this is a plea for survival. Burt Reynolds is ready to do some real acting again.

Burt keeps things short. He tells another story, plugs his production company, thanks everyone for coming out, and pretty soon the room starts to clear. Mitch turns to me and says, "What did I tell you, David? A shameless ploy to get work. Now, if you are so inclined, I am off to Don't Tell Mama, where Stanley Michael Hunthausen will be performing a one-man show. Would you like to join me?"

Stanley Michael Hunthausen is by far the biggest pest in Mitch's capacious coterie of annoying clients. He enjoyed some modest success with his first play, but his recent efforts aren't gaining traction. Why Mitch keeps him on I have no idea, but agents have to feign interest in their clients' work from time to time. I feel roughly the same way about cabaret singers as most people feel about mimes, but I know a good chance to curry favor with my boss when I see one. At six, we leave the office together and grab a cab.

"So, Mitch, a one-man show. Is there a theme?"

"Yes, David. Like many shows of this type, it's based on the life of the singer. Stanley Michael was born to a family of Jews in northwest Minnesota. His siblings were already grown up by the time he was born, and his parents were rather old and distant. Consequently, he spent a great deal of time in his bedroom, making up stories and so forth, pretending to be one singer or another."

"Couldn't have been easy growing up a gay Jew in the Midwest."

"No, David, not a bit easy. Stanley Michael has come a long way. When I first met him, he was the candy boy at the Booth Theatre."

Being with Mitch at MoMA is one thing, but at Don't Tell Mama the man is truly in his element. I hold the door for him and he enters like a king, gives a little wave to the pompadoured host, and then stops dead. I almost run into the back of him.

"Why, Daniel Ramsdale," I hear him say. "How're *you*?"

"Why, Mitch Douglas," replies my dermatologist. "How are *you*?"

Ramsdale is a top doc at NYU, yet there's something twisted about him. He always insists that I undress. The thing is, I don't have any problems down there, but Dr. Ramsdale, ostensibly in the name of medical thoroughness, always has to make sure. I call him the Rammer. "Get down to your skivvies," he'll say in a jocular tone, like a hockey coach. I guess the slang is supposed to be disarming. Then he disappears for several minutes. I always envision him huddled in a secret room, watching me through a hole as I nervously pace around in my tighty-whities.

Seizing the moment, I step around Mitch, clap the Rammer on the shoulder, and say, "I don't care what you say, Dr. Ramsdale, I am *not* getting down to my skivvies."

"David, good to see you," he says, uncomprehending.

"Daniel," says Mitch, "How is it that you know my assistant, pray tell?"

"Oh, he's your assistant, I see," says the doctor, looking slightly less feral. "Er, David's my patient."

"*Really...*" says Mitch. "Tell me. What does he have?"

"Now, Mitch, I couldn't possibly—"

"Oh, come now, Daniel, I have a right to know if my assistant has genital warts, don't I?

"I'm a dermatologist, Hal, why would he go to me for—"

"Well, the genitals *are* made out of skin, last time I checked."

Ramsdale reddens. "Well, he doesn't have genital warts."

"Well *that's* a relief."

"Now, Mitch, I really must be—"

"What about chlamydia? *Haw haw haw!*"

"I vote we change the subject."

"This is tacky, Mitch," Ramsdale says.

"How big is he?"

"Great to see you again," says the doctor, hustling off.

"Thanks, Mitch. That was painful."

"Oh, spare me, David, I did us both a favor. What an odious man. I don't know what in the *hell* I was thinking when I slept with him. *Haw haw haw!* Now come on, let's get *drunk.*"

And we do. We meet up with an assortment of Mitch's salacious friends at a nearby Spanish restaurant and work our way through a great deal of sangria. It helps obscure my mental image of Mitch spooning with the Rammer.

The next morning, I arrive at work to find Mitch seated at my typewriter, clacking away in an obvious huff—sans pants. Presumably he's gotten soaked in the downpour I've just made my way through and hung up his trousers to dry in his office. It's a few minutes before ten, when work officially begins, so he's banking on minimal foot traffic.

"David, what did I tell you?"

"About what, Mitch?"

"*About what Mitch*? About Clause 3 in the *Callanetics For the Legs, Hips and Buttocks* contract, roman numeral 2, subparagraph little 'a.' What did I tell you?"

"That we have to add the language about videocassettes."

"Yes, David, that we *have* to *add* the *language* about *videocassettes.*"

"I was going to add it this morning when I got in."

"When am I meeting with Barbara Guggenheim?"

"This afternoon."

"Did you write it in the book?"

"I came into your office yesterday afternoon and wrote it on a yellow sticky pad and held it up to you and you said 'OK.'"

"Did you write it—don't you get sassy with me—did you write it in the book?"

"No."

"Do you remember what I told you on your first day about the importance of keeping my book?"

"I believe you called it the bulwark of any successful agency."

"David, are you trying to annoy me or are you just *stupid*?"

"We had a good time last night," I said. "Can we not just bask in the afterglow of that for a minute or two?"

"No, David. I've been doing this for twenty-two years and I'm not about to change now. Your job is to obey me."

"I'm not being willfully disobedient."

"I don't care about that. I just want you to obey me."

"OK."

"Say it. Say 'I will obey you.'"

"This is unnecessary, Mitch. I'm here to assist you, and I assist you I will. But 'obey' implies a sort of master/slave relationship—"

"Exactly, David. Egg-*zactly*. Somehow you have managed to stumble upon *le mot juste*."

"I can't say that. It's against my religion."

"You will obey me or you will be discharged!"

Hearing the words "I will obey you" spring from my lips surely ranks among my life's low points.

"Yes, you will. Now David, it never hurts to learn your place in the pecking order. Because some day, Lord willing, you'll have someone who'll obey you, too."

"That's not really what I'm after."

"Really. And what are you after?"

"That's a good question. Did you happen to read yesterday's obituary of Pinky Lee in the *Times*? He had initially planned on—"

"David?"

"Mitch?"

"Go get me my pants. They're on the heating vent in my office."

The phone rings. "Mitch Douglas's office." It's Stanley Michael Hunthausen.

"Ah, Stanley Michael, the man of the hour. You must be feeling well. You were really in command last night."

"Oh, you were there?"

"I had to make a swift exit, but I must say, you actually got me a little misty there when you sang 'Send in the Clowns,' and God knows that one's been done to death."

"Thanks, he says. "I think."

"And I loved your scat singing on 'Green Dolphin Street.'"

"Scat singing?"

"I'll get Mitch."

I print his three names on a yellow legal pad in child-like block letters and hold it up to Mitch's face. He snatches the phone from me.

"Why Stanley Michael Hunthausen," he purrs. "How're *you?*" Then, placing his palm over the receiver, he hisses through clenched teeth: "My pants—now!"

In Mitch's office, I pause to gaze down on lush, green Central Park. I survey the framed thing commemorating two million dollars in sales of *Super Callanetics*, the contracts littering his desk, his leather couch, the bust of Truman Capote. Eventually I spot his pants. A minute later I emerge from his office wearing them.

Mitch is capacious through the middle, so the trou, which are almost dry, fit comfortably over my own, although they end several inches above my ankles. As I slip my coat off the back of my soon-to-be former desk chair, Mitch looks up as he types but doesn't put it together at first. I'm already around the corner and headed toward the elevator when I hear him bellow, "You take my fucking pants off!" I can still hear him as the elevator doors close.

Weeks later, I run into Gordon Kato on Sixth Avenue. I tell him I'm writing short stories and ask if I can send him a few, and he says OK. Eventually, Gordon writes back to say he's not even sure that what I've written qualifies as short stories.

Chapter 22

Like a Lazy Monarch

A *Pictorial Encyclopedia of Aberrant Behavior* (Vol. 1 "Crimes and Punishment") was waiting for me at my apartment, in a large manila envelope that also contained a dinner fork tine with a feather Krazy-Glued to each end, an obituary from the *Times* ("Ettie Mae Greene, Seamstress, 114"), and a Lincoln Log—the short, stubby kind, which appeared to have been gnawed upon. When I opened the book (which was not easy; it was bound with piano wire), an index card fell into my lap. In eyebrow pencil, in that crazy hand of hers, it said, "*If this were a piece of glass, you'd be bleeding now. Still love me?*" She had signed her name in the usual way: with a staple.

Sara's deliveries are her way of making me forgive her latest indignity and start jumping through hoops again. To rectify a previous crisis, she made me a mixed-media portrait of myself [*David at Rest* (1993). Sara Salmus (b. 1969). Sandpaper, paint marker, Tiny-Size Chiclets, frying pan, hot glue gun]. On a different occasion, she dispatched a messenger to deliver a package to me containing a coupon for Pamprin, a tequila lollipop with the worm in it, and an assortment of sticks and leaves.

Sara has this theory about gifts. She says the only gifts worth giving are ones that have never been exchanged in the course of human history. And since so many things have been passed back and forth at this late date, you have to go to great lengths to find a genuine, first-time-given gift. Sure, scores of romantics over the ages have given away a lock of their hair, but how many gave their beloved a single hair? How many have given a toenail painted iridescent gold, floating moon-like over a cobalt blue-painted matchbook? Who has ever taken the time to thread an eyelash through a packet of ground pepper? That moves me.

The first time I saw Sara Salmus, she was making copies of a layout she'd done for the dust jacket of a book of poetry by a Holocaust survivor. She was the newly hired assistant to the art director of Hyperion, and I was trying to get a look down her sleeve hole, which was large enough to allow me a pretty good view of an off-white, almost military-style brassiere sheathing her breast like a siloed missile. With the copier light playing prettily over it, her profile was like an exquisite succession of commas. I began to obsess. There was nothing I could do about it, and her occasional banality did nothing to diminish my debilitating infatuation.

One of my only true life goals is that I want to be the father of a child someday, but at almost thirty, with my peers already starting families, I'm still figuring out what I'm good at. Years will pass before I might be *husband* material. As for breadwinner and eventual dad—Y2K, maybe? That's fine with Amanda, who wants nothing more than for us to continue. She isn't even divorced yet. Goosed by my encroaching thirtieth birthday, the perpetual enticement of Sara Salmus, and the dispiriting knowledge that I can coast in my current relationship, I start to wonder where this thing of ours is going. The feeling swiftly snowballs.

On a chilly Sunday in January, Amanda picks up tickets for a matinee showing of *Until the End of the World* at the Angelika, and I make myself tell her I can't go on this way forever—meaning I can't go on this way at all. We go to the movie anyway. It lasts forever.

A few days later, Amanda leaves a tape with my doorman. Two of the songs come from the *Until the End of the World* soundtrack, so at least our purgatorial experience at the Angelika has an upside. The tape's title is a phrase she cut out from a magazine; otherwise the paper insert is unlabeled. Not that any annotation is needed. If there's ever been a tape where a song lyric that said "you" meant me and those that said "me" meant her, this is it.

Contest of a Lifetime

YOU COULDN'T HAVE COME AT A BETTER TIME - LUKA BLOOM
TELL ME - BOB DYLAN
ALIVE AND LIVING NOW - GOLDEN PALOMINOS FEAT. MICHAEL STIPE
MY LOVE LIFE - MORRISSEY (W. CHRISSIE HYNDE)
YOU TOOK MY BREATH AWAY - THE TRAVELING WILBURYS
LOVE TO SEE YOU - THE ROCHES
CALLING ALL ANGELS - JANE SIBERRY (FEAT. K.D. LANG)
HOW CAN WE HANG ON TO A DREAM - TIM HARDIN
DAYS - ELVIS COSTELLO

The tape ends with the words "Remember me," speaker unidentified. There is no Side 2.

Smacked in the gut by my own native medium, I welcome the punch in a way. I deserve to feel some pain here. My reward, if you can call it that, is that Sara—mercurial, not-quite-broken-up-with-her-boyfriend Sara—can now be my full-time obsession.

Sara's unpredictable, not hemmed in by conventional modes of social behavior or discourse. We'll be walking up Fifth Avenue and she'll think of something funny and start cackling so hard she'll bump right into me. Not for effect, but out of a genuine inability to laugh that hard and still keep walking. Sara has two dick stories. She briefly dated a guy who was enormous, like nothing she'd ever seen. Like a tennis ball can. When she first laid eyes on it, she insisted on calling her friend immediately. "Megan," she said breathlessly, "I'm calling to tell you that I'm holding the hugest penis in the entire world right now." On a different occasion, Sara was out drinking with some friends, and a major Hollywood actor, an Oscar nominee, hit on her. She ended up back at his apartment, and this star of stage and screen had the *smallest* penis she had ever seen. He even made a joke about it. Somehow, Sara managed to resist calling Megan until the next day.

Despite my artistic limitations, I'm inspired to pick up a pen and draw cartoons to amuse her. I find a way to render Sara as a beautiful, blond, urban-dwelling sprite and our various co-workers as pathetic boobs. One night we leave work together and walk to her apartment. We drink some white wine and she lets me massage her feet. But I have to do it correctly, pressing the toes back and applying pressure to the underside with bunched knuckles, just so. It's like treating a prized thoroughbred.

Sara finally lets me have my way with her on the first night of the LA riots: April 29, 1992. Not as a statement of unity or anything, it just works out that way. Work shuts down in the early afternoon, and Team Disney advises its members to proceed swiftly to a secure location in the event that New York City experiences a riot of its own, and... one thing leads to another. She relents more than anything else.

I carry Sara to her four-poster bed, and she gestures for me to remove her boots, so I do. And her socks, and her jeans too, so I do, and all the while she lies there like a lazy monarch being denuded by her manservant after a long day of beheadings and teas. My eyes are not allowed to linger over her nakedness—she shields herself beneath a giant down comforter. And when we're in our final throes, she doesn't whisper, "Fuck me," as one might expect, or possibly even hope. Nope. She says, "Fuck *you*." Afterward we lie there in curious silence, Sara gazing at me as one would survey a lab specimen. Nevertheless, Charlie Brown to her Lucy, I persist, with the occasional result of getting her back into bed, which always leaves me feeling let down, desperate, and faintly ridiculous.

Once I tried to pull this ruse, that I'd gotten myself a girlfriend, thinking that would get me past my unhealthy obsession. I'm a terrible liar, but Sara bought the tale, and it was a tall one—just like my fictitious girlfriend, whom I designed for maximum annoyance.

Her name was Kimberly. She worked at the UN. She spoke eight languages, and she was a yoga instructor whose real passion was sculpting. And not just any old yoga—Kimberly was a practitioner of Bikram yoga, the kind performed in a room heated to 110 degrees, which was new then. And not just any kind of sculpting: she used special clays dug from selected spots because of their mineral count and enhanced tactile quality. Whenever Sara and I talked on the phone, I would drop some new and completely galling trait. Then Sara started calling me "hon."

"I'm so happy for you, hon," she'd say. "Oh hon, she sounds amazing."

What "hon" meant was that we would never sleep together again. We'd have a kind of brother/sister relationship. Why the hell couldn't she just get jealous, or make fun of my perfectly annoying Kimberly? My ruse had worked—but now what? I had neglected to begin with the end in mind. Then the postcard came. Around the edge was a repeating motif of the little icons you find on packages of chopsticks showing you how to use them, only she'd manipulated the images with Photoshop and now the hands made obscene gestures.

Who was I kidding, anyway? Everywhere I looked I saw Sara. Things that shouldn't have reminded me of her reminded me of her. Dropped gloves in the street. Fish tanks in Chinese restaurants. Other women's perfume—because she wore perfume. The sun would rise, and I'd think, ah, daytime. I met Sara during the daytime. And I would sigh.

So I arrange for Kimberly to be transferred to Namibia and ask Sara to meet me for a drink at Bandito's on 2nd Avenue, known for its gigantic frozen margaritas and flammable tortilla chips. Eventually she complies.

Sara's late, which is to be expected, but when she does show up, she's with a guy. A guy! And this guy—sort of beefy, with an impressively sculpted jaw and an air of surly disdain.

"Roight, Dave," he says, extending his hand.

"Right." What ever happened to hello? I draw away, but he holds on to my retreating hand.

"*Liam*," he says, giving a final shake and releasing it.

"Got it. *Liam*," I say, this time with italics. "Friend of Sara from . . ."

"You might say that," he says with a smirk.

"You work together?"

"A bit, a bit. Wot you drinking, geez?"

"Tecate."

"Roight. Sara, margarita for you?"

"Roight. No salt, though. I'm watching my kidneys."

They share a laugh, as if tuned to the same frequency.

"Could I get one of these?" I say, lifting up Liam's pack of smokes.

"Help yourself."

I light one and suck down a huge drag and blow it out luxuriously. "Cheers," I say. "I feel like I've seen you here before. Do you know Nigel? He frequents various watering holes on this block."

"Nigel?" A grin materializes out of nowhere, one that might be described as movie-star handsome were it not for the missing front tooth. "D'you suppose I have but one English friend named Nigel? Or is it that, being British, I must have at least *six or seven* friends named Nigel?"

Sara rolls her eyes. "*Leee*-um."

"Actually, I'd be surprised if you had six or seven friends, *period*. Or, full stop, I guess you'd say." He grins again, a little less wolfishly.

"That's it, boys. Play nice. I'll be right back," she says, heading for the payphone.

Sara is so deathly afraid of being alone that she needs to be on the phone even when she's *with* people. Soon there's a soft knock on my knee.

"Want a bump?" Liam cocks his head to indicate the packet of cocaine in his palm.

That knock has become a familiar sensation. Many of my nights out entail six or twelve beers, numerous knee knocks, and trips to one ghastly bathroom or another. The one at this place is especially cruel. Each wall is a mirror, so your grotesquely distorted features are reflected back and forth infinitely until you fade off into nothing. There's dead water in the soap dish, sodden paper towels strewn in clumps over the damp floor tiles. When Liam locks the door behind him and regards me dead eyes, I feel like I've already had a big cocaine blast.

"Y'alright, mate?"

"Fine."

"Y'sure?"

"Yeah, I'm sure. No problem."

He takes a step toward me and I'm pretty certain something awful is about to happen. He puts his hands on my waist, and I'm on the verge of fight or flight, but he just moves me gently aside, like we're fox-trotting, and slips past me to the urinal.

"We should probably hurry this up."

"You think too much, mate," he says, in the midst of a languorous piss.

"There's just, I hear people outside the door and—"

"Fuck 'em," he says. Liam turns back around without flushing, zips up, and retrieves the coke and a set of keys from his jeans. He scoops out a healthy load of it. I sniff, but nothing comes up. Liam reaches up and places his thumb over my left nostril, as if him touching my nose were the most natural thing in the world. I breathe in, and the hit shoots straight up to my brain.

"Woah," I say with a shudder.

"Wanker," Liam half-whispers.

"Gosh," Sara says when we return. "You two are practically lovers now."

After a few rounds, the speedy coke buzz begins to recede to a tolerable level, as does a portion of my resentment about the intrusion of this Liam character. Maybe he's just a cocky bastard she knows from work. It doesn't necessarily mean they're involved. I slip off to feed the jukebox, but when I turn around, there's a space at the bar where they had been. Her jacket's on the stool, which means they're still here. In that squalid, extremely narrow bathroom. As the minutes tick by, my rage reaches a rolling boil, and I blow out the door in a cartoon huff. Once I find a phone, I put in a call to the bar, whose tender confirms that Sara Salmus has just paid the tab and left with a bloke.

When I get back home, I don't hesitate. I gather everything up: the glitter-dipped pine cone, the molded rubber *Rattus norvegicus*, the faded Old Maid cards, the miniature hangman's noose fashioned from her own blonde hair, the sticks, the leaves, the frying pan—and dump it all down my building's trash chute. But when I reach the fridge to toast myself with a congratulatory beer, I see that in my haste I've missed the eyelash pepper packet, secured to my refrigerator door with a rectangular magnet showing Edith Massey in her *Pink Flamingos* playpen.

Gently sliding the eyelash out, I carry it to the counter and place it under a shot glass while I fetch a couple of vintage guitar picks (Guild, medium gauge, tortoiseshell). I lay the lash down between them, light matches to seal the edges, and place the wedge inside a flattened Dixie Riddle cup (*"Where do cows go on Saturday night? The moo-vies!"*). Encircling it with a bow fashioned from dental floss (Johnson & Johnson, mint, waxed), I place the item in an empty cassette case and call Speedy B's Personal Courier Service.

Those guitar picks—remnants of my teenage years, taking lessons from a part-time Guild salesman—are deeply permeated with my thumb and finger oils. At least our DNA will be inextricably bound, or very close together, for something like eternity. Sara is never going to be mine, but I derive some small shred of peace knowing she'll be the willing custodian of our little fossil, and that we, or the idea of us, will remain, preserved in that mottled, heart-shaped amber.

Chapter 23

The Beautiful People

"Don't you hate it when you have, like, fifty ones?"

Gwyneth Paltrow is perched swan-like at the edge of a glove-soft leather sofa. Only the faintest wisp of annoyance shows upon her silken brow as she surveys the contents of the purse she's just emptied onto my cousin's coffee table. There's not much to say about the coffee table, other than, like every other item in the apartment, it's extremely tasteful. Twenty years later, when asked if she found the original script for *Shakespeare in Love* on this very piece of furniture, Gwyneth will call it an urban myth. But I'm getting ahead of myself. Tonight is the MTV Video Music Awards show at Radio City, hosted by Chris Rock, and there will be parties.

As the cousin who sometimes comes by to hang, I've met Gwyneth before, and she's pretty easy to be around. We're sitting in the sun-drenched ground-floor apartment on Gramercy Park North that she and Noni have been sharing lately. One of New York City's most exclusive neighborhoods, Gramercy Park surrounds an eponymous greenspace that's accessible to a precious few via a very special key. Not that Noni will ever use hers, but I could probably borrow it and go and sit with a crossword puzzle.

Why would two A-list twentysomething actors choose to room together like normal people when they could live luxuriously all on their own? Maybe it's because they understand each other's reality. My guess is that when you're the central figure in an ongoing enterprise where your agent, publicist, media companies, fans, stalkers, and casual moviegoers all have a stake in your career success, it's a comfort to find someone who can truly relate to that kind of pressure.

At twenty-six, Noni is a year older and the more established star, but Gwyneth's been a big name since *Se7en*, and last year she earned raves for *Emma*. Noni and Gwyneth are accustomed to being gossiped about, and they're both in the midst of a non-working summer stretch. Noni's last movie, Woody Allen's *Celebrity*, finished shooting in April, as did Gwyneth's *Sliding Doors*. So they're taking meetings, reading scripts, and plotting next moves.

There's a phenomenon that happens when girls are extremely comfortable together. They share a tactility you rarely see in your guys. Noni and Gwyneth are that way, like sisters. Making a dual entrance at parties and premieres, they'll sometimes hold hands. I admit to feeling a bit ungainly in the presence of such star wattage, but I'm along for the ride. This is going to be fun.

"What do we think about Skysby's shirt?" Noni says.

Gwyneth looks over my duds coldly, offering a flaxen nod of disapproval. Maybe there's a soupçon of empathy, not unlike the immortal frown she'll later give Tom Ripley, who, God bless him, just wasn't born into all this grandeur. Noni turns to her young friend from the West Coast and asks if it would be OK if I wore the shirt he currently has on. Nathaniel, we'll call him Nathaniel, is handsome and slim, and doesn't seem the least put out—like this isn't the first time he's had to part with an article of clothing to avert a fashion disaster in the making.

"Not a *problem*," he sings. "As long as you don't mind it being a little... snug?"

I'm being given a gorgeous, slightly warm but not at all damp, men's shirt by Prada—jet black. But wow, this one hurts. I was totally ready to wear what I'd picked out, a dark, slinky- fitting psychedelic-patterned dress shirt with long cuffs that slipped past my wrists and made me feel vaguely like a rock star. Worse, taking the shirt off another person's back has an ancient, damning implication. Inhabiting the discarded shell of a hermit crab with washboard abs in front of Brad Pitt's ex is arguably worse than being booed by Led Zeppelin, my other peak moment of celebrity humiliation.

As various outfits are tried on, a CD of Fleetwood Mac's *Rumours* plays on repeat. Noni's been on a Fleetwood Mac kick since becoming pals with Stevie Nicks. Now it's all she wants to hear. I haven't made her a tape in ages because, as much as it pains me, she no longer needs my help. My status as resident musical expert is on even shakier ground since I foolishly confessed to having a soft spot for Paula Cole's tear-jerking "I Don't Wanna Wait," which is still a few years shy of finding cultural ubiquity as the theme song for the teen soap opera *Dawson's Creek*.

Rumours is finally quashed, we tune into MTV, and immediately the "I Don't Wanna Wait" video comes on. Noni alerts Gwyneth—*this is the one Skysby has a crush on*—and they share a little chuckle. It's not that I have a crush on Paula Cole, but the truth is even worse. I discovered the song a few months ago on my monthly CMJ compilation, just as I'd been dumped by someone I'd fallen hard for, and Paula's throaty lament was my perfect sad-listen. But they don't need to know that. Better to be thought of as a sensitive guy crushing on a gal who wants to know where all the cowboys have gone.

I'm ready to loosen up a little, but Noni is neither a drinker nor much of a recreational drug user. I see this as almost an act of rebellion. She once confessed to me that her parents were getting after her to take mushrooms and see *Koyaanisqatsi*, the time-lapse Philip Glass-scored art house hit. The world's most permissive parents were finally putting their foot down. They were practically insisting.

"Skysby," she had moaned. "I'm gonna get grounded unless I trip!"

Beck and Jamiroquai rack up several awards each. Fiona Apple, Spice Girls, and No Doubt top key categories. Sting and Puff Daddy offer an earnest tribute to Biggie Smalls, and Madonna offers an earnest tribute to Princess Diana. There's not a ton of raucousness on display. Performing an unmemorable single called "Please," U2 is notably stripped-down. Devoid of eyewear and wearing a dark hoodie, Bono looks like a junior Sith lord. Unquestionably, Marilyn Manson delivers the performance of the night with "The Beautiful People," which is riveting theater—an electroconvulsive Nuremberg rally with butt cheeks that leaves the audience's ears ringing and minds jubilantly assaulted. Then, at a leisurely pace, properly attired, we file into a hired car—spacious but not a limo—and head uptown to the Four Seasons hotel.

We ascend the marble steps leading to the bar, sumptuously lit in tones of deep red and gold, where we find Bono. He's just flown in from Edinburgh for that one song, and he looks a little worn out. Five years ago at Yankee Stadium, U2 was on top of the world. Now the band is supporting a supremely ill-advised venture into drum-and-bass and mired in the much-maligned PopMart Tour. Worse, the musical worm has turned. A pale Scientologist named Beck, whose wry genre dabbling and easy hip-hop fluency seems granted at birth, is all the rage. U2 spent millions commissioning a 100-foot golden arch, erecting a shimmering, techno-fantastic lemon (which malfunctioned multiple times, trapping the band inside), and dragging the world's largest LED screen across every major sports arena in America, looking for a way into the nineties zeitgeist. And as it turns out, two turntables and a microphone are ... *where it's at.*

Bono's gracious despite the circumstances—no rock-star amnesia here. On the other hand, I get the distinct impression Dave Grohl will forget me in seconds. I don't hold this against Dave's lovely mother, Virginia Hanlon Grohl, with whom I yammer everlong while Noni and Dave engage in cozy, beautiful-people conspiracy. Virginia, who will go on to write the essential "rock mom" book, *From Cradle to Stage,* is a teacher, so the conversation flows easily. But chit-chatting about progressive education with the mother of the drummer for Nirvana, while no doubt a nifty thing, still has me feeling like a bit of a heel, rhapsodizing about the smell of Crayola crayons and classroom paste while surveying the room for talent over Virginia's shoulder. Around here is where Courtney Love's Friend's Friend Who Has an Extra Hit of Ecstasy comes into view.

She and I find each other through mutual need. When you're in that plus-one category, you need companionship and conversation. Declaring my Winona connection is always a reliable conversation starter, and I've got another plausibly interesting sounding job, this time at Muze, a provider of digital content to businesses in the music/books/video sphere—which is a very wide sphere. *Green Eggs and Ham*? *Faster Pussycat, Kill Kill!*? The latest in dark illbient? Muze has you covered. And they make those kiosks you see at Tower Records that let you listen to a sample of a record before you purchase it.

Nineties, baby. I'm in metadata now. Doesn't that sound proper?

Noni catches my eye. We're moving to a new location. A group of us—Ms. Grohl & son and various posse members included—fill up a private elevator, and we ride in our finery to the fifty-second-floor pinnacle. The doors part, and we enter a vast nine-room space designed by legendary edifice builder I.M. Pei, bordered by floor-to-ceiling windows and a panoramic view of glittering Gotham.

If the previous party was your basic booze-and-schmooze with industry types, big-name stars, and their parents (I chatted with Beck's mom as well), we've now made it to the hip kids' table. In one room, Leo DiCaprio lounges on a bed with several gorgeous friends, David Blaine pulls cards out of his ass in another, while Jamiroquai, or very possibly the guy from Counting Crows, holds court nearby. Noni and Dave don't mingle. They hang back, discussing. In short order, she lets me know they're leaving.

Now I'm on my own, loosened by drinks, legitimized by Prada, the rising E pill whispering sweet nothings in my ear. Ordinary movements—arm rotations, gnawing gently on a lower lip, *breathing*—feel languorous and delectable, and we lean in closer now, the warmth of skin meeting skin, the mere brushing of an arm or a shoulder, exquisite. And then, just as I'm starting to tingle like a plucked guitar string, the Verve's "Bittersweet Symphony" comes on big over the I.M. Pei-approved audio system.

Abetted by the nervy video in which singer Richard Ashcroft tramps down a busy London sidewalk, knocking into pedestrians and not giving a single shit, "Bittersweet Symphony" is having its moment. That opening fanfare of orchestral strings, which will eventually get the band devastatingly sued, acts as some kind of signal. On cue and with undeniable charm, Courtney Love and Billy Corgan start waltzing. A beat or two later, the rest of us join in, ballroom dancing with playful formality with the whole of nighttime New York City as our backdrop.

As a kid, I experienced some real trauma when a serious injury threatened the sight in my right eye. These days, my roving eye, a completely unrelated condition, does me the most damage. Surely, it's to blame for my presence in a limo with Courtney Love, Edward Norton, Courtney Love's Friend Who Is a Model of Some Kind, and Courtney Love's Friend's Friend Who Had an Extra Hit of Ecstasy Roughly Four and a Half Hours Ago. Still, I tell myself, something good—material for a short story, perhaps—might be right around the corner, or, more accurately, through a hotel lobby and accessible via elevator.

Despite the frazzled state of my synapses, I'm lucid enough to wonder just what in God's name Edward is doing with Courtney. Fresh from his breakout performance in *Primal Fear,* Ed is one of the hottest young actors on the planet. After spending a handful of moments with Courtney this evening, I believe she is not the most well person. Sure, in the two years since she chucked a makeup compact at Madonna, at these very awards, she's gotten sober, secured a role in *The People vs. Larry* Flynt, and earned not just an Oscar nomination but a massive career boost and the veneer of respectability as a result. But I've had a peak behind the facade tonight. Edward, meanwhile, is calm, bright, very good at acting, and obviously not an attention whore. Maybe being nominated for Best Supporting brings disparate people together in some magical way. It happened with Billy Bob and Angelina, right?

Trailing behind Courtney and the gang, I'm mildly disgusted with myself for having sweated through the gorgeous garment loaned to me by Bobby Cheekbones hours earlier. But waltzing in tight-fitting fabric will do that, especially combined with an E pill. Perhaps the opium-den-like setting where I hope we're heading has a dry cleaners. When Courtney reaches the end of the corridor, she raps on the door.

I have to clarify something.

All of the foregoing—everything I've said, even the stuff about Jimi Hendrix and Robert Plant and Marisa Tomei and Miss G and Jethro Tull showing me his nuts—all of it flashed through my mind just exactly as I've explained it to you thus far, in the long minute it took for the door to swing open. Like in "An Occurrence at Owl Creek Bridge."

"Hey, come on in," says Twiggy Ramirez.

Shirtless, with a fur cap nestled upon his head, the bass player in Marilyn Manson's band clutches a white bath towel at his waist and ushers the ladies in, leaving a heady tailwind of baby powder in his wake. Now it's just me and Edward Norton bringing up the rear. Ed can easily keep on walking, but God bless him, he stops and turns to me and says sotto voce, "Don't worry, man. Nobody else has any idea what the hell they're doing here either."

Bolstered by his assurance, his "man," I follow him into the main room, where Marilyn Manson and a striking blond-tressed woman are propped up in a deluxe-size bed, under a quilt strewn with glossy magazines. They wear matching white hotel robes. The woman looks like Cicciolina, the Hungari-an-Italian former porn star, politician, and singer born Ilona Staller, who is Jeff Koons's girlfriend, so I'm pretty sure it isn't her. Edward greets the couple with a few pleasantries, and then I approach the bed and introduce myself to the man who just hours ago had proclaimed to an audience of millions, "We will no longer be oppressed by the fascism of Christianity!" Gazing up at me with a mild expression, as if entertaining visitors at bedside were an everyday occurrence, he extends his hand, and we exchange a gentle six-in-the-morning shake. Without makeup, he's actually less pale than with.

"Manson," he says.

Courtney perches at the foot of the bed, engaging our hosts. Ed relaxes in an easy chair. Crouched on the carpet next to Manson's side of the bed, Twiggy adjusts a small portable record player to an unhearable level. Because the drugs don't work, and we all feel like a scared hamster. As Manson reads aloud from a recent Q and A in *New York Rocker,* we plus-ones arrange ourselves on an adjacent bed, doing our best not to touch.

"The British magazine *Kerrang!* claimed that a girl in Australia tried to com-mit suicide because she was too young to see your concert," intones Manson, in a sober interviewer voice. Then, continuing as himself: "That's the first time I heard the story, but in case it should be true—somebody should have given her a ticket for the show." Chuckles are dutifully rendered, and then the bed conversation turns quieter. Twiggy lowers the music even more, and some perverse mechanism within me decrees that it's my turn to speak. Despite my next thought ("Resist this urge, or at least come up with something worth saying"), I forge on.

"So," I begin, addressing Courtney Love's Friend. "Fashion model?"

Manson detects the weirdness and looks up from his magazine.

"No," she snaps, "I'm a *secretary*," spitting out the final word like a poison dart.

She's being sarcastic of course. There's no greater hell on earth than being a secretary, and I should know. The moment spreads its tendrils, and paralysis suffuses the room. Someday, you will ache like I ache.

I exhort myself into action via simple instructions: "In twenty seconds, you will rise to your feet. You will say it was extremely nice meeting you all. You will place one foot in front of the other..." That kind of thing.

When I close the door behind me, I fast-walk for a few steps, but soon I'm galloping for all I'm worth, and not just out of sheer relief, but because it's just occurred to me that I have work today—an office temp job, which is just another way of saying secretary—and I have about an hour to get there on time. Eva Passaretti, an administrative resource manager in MetLife's HR department, could not care less about who I've been hobnobbing with.

At my apartment, I ditch the sweaty Prada, feed the cat, dose myself with Ibuprofen, Visine, and coffee, and fumble through my closet to find my cleanest dirty shirt. I'll be virtually on time, although my first hour will go to paying for the taxi. Upon arrival, flop-sweating and wincing at the negative pings in my skull and the fluorescent lighting, I swiftly encounter Eva, who greets me with a withering look and a stale exhalation of disapproval. I follow her into a room where a stack of paper the size of a small child is piled on a vast conference table.

"OK, here is what you do," she says. "Sort the cases out by file, then put the active cases in one pile and the pending cases in the other. You can tell if the case is active by the red stamp that says ACTIVE. Got it?"

"Got it."

"Good. And don't be making phone calls in here. This is a conference room, you know. You cannot just be making phone calls in here."

The files turn out to be disputed life insurance claims, mostly drug- and alcohol-related fatalities involving cars and other heavy machinery. Or what I call stellar reading material. I'm especially spellbound by a case involving a military wife, her deep-sea-diving ex-military husband, and autoerotic asphyx-iation. MetLife, which refuses to pay the policy, deems the man's demise "death by misadventure" (sick epitaph). His wife argues to the contrary, that her hus-band was an otherwise careful, health-minded person: a buckler of seatbelts, an avoider of drink and drugs, an inveterate gym goer—someone who wanted to keep on living, in other words. The man, an experienced free diver, had simply made a fatal miscalculation. This was not death by misadventure, but rather a tragic accident.

Fascinating stuff. And great short story material. Despite the brain pops and the unpleasant memory of all the squishy, sensitive feelings I expressed last night, not to mention the Manson hotel debacle, these authentic tales of human foibles, tragic occurrences, and corporate intransigence have me feel-ing like myself again. Taking a pause from my sorting work, I head to the men's room with a trace of spring in my step.

Crouched at the base of a wall of file cabinets with a label-maker at her feet, very much in troll-guarding-the-bridge mode, is Eva Passaretti. Joints pop-ping, she assumes an upright posture and I take a step back, reflexively.

"Need something?"

"Oh, do I have to show you my hall pass?"

"Don't you get loud with *me*, guy."

"Who's getting loud?"

She shakes her head wearily. "You have a bad attitude. I could see that from the very start."

"You see a lot, Dr. Lecter," I say, channeling Jodie Foster. "But are you strong enough to point that high-powered perception at yourself?"

"That's it," she says. "Pack up your gear."

"Gladly. I'll just need your John Hancock on this," I say, retrieving my timesheet from my blazer pocket.

She snatches the sheet and scrutinizes it.

"I'm kind of sad though," I say. "I feel like we were… *Como se dice en español? Simpatico?*"

"No, that's not right," she says.

"*Theeem*-patico?"

"You were not in at nine A.M. this morning," she says, snatching a pen-cil stub from behind her ear, changing my "9:00" to "9:15," and initialing her correction with a flourish worthy of Zorro. She then beelines to a nearby fax machine and sends the sheet through to my temp agency, the number of which is programmed on autodial for precisely this type of shenanigan. As she leans over the machine watching the paper go through, I assure Eva that I know she's just doing her job. "And besides, an extra quarter hour of my salary might have a potentially devastating effect on the company's bottom line," I say. "I mean, six dollars and thirty three cents here, six dollars thirty three cents there, pretty soon it starts to add up to real money."

"That's not the point," she says, her expression defiant. "And that's the sad thing with you. You'll go through your whole life thinking *you're* the one who's being wronged. But your attitude is what's wrong, not the actions of hardworking people."

"Well, I may be morally bankrupt, but at least I floss regularly."

"Janine!" she barks to the firm's newly hired junior associate account executive, who wears an ill-fitting brownish business suit and a mild expression. "Call Security!!"

Janine doesn't, though. Instead, she looks up at me with soft eyes and says, "Maybe you should just go."

Maybe you should just go.

I can barely suppress the urge to lean down and kiss her slightly damp forehead and gently push away the strand of stray hair that's plastered slantwise across it. I want the world to go all foggy and soft-focus and the music to swell, and I want to fluff up her hair and take her glasses off and say, "See, I always knew you was pretty."

Instead, summoning my best Veronica Sawyer in *Heathers*, I tell Janine, "You're beautiful."

Chapter 24

People Need to Party

Stephen Mailer may be the funniest human being I've ever met—and I've met Joey Bishop.

In high school, my pal Pete was dating the daughter of Corbett Monica, a former Borscht Belt comedian who'd enjoyed moderate fame opening up for Sinatra, guesting on *Johnny Carson* and *Ed Sullivan,* and serving as the sidekick on *The Joey Bishop Show.* His heyday was behind him by the late seventies, but he was still performing. Here's a typical Corbett joke: "We had nine kids—nine! We all slept in the same bed. I never slept alone till I got married!"

So one day Pete and I go to pick up Corbett's daughter, and Corbett's in his sunny suburban kitchen with some of his comedian pals, noshing on drinks and sandwiches, and I'm introduced to Joey Bishop. Joey says to me, "What's your name?" I tell him David. He says, "How old are you, David?" I tell him eighteen.

"Eighteen?" he says. "I have ties that old."

I first encountered Stephen Mailer at the screening of *Cry-Baby* where I first met Johnny Depp. Stephen had a featured role as Baldwin, the smug preppy nemesis of Johnny's Cry-Baby Walker. A few years later, Stephen and I met for real, when Tommy Morgan began regularly hosting late-night poker games at the apartment we shared on Mercer Street. Now Stephen and I are flying down to Rio to serve as co-best men at Tommy's wedding.

Stephen has a quick and dancing mind, superior vocal and physical mimicry skills, the ability to slip effortlessly into a newly invented character, and the sheer force of will to make a bit work that would fail mightily in the hands of less committed souls. One night at a blackjack table, according to Tommy, he did Tony Montana's *"Now you're talking to me baby, and that I like,"* every time he won. Into the wee hours.

Tommy's finagled an excellent rate on a block of ten rooms at the beachside Marina Palace hotel. Stephen and I will be sharing one out of economic necessity. Spending a week in Rio will require some strategic frugality on my part, but I'm at least semi-solvent. As for my seatmate, the son of one of the twentieth century's most celebrated novelists, Tommy noted in a recent email that "Stephen is feeling very stressed about having $24 in his savings account."

Stephen's acting career was at its peak a good five years ago, when he was on Broadway alongside Nathan Lane in Neil Simon's *Laughter on the 23rd Floor,* portraying young Neil Simon. But the play didn't run very long, and in the ensuing years he's only had a couple of small roles, playing a fed in a TV movie about the Waco standoff and a brief scene in an upcoming Ang Lee movie. Stephen the actor has pretty much shifted to Stephen the husband—and, as of a few months ago, Stephen the father.

Tommy Morgan found the love of his life on Ipanema Beach. Just like in the song, he'd watched an enchanting someone *walk to the sea* and *look straight ahead not at he.* But on that exquisite day, in his beloved new home, Tommy summoned the moxie not only to rewrite an enduring classic but family history as well. For, in his youth, Tommy Morgan *Senior* had befriended a Brazilian textiles magnate (as you do) and was *this close* to marrying the man's sister, a beautiful and gracious Carioca. Eventually he backed off and married Tommy's volatile American mother, to what I suspect was his lifelong regret.

Rising to his pale, possibly sunburned feet, Tommy approaches this sumptuous vision on the sand and starts speaking to her in his undeniably excellent Portuguese. Tommy's a praying man, especially now, in the twelve-step era, and when the tall, tan, and impossibly lovely Isabella responds with an easy, and it should be said, flawless smile, and agrees to join him for dinner that night, it's the miracle he's been waiting for. From there, things escalate fairly quickly, although not without a hitch. They survive a brief breakup and enjoy a sweet reunion tempered by realism. In subsequent lengthy emails, Tommy assures me that his mind is right; he just needed a little time to come to terms with things that weren't perfect about her.

Our flight takes off at midnight from JFK with a mid-morning arrival in Rio. Stephen and I are amped up, talking like crazy, ready for adventure. Stephen orders a Diet Coke, I opt for red wine, and he mentions that Philip Seymour

Hoffman, another regular at Tommy's poker games, will be joining us in a few days.

Thanks to Tommy, I've had an insider's view of Phil Hoffman's career, from, "Check it out: Phil's flying to Texas to film a movie with Steve Martin, Debra Winger, and—this'll crack you up—Meat Loaf!" [*Leap of Faith*, 1992] to "You're not gonna *believe* who Phil just auditioned for—Al fucking Pacino!" After *Scent of a Woman*, in which he was still billed as Phil S. Hoffman, his rise became easier to chart on my own. I'm dying to grill him about his recent performance as the chronic masturbator Allen in *Happiness*.

"So Stephen, how did you all find each other? Like, how did you meet Phil?"

"Me and Phil go back a long way," he says. "Summer of '86. You ready for this?"

"I'm ready. Belted in. Tasting tannins."

"I'm in the NYU theater program, in the Playwrights Horizons wing because I'm interested in directing and playwriting. I'm doing a summer program through NYU with the Hangar Theatre in Ithaca, and so is [*Capote* director] Bennett Miller, who I know from NYU. Bennett had been at theater camp with Phil in high school, and he and Phil became fast friends while Bennett was at Hangar. Phil lived in Rochester, and one night he came to visit with his girlfriend—and we got drunk together. And I couldn't really stand him."

"Really. What was it?"

"Something about him. He was really intense. He was just fuckin' angry. Whenever Phil and I saw each other, we were always drunk, and we didn't really like each other. Especially in the NYU dorm. Bennett and Phil were friends at Weinstein as sophomores. One night we were in Bennett's room partying and we were playing the Eagles, and Phil turned it up really loud and faced the speakers out into the quad—just blasting it. And Phil's like, "It's Friday night, man! *People need to party*! They need to hear this!""

"Really? The Eagles?"

"Yep. Full blast."

"Good God. But seriously, I'm having difficulty imagining you drunk, Stephen. I mean, I've never seen you not sober. What were you like—some kind of a silly drunk?"

"I was a self-centered drunk. Opinionated. I had a chip on my shoulder. I thought I was a genius. All that bullshit."

I still can't quite fathom it. Stephen seems like he would have been the ideal person to have a drink with when he was drinking.

"And so Phil was an angry drunk?"

"I thought Phil was crazy. We were basically the same animal, fused by alcohol."

I sip my wine and let that wash over me.

"So, a few years go by, and one night Phil and I both show up at Bennett's house, at separate times—really drunk. And Bennett thinks, wow, those guys really need help. Phil went to rehab in November '89, me in April 1990. I got six months, but I wasn't really invested."

"How do you mean?"

"I went to forty-five meetings in ninety days. You're supposed to go to ninety. I didn't work any of the steps, didn't have the fellowship at all. But during that time I was at an audition, and I ran into Phil. And Phil says, 'So I hear from Bennett that you aren't drinking. You going to meetings?'

"And I say, 'Not *really*...'"

He says, 'I'm gonna go to a meeting later. Wanna come with me?'" And he was really sweet. It was like a whole new Phil. I said, 'No-o-o-o... I'm fine.'

Then another time, I'm coming out of the subway at Columbus Circle, and he says he's on his way to Fireside, the meeting in SoHo. 'Ya wanna come?'

And I said 'No-o-o-o... I'm fine.'

"And again, he was really sweet, a new dude. And *then.* Then I was riding in a cab in SoHo, on Prince Street, and I saw him in the distance. He was playing stickball. It was like the universe was trying to connect us."

"Oh, man. So that was the moment?"

"Nope, I drank again. I went back to A.A. on November 4, 1990. After that, I was at Fireside every day. The Program opened up a whole new relationship with men—for all of us. It was loving. We would, like, hug each other. That was the thing—I never had male friends who I hugged. My dad was never affectionate like that when I was a little boy. And I needed it desperately. All of a sudden, I've got these friends. We're hugging, we're saying 'I love you,' and eventually we would, like, kiss each other on the cheek. And I brought that into my family. I would hug my brothers, and my dad would sort of give the push-away hug. You know that one? You move in for a hug and he sort of pushes you away?"

"Well, my father learned to hug from a how-to manual—"

"So you know what I mean! Yeah, man. The push-away hug..."

Stephen has many talents, and sleeping on planes appears to be one of them. The aircraft has long since transitioned to nocturnal mode, yet I'm up for hours in the darkened cabin, listening to Caetano Veloso and Jobim on my

Walkman and taking a strange delight in the guileless expressions and childlike vulnerability of the assembled unconscious. I doze a little, and pretty soon it's morning, the plane descending through papery light, and I'm nudging Stephen awake.

Once we land, it's clear that in Brazil, everybody has a great ass. Meaning the baggage handler, the person on the payphone, airport security—all the callipygian ideal. Right past baggage claim, just as Tommy told us, is the duty-free shop, where we purchase cases of scotch, vodka, gin, and rum, a bottle of aged cognac for one of Isabella's uncles, and some top-shelf Champagne. The man has a big Brazilian wedding to throw and wants to keep costs down. He'll pay us back later with folding money.

I feel a tap on my shoulder: Tommy, in a white polo shirt tucked into belted khakis, his hair thinning a bit but Irish eyes full of twinkle, greets me with "Daveed," an ancient nickname. We exchange a heartfelt *abrazo*.

Stephen's greeting, a small theatrical event in itself, involves outstretched arms, a quick glance to the right, outstretched arms, a look the other away, and then—sudden, rapturous recognition. Followed by a leap into Tommy's surprised embrace, like Yogi Berra and Don Larsen after the perfect game in '56.

We load our stuff into Tommy's sedan and take off, highway driving under brilliant blue skies on a winding asphalt freeway, catching glimpses of palm trees, pale-hued apartment buildings, and mountain shapes in the distance. We zoom through a tunnel cut into blackish stone, Rebouças ("Hey bo soos" says Tommy), and across a bridge. To the right is a pedestrian walkway teeming with bicyclists, joggers, walkers, and strollers. Beyond it is the glorious sea.

"My God, the water," I say. "So blue."

"It's polluted," Tommy says, retrieving his cigar from the ashtray and lighting it. When he's done, I push the dashboard lighter back in and retrieve a joint from my shirt pocket, singing, *"Rio! Rio by the sea-o!"*

"Still smoking that shit?" Tommy says.

"Stephen," I say, turning to the rear. "You don't mind, do you?"

"I don't mind," he says mildly.

"Smoking seventeen years, Klim," Tommy says, employing an even more ancient nickname. "That's almost half your life. You could at least, you know, check out life without it."

"Everything in moderation," I say. "You just couldn't pull off the moderation part."

"You just hide it better. I always got caught—that was my thing. Remember? That first time, when I stole Betty's Buick and got chased home by the cops?"

"And you took a hard right into your driveway and crashed into the back of your dad's Seville? That does ring a bell, now that you mention it."

Stephen cackles from the backseat.

By the time his driving put the kibosh on his drinking, Tommy had amassed an impressive history of automotive malfeasance. In an echo of that formative police chase in Tenafly, his final act of drunkenness also involved Betty's Buick, albeit a later model. History may not repeat itself, but it sure as hell does rhyme sometimes.

Tommy would borrow Betty's car, stash it in the parking garage located beneath our apartment, and break it out on Saturday night—all the better to hit the circuit of bars and pubs dotting the East and West Villages. He knew he wasn't exactly flawless behind the wheel once he'd had a few, but if the choice was between operating a private vehicle or heading from bar to bar on foot—or blowing good money on a cab—Tommy would invoke his God-given right to drive (while impaired) every time. Until the night he ended up in the Tombs, New York's notorious house of detention, on a DUI charge.

Tommy spent thirty hours in police custody, five of them in a holding facility, tightly handcuffed. The pain lingered for months. He spent the bulk of his time in the Tombs, free of cuffs but shackled and stripped of his shoelaces, in a dark, dank, dangerous place. As fights broke out, he shrank back into a corner, struggling not to pee his pants and to accept that he had only himself to blame for the mess he was in. Here he was, corralled among people for whom he had nothing but abject disgust—no empathy, just contempt. These were the scum of the earth, as far as Tommy was concerned, not the meek who would inherit it, and he was wholly unprepared for the dissonance between how he saw himself and these piss-stinking circumstances. The shame of it. The not knowing when it would end. It shook him to his Catholic core.

While agonizing, the crawl of time enabled Tommy to take stock: of the half-dozen bars he'd hit before making his way, unsteadily to be sure, out of that dive on Avenue A between Fourth and Fifth, whose name he could not recall; of climbing into his car, turning the key in the ignition, and imagining how good it was going to feel to stretch out in his king-size Sealy Posturepedic; of the times he'd gotten behind the wheel in a similar state and managed to get home in one piece; of things he'd done and said while extremely drunk, bad acts he'd justified doing while completely hammered. Surely, he ruminated on how he would explain all this to Betty, who expected her car back on Sunday by early afternoon for shopping purposes, per the agreement she had made him sign. And who knows, maybe even the Eye Incident penetrated his consciousness during those hours of incarceration.

Not that the eye thing was alcohol-related—we were in fifth grade—but it took fifteen years, during a bender at my college townhouse over Christmas break, for Tommy to fully own up to the deed. He'd always maintained that he only shot a rubber band at me that day. Though I knew better, and Dr. Seligman had confirmed that something pointy and sharp had pierced my eyeball, I never pressed Tommy on the issue. Hearing him blurt out "It was a paperclip," even in a fever dream of coke and booze, meant a lot to me. That year, I wrote a paper about Tommy's personal evolution for my developmental psych seminar and got a B-plus.

We emerge from another rock-hewn tunnel into a postcard-worthy vision: pale sand and turquoise water under an immense blue sky to our left, a swanky spread of gleaming white hotels, multi-hued shops and cafés, and a flow of scantily clad passersby to the right. Straight ahead, many miles in the distance, a pair of mountains—their upper halves obscured by a heavenly mist—are all that restrict our view westward toward the horizon. With no small trace of pride, Tommy welcomes us to the most expensive real estate in South America.

Being a businessman in Brazil is all this Irish American ever wanted to do. He'd visited a few times as a kid with his dad, spent summers during high school learning his warp from his weft in textiles factories, majored in international business, and cultivated connections with his father's friends, including the owner of Brazil's largest sugar cane plantation. Arriving here five years ago, Tommy was determined to make good on a lifelong ambition.

His first big score was claw crane games, those arcade and bowling alley coin-sucks where you try to pick up a prize with a clamping device suspended from a chain you jerk around with a joystick. He had these machines in locations all over Rio, and people would line up to stuff them with tokens purchased with their hard-earned *reals* in hope of retrieving a plush toy or other low-cost novelty. It was, as they say, a license to print money. At the height of the operation, Tommy had twenty employees, including an armed guard to ensure safe delivery of the weekly earnings to the bank. But that was a few years ago. These days he's into import/export. No armed security required.

Tommy pulls over and we duck out of the car and into the dazzling light and seductive heat of Rio—a warm-weather city with warm-weather natives. There's an expression here for days when the temperature drops below 70 degrees Fahrenheit: *frazer frio.* Not today though, and not any time soon.

As Tommy arranges for our luggage to be brought up and parks the car, Stephen and I push through the revolving door and into the lobby and are instantly chilled. Filtered through the hotel's thick, smoked-glass exterior, Rio's impossible daylight is reduced to a mere suggestion. Oliver, Tommy's sponsor, is here to greet us. He has a firm jaw and a fierce look-you-in-the eye delivery. I can see why Tommy looks up to him. Tommy returns from parking the car, finishing up a call. This portable phone of his, a recent purchase, has become indispensable, especially in light of the complexity of matrimonial logistics. His appearance inspires all of us to lean in for a long hug, and more than a few cheeks are kissed.

That night, we take in a lengthy, decadent dinner at Porcão, a *churrascaria* where cuts of meat are cooked on spits and served tableside by eager waiters. You communicate to them through a two-sided plastic disc marked with the restaurant's mascot, a pig of course, to indicate either "Sim Por Favor" or "Não Obrigado." Leave it on the affirmative side, and your plate will never be empty.

In the bad old days, Tommy's typical evening started with him sitting at a desk arrayed with a six-pack of Heineken (three darks, three regulars), a half ounce of reefer, a bottle of Johnny Walker Red, a pack of Winstons, and maybe some blow on a good night. He'd have the TV on, Pink Floyd cranking. The variety was what mattered, the mixing, matching, and ping-ponging of effects, and the attainment, usually anyway, of that perfectly calibrated buzz. He's been sober for years now, but Tommy hasn't lost his love for a large, multicourse meal, and Porcão is like an opium den for carnivores. Rejecting the cuts that don't quite move him, Tommy fills up nonetheless, cueing me along the way to try the lamb chops, get some brisket, make sure to get a return trip on that lobster tail. My yoga practice has been going great guns lately, and I'm eating a lot of tofu and broccoli, but, loosened by a few caipirinhas, I indulge in the meat-athon with little prodding until I just can't anymore.

Tonight is the closest we'll get to a bachelor party, so Tommy takes us to an upscale nightclub frequented by prostitutes. Organizing this sort of thing usually falls to the best men, but Stephen and I are out of our depth, and it's up to the man himself to throw some sin into the evening.

My image of prostitution, starting with the phrase "the world's oldest profession," is based on a cliché, of sad cases selling their wares on the seedy blocks bordering the Hudson River dockside. But none of that desperation is apparent tonight. Prostitution is legal in Brazil. In this pleasingly dark and picturesque venue, I see no sad cases, only alluring women who don't look away. Independent contractors. Sure, some will take you for all you're worth if you give them the chance, but a plumber will do the same thing. That's what I'm telling myself, at least.

In the time it takes to order a round of Bucklers and a real beer for me, Oliver, who's built like a fit cop, is deep in conversation with a woman in a pale blue gown. Tommy, Phil, and Stephen circle the wagons, unwilling to tempt fate with a potentially scandalous dalliance. I scope the room wide-eyed. Soon I'm chatting with Jessica, who is about twenty, mostly in Spanish, and it's easy. She wants to know why we're here, and I tell her the whole story—how Tommy met Isabella on Ipanema Beach, just like in the song, and how Phil's a famous actor, and Stephen's also an actor—and I'm from Nueva York and this is my first time in Rio.

She's no elegant sylph like many of the women in the room. The one Oliver's making out with, for example, has several inches on him. Almost pale, with shoulder-length reddish-blond hair, she comes up to my breast bone and has the vibe of a genial college girl, which is what she is. She's studying textile manufacturing (small world) at a local college, and her real name is Morgana. Much too soon for my liking, the guys signal that they're ready to leave this den of iniquity. Morgana and I share a lingering kiss and make a plan to meet on the beach across from Marina Palace, two days from now.

Back in our air-cooled home base, still stuffed from dinner, Stephen and I kick back in our twin beds, and he demands the lowdown on Morgana, whom he keeps calling a *hoo-ah*, like Ralph Cifaretto on *The Sopranos*. I oblige, although there isn't much to say beyond our talking in Spanish, the kiss, and the meet-up on Wednesday.

"*Tall and tan and young and lovely,*" he croons, "*the chick from Ipanema goes walkin'*"

I cut in with, "*Tommy saw her on that beach, and he said… wow.*"

And just like that, Stephen and I set about rewriting "The Girl from Ipanema" from a Tommy-centric vantage.

Legendarily sung in English by Astrud Gilberto, "Ipanema" was a worldwide hit in 1965 and now ranks as one of the most recorded songs in history—right up there with "Yesterday," another song in the key of F major about longing for the unattainable. Hell, the song's been covered by everyone from Lou Rawls to Detroit Tigers pitching ace Denny McLain, so why not us? Verse 1 comes quickly:

Five foot ten and oh so Irish
She's a knockout, Brazilian and stylish
He saw her on that beach, and he said… wow

Verse 2 is tougher; the opening we really like, but what to rhyme with "lawyer"?

He's in business, she's a lawyer
And just like Becky and Tom Sawyer
They were meant to be
Oh my, and how…

At the bridge, we dispense with the laudatory tone in favor of slow-roasting Tommy in the time-tested tradition of rehearsal-dinner smack talk. Perhaps it's all the red meat we've just consumed at work.

Woah, woah woah, Isabella
Tom's one lucky fella…
To end up with a lady like that
Not too bad for a Tenafly brat
[that's right!]

Tommy he grew up in Jersey
He raised hell and Lord have mercy
He was not always as you see him right now…
Doo-doo-doo Doo-doo-doot

Tom got drunk for his Little League tryout
Crashed the car and he put my eye out
And for your patience, Betty dear
Please take a bow…

I flip off the lights, and we give it a final run-through. Just as we reach the end, Stephen farts a trombone blast and it's right on key. We guffaw like dorks.

Chapter 25

All That Glitters

Tommy's brother-in-law, Max, who'll be joining us in Rio, loves nothing more than to travel by limo to the Foxwoods Casino in Connecticut—his wife, Christina, and two kids in tow—and spend the weekend gambling. On one such weekend eight years ago, under the pretext of wanting to watch the Knicks game on their primo TV setup, Tommy secures the keys to their place.

With a wraparound terrace overlooking Gracie Mansion, Max and Christina's apartment on East End Avenue is at the pinnacle of elite Manhattan real estate. Yet the place has the unmistakable feel of a relic—a sixties-era bachelor pad retooled for the seventies, at which point time seems to have simply stopped. Mirrors are everywhere, like in a dance studio, and each room is keyed to a particular piece of very expensive 100 percent wool carpeting purchased from Einstein Moomjy. In the master bedroom ("the Leopard Room"), an ultra-king-size bed raised on a two-foot platform allows Max an unfettered view of the Triboro Bridge, or its reflection anyway, in the East River. Taking up more than half of the apartment's 3,500 square feet, the centerpiece Zebra Room is relatively low-ceilinged but horizontally vast; it's wide enough to accommodate a couple of oversize white leather couches, some splashy space-age plastic end tables, and a mother-of-pearl-inlaid three-cushion billiards table right smack in the middle of it all without feeling the least bit cluttered. The kids' rooms feature tiger motifs.

Tonight, Tommy and I happen to possess every illegal substance we've ever ingested. Around dusk we gobble down some mushrooms and pop open a bottle of Max's Cristal and smoke a few joints out on the terrace. That really gets us going. Then we do a few lines of blow and shift into manic, everything-you-say-counts-double yapping. We've got Talking Heads righteously cranked up through Bro-in-Law's primo Kenwood audio setup, the orange POWER BOOST button set to the ON position for the first time in its life, and our energy is boundless. Like Lego David Byrne figures motoring through an enormous grid, we're doing laps around Max's pleasure palace—in opposite directions, to the beat of "Life During Wartime"—and each time we pass each other it's more hilarious and absurd and fantastic.

Many hours later, I call Amanda to let her know I'll be heading downtown in a cab. Amanda lives on a lively party block in the West Village. When we get there, I crack open the door and it's like letting in the circus—a roar of street noise, the sidewalk swimming with people, jarring street lights that end in sharp points (a legacy of the shrooms). But I'm good. I even have the right amount of dollars all sorted out. I shove the door open and step outside.

Into a huge pile of dog shit.

Just as the sickening sensation hijacks my remaining senses, the gas-permeable hard contact lens I wear in my right eye detaches from the surface of my eyeball, which is bone-dry, possibly from the dehydrating effects of booze and blow and high-end California Cabernet, and pops off into the ether. A wave of bodily paralysis and visceral revulsion passes through me, but I manage to hop half a block to Amanda's building, buzz her buzzer, and relate the kind of help I need. In minutes she's sponging off my Chuck Taylor as I lie supine, lamenting the loss of my lens. My vision is like 20/3000 in that eye, a rarified setting that requires a special order and takes a few weeks to arrive. I should keep a few spares on hand. Really, I should.

In the morning, just for a laugh, I return to the scene of the crime—and there it is. Less than a foot from where I'd been let off, at the base of a stop sign, surrounded by napkins, coffee lids, and a half-eaten Mamoun's falafel sandwich, my lens is intact and untouched. Like a winning horseshoe toss, it had landed so close to the post as to be protected from a nightlong parade of passing feet, and evidently breezes had been minimal. Scooping up this precision-made piece of human ingenuity, I wrap it up in a tissue, tuck it in my pocket, and give the thing a good cleaning when I get home. And by God, it works!

I tell you all this because mere weeks after jogging at Max's and the miracle on McDougal Street, Tommy foreswore drinking and drugs for good.

If you can possibly avoid it, do not take part in a lavish Brazilian wedding without a date. A dance partner is crucial. Failing that, having a few familiar faces in the crowd to exchange pleasantries with goes a long way. At these nuptials, I'll have neither. Stephen and Phil will be making the rounds and everybody will want a moment with them. Sure, I'm familiar with a couple of Tommy's college buddies who'll be attending, notably Kenny Crowley, whose PR firm does work for Big Tobacco, and the odious Jared Stiegenthaler, who inherited his father's business manufacturing mechanical fasteners and owns a $15,000 Peter Max print of Lady Liberty, of which he is extremely proud. One time I gave him a lift somewhere and one of my cassettes was playing in the car—the Screaming Blue Messiahs. After a few seconds, Stiegs turns to me and says, "Why would you even listen to this?"

I said "OK, who should I listen to?"

He says, "I dunno, man—Crosby Stills & Nash?"

My only hope for a non-ignominious wedding experience is Janaina. As best men, Stephen and I will take part in a procession down the church aisle, arm in arm with a female participant, per an ancient set of house rules. I'll be paired with Janaina, Isabella's maid of honor and a fellow law student. Tommy assures me she's definitely cute and, as far as Isabella knows, single. Her name means sea goddess. Who knows, maybe we can find some of that special wedding magic. Things do happen at weddings, and I am the co-best man, and this *is* the best tan I've ever had. That has to be worth something, right?

Phil, Stephen, Oliver, and I assemble on the beach mid-morning on Wednesday—Morgana Day—before it gets too hot. We're all clad in basic U.S.A. swimwear: knee-length trunks and hokey flip-flops. Far more chic and skimpy is the local beach attire. Tommy arrives in a different polo shirt, phone glued to his ear. To a man, their circumstances are complex: Tommy, a budding master of the universe, is about to be married before God and family; Stephen, a new father with money problems and his own complicated pop; Phil, a renowned actor on the verge of A-list stardom. With so much shared history among them, it's easy to just lie back and dig the banter. There's little of the piss-taking you see among groups of garrulous straight men; instead, there's a sense of mutual, sincere engagement.

In turns, we all reach our heat saturation point and traipse sun-dazed toward the shimmering blue. Phil, with his hockey-player shoulders and unapologetic paunch, trudges wetly back from the sea, his hair shining bright orange in the brilliant light of Rio. He plunks down into a beach chair next to mine and lights a Marlboro red. Then, eyes closed, holding up some sunscreen and chin-motioning toward his freckle-y shoulders:

"Hey, man… would ya mind?"

I'm happy to oblige. It's clear he burns easily.

As my meeting with Morgana approaches, I just can't seem to get past her line of work. It certainly *feels* like something other than a financial transaction involving sex. She told me her real name, and I presume our meeting is *maybe* off the clock. But with Ed Koch's warnings on the fallibility of condoms still echoing around in my head from the eighties, the feeling that *something* bad will happen if I go through with this just won't leave me. Still, the blood rushes to my head to see her coming toward me, right on time—in a black bikini, small triangles just barely there—wearing a gentle smile.

We take a dip, sit in beach chairs with ice pops, kiss on our blanket, space out in the sun. We while away an hour or more, sometimes speaking, sometimes not, taking in the warmth, listening to the waves lapping. I ask her if she's free later tonight, and it turns out she is.

Oh shit.

Stepping into the all-encompassing chill and permanent dusk of Marina Palace's main lobby temporarily obliterates the memory of Morgana and her luscious lips. Tommy's at the front desk, in deep discussion with his brother-in-law, a debonair-looking man in his early seventies, and Christina. As discussed much earlier, Christina was a foundational early crush of mine, the ideal 1970s girl next door, with long, straight, center-parted blond hair and eyes like the sky. When at twenty-three she married Max, a wealthy financier with grown-up kids who was, yes, old enough to be her father, it was hard to know what to make of it. Still is. What's never been in doubt is that *they* don't care what we make of it. They seem supremely content with the age difference and their opulent lifestyle. And their tween-age kids—Maxine and Trevor—are lovely and show no signs of spoilage.

Anyway, they're leaving. Max doesn't like the look of the place. Tommy's on the cell phone, reserving them a suite at one of the five-star joints down the block. I get a warm hug from Christina, and Max and I shake hands. He looks me over, takes the measure of me, you might say, and then, in a subdued rasp:

"You look good—keeping slim."

Aha. So it's not just Upper East Side *ladies* who value thinness above all else…

Max recounts the day's sundry woes, chiefly a tardy limo and various nettlesome aspects of international travel, until a car shows up to whisk them away to the Copacabana Grand Rio. Finally I can apprise Tommy of the Morgana situation.

"Oh yeah? She's coming back?"

"Yup. Like 9:30."

"Oh, *Da-VEED*...." he says. "*Tesao*..."

(*Tesao* is an obscene Brazilian expression that means "boner.")

Evening falls, and after a luxurious nap I avail myself of hotel-issued shampoo and conditioner, take a rare evening shave, and apply more than enough hair gel. I want to look good for her. Stephen has assured me he'll be staying out of the way until midnight, and pinched my cheek for good luck, so I have the place to myself and some time to kill. I do a lot of pacing and try not to sweat.

A little before 10 P.M., the hotel phone rings. Morgana's downstairs in the lobby, but they won't let her up. They just *know*. In order for her to come up, I have to come down. I dash out into the hallway and take the stairs rather than wait for the elevator. Now, I completely understand hotels wanting to discourage guests from partaking in assignations with sex workers. The question is, how do you enforce it? They can't just not let her in, so they make their point by forcing—I guess you'd say "the john," i.e., me—to show his face and, in effect, escort the escort.

Morgana stands at a kiosk beside the hotel's front entrance, looking stylish but subdued in a black halter top and jeans, her hair redolent of shampoo and spilling over her shoulders. A compactly built concierge in a dark suit eyes her warily. How can he tell? It's not like she's wearing hot pants.

"You are Mr. Klein in 622?" he says.

"That's correct."

"And this... she is your guest?"

"Yes."

He gives her a final once-over. "Very well then, Mr. Klein."

We start heading toward the elevator, and I spot Jared Stiegenthaler and his wife standing at the front desk with an impressive array of designer luggage. Jared turns just as we pass by, the sight of me and Morgana jolting his heavily lidded eyes into a rare state of turgidity. Did he just give me a thumbs-up? At the elevator bank, I punch the button and smile at Morgana, who's just taken my hand. The doors part and out steps the mother of the groom.

"Well, David Klein," says Betty Morgan. "As I live and breathe. Look at *you*."

The two of us are doing that thing where you shake hands with both hands. But it's almost aggressive, like she has me.

"You know what?" she says.

"What?"

"You haven't changed a bit," she says, finally letting go. "Not one bit."

Turning to Morgana, Betty appraises her. "And you are?"

"Oh, of course. Sorry," I say. "This is… Jessica."

"How do you do," says Morgana, extending a hand.

"I do very well, thank you. *Obrigado*, I should say. Now David, was that polite, not introducing me to your date?"

"You're right. That was rude of me. It's all been such a whirlwind. We met on the beach just the other day."

"Now isn't that romantic. You've found yourself a little Carioca."

"Jessica is studying textiles."

"Of course she is," Betty says with a theatrical wink, then heads off to the lobby.

Which pretty much puts the kibosh on my *tesao*.

We go up to my room, and as I start to sputter out my ambivalence, Morgana takes my hand and shakes me off with a patient expression.

"It's OK," she says. "Really."

"But I feel like I should at least… you know, for your time—"

"I don't want your money. My own time is my own time. It's fun being with you."

"It's fun being with you too."

She reaches for my Brazilian phrasebook and finds a blank page, fishes out a pen from her handbag, and writes her name and home address.

"When you get back to Nueva York, will you send me a postcard?"

The next day, on the way to be fitted for our wedding suits, I fill in Stephen and Tommy on my failed tryst, and they don't even question my manhood or ability to perform. I mean, barely at all. The drive takes us out of the posh Leblon neighborhood and into less picturesque highway driving, with little color, much concrete, and not a single postcard-worthy vista. Eventually, Tommy pulls into a nondescript mall where I assume he's scoped out a good deal. He'll be footing the bill after all.

Stephen and I stand still and respond to commands delivered in primitive English as Brazilian tailors huddle around us, checking our inseams and neck widths and such. We'll be wearing black jackets made of heavy wool with a monochromatic palette: light gray vests, dark gray trousers, white shirts with silver, slightly iridescent ties. I'm sweating already.

On the way back, Stephen and I lay "Ipanema" on Tommy. I'm a little nervous about the "put my eye out" line, and he does wince at it, but the final verse elicits that great laugh of his. That evening, Phil stops by our room before we meet Ollie downstairs in the hotel restaurant for a nothing-special kind of dinner. The guests have started to check in, so Tommy's got a lot of meeting and greeting to do. Knowing our unfettered time together is almost at an end, I ask Stephen and Phil if I can take a photo of them. Their eyes fairly glisten at the prospect, both seeing it as an opportunity for some improv.

Stephen does that thing where you crack your knuckles all at once, in the tough-guy style with interlaced fingers bowed outward, then he lifts the edge of the bed sheet, crawls under, and yawns coquettishly. Phil, in contrast, plays it straight. He spoons in behind him, his right arm tossed casually over the declivity of Stephen's hip, the other curving around the top of their shared pillow. Phil looks asleep, his lips slightly parted; Stephen wears a beatific smile.

Without warning, Phil's right hand darts downward and clasps the sheet where Stephen's balls would be, and the two figures—"the same animal fused by alcohol," in Stephen's memorable phrase—are transmogrified into a single spasm of laughter, Phil's face flushing red and Stephen emitting a high-pitched yelp.

And that's a wrap.

"Hey Phil," Stephen says. "We finished our song. And Choppy says we can sing it tomorrow night."

"Oh yeah?" he says, cracking a grin. "Well let's hear it then."

We've really put some time into this thing by now. After hearing us for three nights running, Tommy's Navy SEAL cousin, staying in an adjacent room, was moved to ask Tommy what the deal was with the two *maricons* at the end of the hall. He'd simply assumed that Stephen and I were a gay couple, because what straight couple stays up at all hours singing bossa nova?

Leaning together over the lyric sheet, we run through it for Phil, including the final verses we nailed down just this morning:

Oooohh, ooh ooh ooh Isabella
Doooooo . . . you real-ly want this fella?
Oh, relax! This guy's learned a lot
He gave up the crack and the pot
That's right!

Now Tom's on the straight and narrow
He's serene right down to the marrow
He called us up Wednesday night to say

Don't lose the love!
He said don't lose the love....
That's right
Don't lose the love!
Oh yeah
Don't lose the lo-o-o-o-o-ove...

Phil nods approvingly. Then, to my amazement, one of the premier actors of our generation asks if he can perform with us. *Asks.* Sure, it's a song parody, not a deep theatrical work, but I know one thing for certain: Phil genuinely likes the material. I know because the other day I said something to Stephen like, "Phil must have done *Patch Adams* for the money."

And he said, "Nope. Once Phil is past the audition phase, he chooses work based on interest."

And I said, "Even *Patch Adams*?"

And he said, "Even *Patch Adams*."

So I know Phil wants in because our song has quality. We waive the audition. Guy's off to do a Mamet movie at the end of the month and we don't want to tax him.

The following night, fifty or so of the wedding's main participants gather for a rehearsal dinner, although there's no real rehearsal. We'll all just wing it tomorrow at the church. Drinks are served, and I make my way around the room, stopping to banter with Max and Christina and the kids. Maxine, all of eleven and a compulsive reader, has a doorstop copy of the latest Harry Potter in hand for the boring parts of the evening.

Isabella greets me with a warm hug and introduces me to her maid of honor. Janaina is petite, with a doll-like delicacy and the softly sculpted features of a tabby. And like a cat, she seems both poised and ready to jump at the same time. We exchange a few words, but I can't get any kind of meaningful conversation going. Animated voices fill the room, but our talk is subdued. It's a start anyway. I'll have my chance to make a more lasting impression after dinner. Meanwhile, I make sure to avoid the gaze of Betty Morgan. I can hear it now: "Where's your date, David? Off studying textiles?"

Once coffee and dessert have been served, people rise from their seats to toast the happy couple. Oliver's up first, and he gives a lighthearted yet earnest rhyming summation of the last ten years of Tommy's life, name-checking the Friday night poker games and various twelve-step milestones as well as a couple of Tommy's Brazilian money-making schemes that were new even to me.

This gets a deep round of applause, because even if you don't understand the Program, the personal growth parts hit home. One of Tommy's college pals delivers an Irish proverb of the "May the road rise to meet you" variety, and then Tommy stands. He thanks everyone for coming and cues us to take our places at the front of the room.

The three of us stand shoulder to shoulder, clasping our lyric sheets, with Phil in the middle. Having him with us adds some extra vocal power and a touch of gravitas to this undeniably goofy maneuver. The audience, many of whom do not speak English, seems amused by the spectacle, and Betty Morgan looks appropriately shocked when I sing "And he put my eye out"—solo, of course.

And just like that it's done. Being one of the three musketeers, even this briefly, is going to be hard to top.

The following afternoon, decked out in our wedding duds, we load into vans and set off for Igreja da Glória, a prime example of eighteenth-century colonial architecture positioned in the mountainous upper reaches of Rio. Stephen and I sit in the rear with Phil.

"I'm still trying to get over *Happiness*," I say. Phil chuckles.

Directed by a fellow New Jerseyite, Todd Solondz, *Happiness* features Phil as the pasty, repellent, mouth-breathing Allen, who jerks off during phone calls to random women culled from a well-thumbed phonebook. Phil's full commitment to embodying this creep without even the slightest attempt to make him sympathetic is what keeps you from turning away in disgust, and what distinguishes Phil from the average rising Hollywood star.

"That must have been hard," I sputter. "Just one deeply humiliating scene after another."

"Wanna know the hardest part about that role? I had to put on, like, fifteen pounds."

"Seriously? That was harder than finding the humanity in a sick fuck like Allen?"

"Oh, much harder."

"So how'd ya do it?"

"It was filmed somewhere in New Jersey and there was a college nearby, I forget the name. All I did was eat there, filled up on cafeteria food for a few weeks.

"That's all it took?"

"Yup. It was brutal, man. Institutional food. It'll kill ya."

The talk turns to summertime jobs and things we've done to earn money over the years. "I worked as a handyman for my father," says Stephen. "He'd pay me by the job. You know, fifty bucks to clear out a crawlspace, maybe a hundred for bigger projects. One time he wanted to lay some pipe and had me dig a four-by-four foot ditch, ten feet deep. And as I was cutting through, I must have hit some poison oak or poison ivy weeds and, whew, what a rash I got!"

"Oh, that's nothing. One time, Betty Morgan hired Tommy and me to remove all the rotting asbestos insulation from their basement crawlspace. You know that stuff? Silver, with pink stuffing inside? Causes cancer? So we're in this dank cellar, peeling off these toxic strips with no protection, no face masks, getting this shit all over our arms and hair in ninety-degree heat. We probably lost five years of our lives that day."

Then Phil pipes up. He says he had a job working as a lifeguard at an Upper East Side rooftop pool that nobody ever swam in. One afternoon, the place is deserted as usual, and in walks Miles Davis wearing nothing more than a Speedo and dark sunglasses.

"I mean, he's Miles Davis. I'm not gonna say anything to him," says Phil. "So he starts doing laps—"

"Cigarette?"

"No cigarette. Keeps his shades on though. After a few laps he gets out. He dries off, comes over, and we start talking. He starts telling me stories, all kinds of stories. The two of us are looking out over the city and he's pointing out buildings he owns, accidents he got into, girlfriends' apartments…"

"Wow… amazing. What about music? Did that ever come up?"

"Nope. That's probably the one thing we didn't talk about. And then he just says, 'I'm Miles' and walks away."

Phil will eventually recount this story ten years later in an interview, but we heard it first.

Traveling up a narrow street on a steep incline, we start catching glimpses of the church. From a distance it resembles an intricate Christmas ornament plucked by some giant hand and placed atop a fluffy nest of trees. With its whitewashed walls, stone columns, and onion-shaped dome atop a central tower, the structure seems to get smaller as we make our approach. We disembark and make our way toward a pair of enormous wooden doors that lead straight into the church's central aisle. The walls are arrayed with a series of luminous blue and white tiles depicting religious scenes. Ornamentation abounds—carved stone columns and intricately sculpted wooden altars are at left, right, and center. It's a narrow space, but the balcony level and vaulted ceiling evoke the intended sense of majesty.

Janaina stands amid a small throng on the far side of a row of chairs bordering the aisle. I try to catch her eye, but she doesn't notice. When I reach her, she gives me a quick hello and picks up her conversation, in Portuguese, of course. The cold shoulder (*ombro frio*) is immediate and unmistakable. She responds when I speak, but quietly and without inflection, and her eyes are everywhere but meeting mine.

An immaculately put-together woman pins a carnation on the lapel of my jacket, and we're nudged into queue formation in the time-tested fashion (the lady to the man's left, in case he has to draw his sword). Some sweet church organ kicks in, and a spasm of collective movement spurs me into action. I feel her slender right arm weightlessly encircle the crook of my elbow, and we proceed two steps at a time to the altar, where we sit and stand (and sit and stand) in awkward unison. Cued by a berobed priest, prayers are offered, hymns are sung, Jesu is thanked. The congregation, well versed in these age-old dance steps, murmurs at the appointed times.

This is only my second Mass, and Tommy has been the catalyst each time. The first one took place after a rare sleepover at his house. We awoke on a Sunday morning, and the Morgans invited me along to Mass at their church, known as the Mission. I figured why not? More time with Tommy. And I was curious about the Mission, which sounded a lot more mysterious than Temple Sinai. What stands out is the moment the priest instructed us to kneel on those leather-covered fixtures that fold out from below the pew in front of you, and everyone held their palms together in prayer—Christian style. I'd only seen that in movies.

Head bowed, I whispered to Tommy, "What should I do now?"

"Pray for Vince Lombardi," he whispered back.

It's time for Tommy and Isabella to exchange their vows, which the priest reads in English and Portuguese. About midway through, Isabella accidentally responds to one of the English vows in Portuguese, and a big bark of a laugh rings through the church. It's Phil.

The sound snaps me to attention, and in a flash, it hits me that divine intervention in the form of a love spell cast by the sea goddess Janaina will not be forthcoming. But, hell, what was I even expecting? I'm thirty-seven, not super young anymore, at least not to Janaina, who's twenty-five, if that. I have no great story to tell, no impressive six pack and bad boy charm to purvey. I live paycheck to paycheck, work at an online "content provider," and while I'm getting into yoga and tiring of my bar-centric social life, I still leap too quickly with women I meet at parties, only to have to awkwardly extricate myself from these entanglements in the ensuing days, weeks, or months. Hoping for romantic sparks to fly with Isabella's bridesmaid is pure magical thinking. She probably took one look at our act last night—three American guys singing an all-too-familiar Brazilian song in complicated English, thinking themselves hilarious—and said, "Really, I have to walk down the aisle with *that guy*?" You know, but in Portuguese.

After a half-hour van ride we arrive at a place called Casa das Canoas, and I have to say, Tommy's really pulled it off. The former home of the Brazilian Frank Lloyd Wright, this magnificent structure is set atop a slope of mountain-side overlooking a bay, sort of nestled into the earth itself. Now an events space, it sprawls before us as we follow a stone hallway leading to several large rooms, each seductively lit by theatrical spotlights, bedecked with floral displays, and flanked by crisply attired staff. Balmy air flows through from the open-ended far side of the building, which offers a striking view of the distant water and sky.

Last night's rehearsal dinner was a relatively intimate affair, but it had a sort of ripple effect on today's social dynamics. In those initial conversations with people you haven't seen in years, at least you have the years. You're guaranteed of a few things to catch up on. Encountering these same people twenty-four hours later, what else is left? You have to work at it. You remark on how beautiful the ceremony was and you're out of ammo. Tommy's freshman-year roommate at GW and I have already had a big laugh about the walk-in closet Tommy claimed as his own and lived in for two semesters. (What? There was room for a bed, a night stand, and a bong.) As for the rest of the attendees, I imagined my basic Spanish might help somehow, but it doesn't in the least. Portuguese is as beautiful as it is incomprehensible.

After dinner plates have been cleared, a party-hearty groove kicks up and the dancing begins. Elegantly dressed Brazilians of all ages, all with that great ass, join together in what seems a familiar ritual. Everyone knows everyone else, everybody knows the dance, and with the volume turned up and the room erupting in motion, it's like the evening's final act has begun. There's no standing still. You're either in or out. My wool suit pants and I take regular breaks on the candle-lit veranda and around the perimeter of the parking lot to cool off.

Back inside, Stephen and Christina are at the center of a gyrating circle of revelers, and everybody applauds because Stephen is such a perfect ham, shifting from vaudeville poses to Travolta-worthy disco moves to that Russian thing where you dance while squatting like a catcher. Somehow amid all the dancefloor action, we catch a moment together around a table, just Tommy, Phil, Stephen, Ollie, and me, with cigars and non-alcoholic beers and some laughs at Tommy's expense. But soon enough the crowd's got him, and he's being carried around on people's shoulders and I'm back to being a fly on the wall.

Sometimes a DJ saves your life with a song. In this case, not necessarily a great song, but a damnably catchy one at least, and one at the very peak of its, let's say, initial ubiquity. Everybody in the world, or certainly in this vast and impressive room, knows "All-Star" by Smash Mouth, and *Shrek*'s still two years away.

Tommy's niece lights up when she hears Steve Harwell's opening line: "Some*body* once told me the world is gonna roll me / I ain't the smartest tool in the shed." Maxine, still in her white flower girl gown from earlier and all hopped up on Guaraná—a traditional Brazilian soft drink with a pronounced caffeinating effect—knows every word, and now she's doing the shape of an L on her forehead, and the sight of her is just so joyful and unaffected that my throat tightens for a second, then un-tightens, followed by the feeling of a weight being lifted.

With my blues briefly banished, I bop on over to Maxine, and we do that oddly evocative wedding dance between people of vastly different heights who see nothing funny about the disparity. I don't even mind that Janaina is shaking it on down with the Brazilian Bobby Cheekbones, unleashing a dancefloor abandon that I, no doubt naively, never imagined the maid of honor had in her.

Because this is pretty perfect right now—this moment.

And when I say I don't mind, I mean... not really.

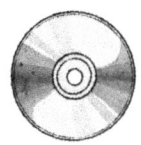

Chapter 26

Society for Modern Myths

In "Mysterious Ways," when my close personal friend Bono sings, "If you want to kiss the sky, better learn how to kneel," he's not suggesting people do so at his own feet. But for the guru, whose feet—like Bono's hands, come to think of it—are dry and slightly calloused, kneeling is standard and kissing is encouraged. Once again, as prophesied by David Byrne, I have to ask myself, Well, how did I get here?

It's the summer of 1998, and yoga-mania has reached critical mass. Lululemon debuts. Madonna's *Ray of Light* rides high in the charts. Sales of harmoniums and nose-jewels are through the roof. Part of the phenomenon is due to people like Sting, Christy Turlington, Mike D of the Beastie Boys, and Gwyneth Paltrow loudly singing the praises of this ancient but recently modernized practice. But their endorsement is not just for yoga; it also speaks to the power and prowess of Sharon Gannon and David Life, founders of the Jivamukti method.

Heeding the call of charismatic self-help gurus offering physical and spiritual advancement is par for the course among the rich and famous. But I've never been a joiner or a gym goer, nor am I spiritually minded in any but the loosest sense. So how the hell did I fall for it?

In 1982, David Kirkpatrick, a fine arts major from Lansing, Michigan, lands in the East Village with his wife, Kathy, after a few years of knocking around the country with three greyhounds. They move into a rented storefront at the corner of 10th and B, on the northern edge of Tompkins Square Park, a no-man's-land of abandoned buildings and shooting galleries. The intent is to open an antique shop where they can showcase David's work, and people do stop in, but not necessarily to buy anything, just to warm up and hang out. So David and Kathy brew up some coffee, bring in some baked goods, and voilà, they own a coffee shop.

By way of decor, David lacquers images from *Life* magazine onto the venue's tabletops and mounts items plucked from the surrounding mean streets—broken toys, discarded plumbing, the occasional mask—on the walls of the place, which he names the Life Cafe. And he starts going by David Life.

With its homespun, inclusive vibe and fifty-cent vegetarian chili, the place becomes a haven for local starving artists and musicians. Jonathan Larson writes *Rent* there, and even features it in one of the show's big numbers, with actors belting out the song atop facsimiles of David's collaged-up tables. David, a performance artist, presents his work in the space, as does a parade of poets, visual artists, jazz musicians, comedians, and avant-garde performers. One of the latter catches his eye.

Sharon Gannon, who waits tables at the café, is a dancer, poet, and performer. She plays violin and sings in an experimental duo called Audio Letter with a songwriter/multi-instrumentalist named Sue Ann Harkey. Originally based in Seattle, they're new in town and have just self-released their first cassette, comprising twenty-four completely improvised pieces including "Iguana Eggs" and "I'm Not a Sandwich, I Know Who the Bee Gees Are." Mixing art song, screed, and first-thought-best-thought improv, Sharon intones bone-chilling sprechgesang over a maelstrom of chaotic prepared guitar effects and disjointed percussion. David is smitten.

Eventually he and Sharon start performing together. This adds extra strain to a marriage already stretched thin by the challenge of keeping the humble café afloat in a scary neighborhood that most New Yorkers steer well clear of. By 1984 the couple splits. David wants to sell the restaurant, but Kathy refuses. David and Sharon continue their artistic pursuits, performing a piece called Festival of Lights and putting out a cassette recording of it on Sharon's label (City-zens for Non-Linear Futures) in 1985. Meanwhile, around this time—accounts differ, but *sometime* between 1984 and 1986, these committed avant-gardists with day jobs and night gigs come up what they call "a path to enlightenment."

This is the part of the story that has never made sense to me.

At this point they were exploring yoga on their own as well as in their performance work, but they had no formal training. Wouldn't it make more sense if they had come up with their method after, say, going on a spiritual quest and studying yoga with a master? Oh, they did that—but this was two or three years *after* they came up with Jivamukti. According to all accounts, Jivamukti, which means "liberation in the body," was established before they embarked upon their own true yogic education. One thing that seems indisputable is that they bonded over yoga, at least in part, because they were both very good at it.

Also not in dispute is that David and Sharon traveled to India in 1986 for the Sivananda training program and returned in 1988 to study with a man named Swami Nirmalananda. He ordained them as teachers and bestowed upon them new names (Deva Das and Tripura Sundari, respectively). David even became a monk, a renunciate, with shaved head and robes. Eventually they returned to New York, the renunciate renounced his vows of celibacy and poverty, and the couple married. Sometime in the early nineties, they opened the first Jivamukti Yoga Center.

David is all sinew, with deep-set eyes and handsome, gaunt features not unlike Willem Dafoe, who happens to be a hardcore Jivamukti devotee. Sharon is striking—impeccably kohl-eyed and Kabuki pale with glossy black hair and a dancer's grace. The brand of yoga they espouse is a different animal because it places the teacher at center stage. No longer a mere facilitator, the teacher is the prime mover, pushing students, sometimes literally, to the extreme through a multisensory approach. You can practice yoga farther uptown at Dharma Mittra's walkup studio, and you'll be guided through a series of movements in a fluorescent-lit, shag-carpeted room, with Dharma calling out postures and performing them right there on the floor with you. Doing those same asanas in a softly lit, wood-planked space, with Sharon and David orchestrating your every breath and the Beatles and Ram Dass supplying the soundtrack, is an entirely new concoction: a radical mix of the ancient and the modern.

Yoga is the one thing I do for my health. Thanks to Amanda's long-ago gift of *Richard Hittleman's Yoga: 28 Day Exercise Plan*, I've maintained a steady home practice for about five years. But even though yoga is all the rage, entering a yoga studio was never in my plans until my friend Julie, knowing I'm a home practitioner, drags me to Jivamukti so I can "see what a real class is like."

The center has outgrown its former space on Second Avenue and relocated to a hip stretch of Lafayette Street that's home to the Public Theatre, the Blue Man Group, and Indochine, exactly the sort of half-block where a male model cum international assassin might begin to lose his shit in a lesser Bret Easton Ellis novel.

As Julie and I mount the stairs leading to the studio, we have a downward view into the street-level Crunch gym, with its over-bright lighting, rows of exercise equipment, and scores of Lycra-clad fitness freaks straining for the hard body de jour. At floor three, we push through a purple door. Incense is in the air, a fountain trickles, and sitar music plays faintly in the background. The neon "Om" sign is just icing on the spiritual cake.

Inside the enormous fuchsia-and-turquoise room at the center of what the *Times* calls "the white-hot center of New York yoga," we're hit with an uptick in humidity and the rich redolence of Tiger Balm, patchouli, and proudly unchecked perspiration. Forty or so skimpily attired people—variously tattooed, dreadlocked, sarong-clad, and toe-ring-wearing—have arrayed themselves in tight rows on multihued mats. Some assume extreme postures. The men wear the tiniest of shorts.

I find a place at the front of the room, at the edge, near the street-facing windows, so I can block out most of the others. Sharon Gannon appears and the room quiets down. With a regal air, she makes her way to a central spot where a small rug and a harmonium await. She assumes a lotus position, and, at her cue, we all intone "om." Her harmonium begins to drone, low and quavering, and she chants a phrase in Sanskrit, in a tone I find a little unnerving this close. She pauses—well, at least it was brief. But no, the room responds right back, a God-bless-you to her sneeze. She chants again, then it's our turn. Aha.

Well, this sucks. I'm right back in Hebrew school and she's the Jewish Joan Baez reincarnated in Indian garb. I glower for all I'm worth, because this is not what I signed up for. I steal a fierce glance behind me to make sure Julie knows how I feel about being subjected to all this holy hoo-ha. But Julie's got her eyes clamped shut and she's chanting with gusto. She knows the drill.

The chanting ends, and Sharon has a speech to give—a dharma talk they call it. Her subject is ahimsa, or non-harming. The first responsibility of any yogi, she says, is to become a vegan without delay. You can't get enlightened unless you're non-harming to all living beings, and why would we have come to yoga class unless we were seeking enlightenment? That's the essence of it anyway. All this and we hadn't even moved yet.

And when we *do* move?

Imagine you're at a square dance and the man keeps calling out commands faster and faster. Most of these positions are familiar, but I can't seem to catch up to the beat. And the sweat. The sheer amount of sweat. It's everywhere: in my eyes, cascading over my nose, pooling in my ear. As beads of perspiration course down my up-stretched arm in triangle pose, I hear Sharon's voice getting closer. She's right behind me now, counting out breaths ("Inhale three . . . "), and I feel her take hold of the fingers of my slightly quaking hand and pull upward so my arm is perpendicular to the floor.

Like this, you imbecile!

The quick-switching segment comes to a merciful end, and Sharon prompts us to do a headstand. Relieved to finally be off my feet, I lay my forearms on the rented mat, nestle the crown of my head between interlaced fingers, and scan rearwardly, noting with some smug satisfaction that Julie isn't even attempting what Richard Hittleman calls "the king of all yoga poses." I hope Sharon will notice that I have this one nailed, but she's occupied with Willem Dafoe—who needs no help whatsoever. Hands placed *just so* on Willem's narrow hips, she surveys the room with a rapturous expression, mere inches above the celebrated actor's arches. Savoring my prowess, I remain triumphantly upright for a good minute as Sharon extols inversions.

"Physically elevating our hearts above our heads has a profound psychological effect," she says, "as our intuitive feeling brain, situated in the heart, takes precedence over our rational intellectual judging mind. Because inversions reverse the action of gravity on the body inside and out, they provide a powerful toning massage to the internal organs."

I'm about ready to come down.

"Yogis," she says, "if you don't hold *shirshasana* for a minimum of five minutes, you will not get the benefits."

I'm wobbling now.

"This needs to be a daily practice. Not a day should go by without turning upside down for at least five minutes—unless you're menstruating."

A vein I never knew existed is doing the mambo across my forehead, and I'm calculating how many two-minute headstands I've done in the past five years—hundreds at least—and all of them worthless, apparently. I come out of the pose and rest my forehead on the mat, raining rivulets, while the others around me remain steadfastly vertical for a good thirty seconds or more.

Class ends with you on your back—spent, whipped, run over by a cosmic truck—in corpse pose, because you end up as a corpse and you may as well learn to accept it.

I return to the center again and again, usually on weeknights after work. These classes almost feel like happenings. They bring in the most passionate devotees and are taught by the center's most popular teachers. Uma Nanda Saraswati (real name: Tara something) is a Californian in her early twenties who has been on a spiritual path since her teen years and has clocked time with the Hare Krishnas and the qawwali singer Baghavan Das. She chants in a spine-tingling voice, possesses contortionist-level flexibility, and likes to tell stories about the elephant god Ganesh, or about concentrating on the death goddess Kali with such pure intention that she felt no pain during a root canal.

Unremitting abrasiveness is a rare characteristic in a yoga teacher, so Kelly has a rabid following. "Third row, guy in the green T-shirt—spit out the gum," is how she began one of her packed-to-capacity classes. In another, at the same early juncture, she shamed us for not quieting down with suitable alacrity when she started pumping her harmonium. The appeal of Kelly's class is analogous to the famous experiment where a baby monkey is separated from its mother, which is replaced by one of three types of mechanical monkeys. One of them vibrates warmly, one beats the baby monkey, and one ignores it. As it turns out, monkeys prefer the mother that beats them to the one that ignores them. Kelly may be a yoga bully, but at least she's funny. As she stood bestride a woman doing a supported push-up—on all fours, lower back arched—Kelly tried to get her to lift her butt higher.

"Come on, girl," she exhorted. "Don't *tell* me you've never been in this position before!"

Ruth's class is hardest of all—no music, no child's pose, just long holds and greatly challenging sequences. "Keep your voice out of your breath," she'll say, when something like a moan escapes from the lips of a practitioner being pushed to the very edge. Ruth came to yoga as a way of healing after a car accident. She's older than the other teachers, and she doesn't radiate physical health the way they do. Almost wan, not carefully kempt or attired, she's nothing like the perpetually costumed Sharon and Uma. And while their dharma talks tend toward the Hindu gods and energy flow and karma, Ruth's stories are earthbound. She'll talk about her husband, who works selflessly as a nurse at a busy hospital, or about stopping her car to tend to an injured animal—all delivered in a soft New York accent. You might take her for a flaky college professor if you met her at a party. But unlike the average college professor, she has a guru. Ruth believes that her teacher is a holy being. A fully realized master. Divine.

"Practice and all is coming," she quotes the guru as saying, and the room responds with a wordless murmur of assent. Because that's supposed to be *it*—all is coming.

Ah—but of course. That changes *everything*.

Gradually, all the chanting and the God talk ceases to stick in my craw. I want to be part of this world now, and when I show up for kirtan one evening, it's the first time seeing all these people I'd only sweated with, in their street clothes—albeit street clothes that favor sarongs, saris, and dhoti pants. This is a new frontier for me. You can usually find me at the bar.

I find a place among the crowd and assume a cross-legged posture. When it gets uncomfortable, I'll shift to kneeling. A spotlight picks out the kirtan leader, Krishna Das, who's seated in front of a burnished russet-hued harmonium and flanked by assorted rhythm players. Krishna Das (born Jeffrey Kagel) sings traditional Hindu chants in an Eddie Vedder[13] baritone and has duetted with Sting (born Gordon Sumner). Heads turn as the colossal Bhagavan Das (born Kermit Michael Riggs) enters the room. A qawwali singer who's spent years wandering the world as an ascetic, he's in a floor-length kaftan and trailed by a throng of young, berobed female followers, like a harem owner in ancient times.

Then Sharon arrives, resplendent in a white sari, and people scurry to create a path for her. Several acolytes in my vicinity greet her worshipfully by name, some with the honorary "Sharon-ji" as they press their palms together prayerfully and bow their heads. If Sharon hears or sees them, she gives no indication. She does not acknowledge them in any way. Having scanned the room, she begins to make her way toward the spotlight.

It's just a feeling, but it's like I've just seen something I shouldn't have—peeked behind the curtain and glimpsed the real Sharon, as opposed to the one who preaches humility and compassion. The feeling returns a few weeks later, when I accidentally witness one of her flock creating a scene in the Astor Place K-Mart after being called out for cutting the line—the feeling that these people aren't who they say they are.

Still, the power of these classes, sometimes having merely withstood them, delivers like nothing else. Sure, the teachers are full of human foibles, favoring the famous and the familiar, talking about Indian gods as if we all believe in them, lecturing us about animal rights at every turn, yet they orchestrate the

13. Born Edward Louis Severson III.

magic feeling. And some of them are warm, wise, and relatable. I've done yoga in my living room for years and it's not the same. If there is a divine spirit, I'm more in touch with it than I've ever been, and I have these teachers to thank for it.

My principal hangout is the Telephone Bar, an English-style pub on Second Avenue with three authentic red London telephone boxes out front—as it happens, directly below the site of the original Jivamukti Yoga Center. The bar's dominant clique is a British bloc, a loose confederation of blokes, lads, and Petes. Blokes are painters, plasterers, demolition guys. Lads work in advertising or graphic design or finance. Petes are five guys named Pete: Sneaky Pete, Creepy Pete, Manchester Pete, Pete the Greek, and Pete Mullan. The subject of conversation rarely strays far from English football and drunk tales, and there's a lot of taking the piss. Bumps of Charlie are snorted in the downstairs men's and cigarettes are smoked copiously at the bar. Despite the occasional decadence, the fellowship that comes from sharing a few pints among a few like-minded souls keeps me coming back. Until I become zealous about yoga, and the warts begin to show.

Doing a downward dog while hungover is nauseating, and since Saturday morning class with David Life is the best there is, a big Friday night is now out. I want to show up for David lucid and motivated. He has a way of talking about esoteric stuff like chakras and regulating the flow of prana and making it seem totally plausible and not like a bunch of spiritual claptrap. He tells good stories, like the one about the outspoken monk who's imprisoned for ten years, and when he's finally set free his first words are, "Now, as I was saying…" And David harnesses the audio component with a DJ's finesse. One morning, after an especially dynamic dharma talk, he prompts us to rise to our feet and hits us with "The Immigrant Song" by Led Zeppelin, full blast. This man speaks my language! And sometimes, after an evening class, there's something so magnificent in the mere act of walking down the street on strong legs that it's tempting to just keep going when I reach the bar. Beer is still beer, but a pint or two is all I want or need.

Some of the regulars find my newfound moderation and attitude bewildering. Like Chaz Bennett, a blond, blue-eyed Patrick Bateman type who once litigated for Skadden Arps but is now lawyering on his own. Chaz always has a different hot-looking not-quite-girlfriend with him and a strong opinion to express. One night, he chances to hear me mention that yoga is doing good things for me.

"Don't give me any of that shit, Klein," he barks. "You're just there to get laid. Just fuckin' admit it."

"Of course you don't get it, Chaz. You have no soul."

"Oh, don't give me any of that soul crap, Klein."

But even Chaz, a sociopath who will go on to swindle three of the Petes out of their life savings, is not completely off-base. I'm not *not* trying to get laid. Several small friendships develop, along with a crush or two. Nothing clicks until Piper.

She could be from another century. With her alabaster skin, eyes like blue snow at dusk, hair copious and flowing, Piper is like the title character in a Kate Bush song. Even in a packed yoga room she's unmissable, always in the same spot at the back, on the slightly raised platform that also serves as a stage for musical performances. Piper is nothing if not graceful, but she tends to rely on the wall directly behind her during headstand.

After months of friendly in-class joshing, we get to talking one evening, and she tells me she works in film, doing hair and makeup. She gives me her business card, but it's short on specifics: just a Mercator projection and the words SOCIETY FOR MODERN MYTHS.

So I start to get a little fascinated. Wouldn't you?

Piper is close with Sharon and David. She and Sharon traveled in some of the same artsy underground circles in the early nineteen-eighties, so she's a true insider, even has keys to their apartment so she can feed their cats when they're off doing holy stuff. But Piper's not above dishing about them. She tells me Sharon despises the singer Diamanda Galas. Galas, a groundbreaking, critically lauded shrieker who works across multiple genres, is exactly the kind of performer Sharon would have been had she opted for a career in the arts, so her antipathy makes perfect sense. I press Piper on the depth of Sharon and David's devotion to ahimsa. Does it extend to household pests? I mean, you can't kill bugs and not cause harm, can you?

Well, she says, they're not *that* fanatical—which comes as a relief. And hearing that David took a bunch of magic mushrooms up at their 125-acre farm/sanctuary in Woodstock to celebrate his fiftieth birthday, and capered around like a madman, endears him to me all the more. Piper also has some scuttlebutt about Bhagavan Das, but she's less forthcoming about herself. She says she was born in British Columbia, grew up in Arizona, and once played keyboards in a band called Das Teardrops.

Proximity to Piper and my regular presence in class and at the center's gatherings brings me closer to the inner circle. I start proofreading the Jivamukti website in exchange for classes, which earns me a place on the company mailing list and makes me privy to things like Sting and Trudie's yearly springtime retreat in Tuscany. At six grand, a week at Il Palagio is out of my range, but Piper goes. Much to my *shagrah*, as Sting pronounces it, she has nothing scandalous to report, but I do get invited to a small get-together at her place on Easter Sunday.

Bundled in a thrift store peacoat and an emerald green scarf from Charivari, my sole bit of chic, I make my way to Piper's light-filled walk-up on East Tenth on a frosty April afternoon. David and Sharon are there, and so is Uma and a few others, including a pretty well-known actor whose movies I've seen. David knows me by now from my staunch attendance of Saturday morning classes, and I'm pleased that his greeting seems to acknowledge this. Weeks later, I'm at Mitali East, an Indian joint on the restaurant-packed stretch of East Sixth Street known as Curry Row, and I see David and Sharon again. My dinner companion is a guy named Chinnah, a garrulous, big-bellied Indian man in his early fifties who I know from Telephone Bar, and as I wave to them from across the room, I have a fleeting thought that my association with a guy who resembles the elephant god Ganesh in human form might imbue me with some proxy spiritualism. So what if Chinnah's just consumed six drinks, each one a different color, during happy hour at Telephone Bar? David and Sharon don't have to know that. He looks like a goddamn swami.

In time, I become familiar with the center's newly minted teachers and their circle, among whom veganism, sobriety, and clean living are all a given. Some have turned to yoga to free themselves of their addictions. Hanging out with this crowd takes some getting used to. Without the release of alcohol or other substances to loosen inhibitions, time spent with these extremely fit and flexible men and women can feel strangely formal, a bit tame, even a little boring. But I stick with it; socializing with people whose great passion isn't hanging out in bars has to at least be worth a shot. If anything gives me pause, it's the whole guru-disciple thing.

Sharon and David ardently espouse the Hindu and Buddhist tradition whereby a spiritual teacher facilitates the awakening of consciousness in students. If you're serious about yoga, they say, you should find a guru. And the people who pass through their training program seem to accept this principle. During the months of initiation into the Jivamukti way, they grow accustomed to bowing at the feet of Sharon and David. By extension, it's an article of faith that the man who brought the vigorous, flowing vinyasa-style yoga to the West—one Krishna Pattabhi Jois—is a divine being.

Jois (the "All is coming" guy) is an octogenarian yoga master from Mysore, India. He looks like a giant teddy bear and is viewed by the faithful as both a cuddly, benevolent father figure and a living saint. David Life keeps a picture of him on his home altar and prays to it every morning. The Jivamukti founders' endorsement of Jois has made him an object of fascination for the center's teachers, and traveling to Mysore to train at his Ashtanga Yoga Research Institute is seen as the mark of true devotion. Teachers refer to and quote him in their classes. They'll chuckle at how he'll call you "bad lady" if you slip out of a pose too soon, or go into a new one ahead of his count, or are somehow less than compliant in your response to his forceful adjustments. I myself have looked on in disbelief as vibrant women in their late twenties cooed over a framed photograph of Jois like he was Mickey Dolenz.

David Life once told an interviewer that he never wanted to be a guru, but everything about the studio, from the framed photos of the founders striking iconic poses to the worshipful behavior they encourage in their students, speaks to the contrary. Each of the center's two rooms is equipped with an altar bedecked with framed faces: Hindu deities, St. Teresa of Ávila, Jesus, Gandhi, Martin Luther King—and Sharon and David.

"To find a guru, be a perfect disciple," Sharon likes to say. She'll hasten to add that a guru might not be a person, but a *force*—so as not to leave behind those who just can't get with the guru idea. But pretty clearly, she and David advocate for a human guru.

The inner circle at Jivamukti often gathers for communal meals at the apartment of one of the teachers I've gotten to know. Eventually Kristin invites me to a potluck in the small tenement apartment she shares with her boyfriend. Dinner consists of an assortment of lentils, grains, and greens, and a bottle of red wine, split twelve ways. Before we eat, we all join hands around a table. David Life speaks a small Sanskrit prayer, and this doesn't bother me at all. I'm into all this holy hoo-ha now, and being part of this circle and open to all this new stuff feels good, if not quite qualifying as fun. At meal's end, an impossibly lean and flexible Jivamukti teacher who can carry on a conversation while lying prostrate with her feet tucked behind her head announces that she's brought dessert: "Guru balls!"

Guru balls. Let that sink in.

Guru balls can almost pass for small chocolate orbs with coconut on the outside, but since they're made with only the most righteous ingredients, they taste strongly of raw ginger and cardamom and flax seeds. I choke one down and make my exit. On the way home, guru balls still taunting my tastebuds, I run into Piper.

She says, "Hey, I'm on my way to see *Blood Simple*. Wanna come?"

Anyone with the self-possession to go see a movie on their own is more than OK in my book. It's the mark of a person who's content in their own company. So Piper and I take in *Blood Simple* at the Quad, both of us for the second time. We chat over some wine afterward, and then I walk her home. There's no indication of a romantic vibe. We're just two people who saw the same movie together, saying goodnight. But a few weeks later, I'm coming out of a yoga class and she's walking out of a different one.

She says, "I was thinking of you earlier."

"Oh really. What were you thinking?"

"I was thinking, I hope I see that man."

That man. It's like something Betty Boop would say.

Over dinner, I tell Piper about my current entanglement with a not quite divorced woman who lives in Texas, and she listens to my romantic woes in a way that feels supportive and wise and mature, like a sexy big sister. She even offers something completely unexpected.

"You're what every woman wants in a man," she says.

"So what about us?" I say, once I can speak. "We've been out a few times—did you ever think about... us?"

"Well," she says. "You need to figure out what's going on with you right now."

I walk her home, and when we reach her door and she invites me up, I'm thinking, Wouldn't it be weird if this is when it happens? For a moment at the top of the staircase, we do seem right on the verge of about to kiss, but then it's gone. She backs away, or I do, or maybe it was never there to begin with.

Acting on instinct, I get to work on a mix, but not with the usual seductive intent. This is a vaguely summer-themed set meant to dazzle her with the breadth of my clever selections, and maybe make her laugh, rather than to confess a deep romantic longing. Because I'm not entirely sure that's the message I want to send.

And this is a CD mix. I've used my Nakamichi tape deck as recently as six months ago, for a New Year's Eve mix titled (what else?) "Y2K," but since then I've gone digital. Well, sort of. A CD player/burner allows me to work in my preferred way—playing the song in real time, as opposed to moving files around on a computer. My brother finds this ludicrous. CDs are passé, he tells me. When am I gonna wise up and get into MiniDiscs?

Piper's Summertime Swoon

SUMMERTIME/SOMETIMES I FEEL LIKE A MOTHERLESS CHILD:
  MOCEAN WORKER
DON'T LET ME DOWN: CHARLOTTE DADA
SHE LOVES YOU: PETER SELLERS
SOUNDPOOL: DIF JUZ
NOBODY BETTER THAN US: LEADBELLY
WHEN I TURN OFF THE LIVING ROOM LIGHT: THE KINKS
DON'T YOU MAKE ME HIGH: BLUE LU BARKER
HELLO STRANGER: THE CARTER FAMILY
RENO DAKOTA: MAGNETIC FIELDS
I'M TIRED: MADELINE KAHN
ALOHA LA NO O MAUI: THE KAHAIALII FAMILY
OCEANS IN THE HALL: LADYBUG TRANSISTOR
WATER INTO WINE: HOUSE OF STRANGERS
LEBANON, TENNESSEE: RON SEXSMITH
SANCTUARY: GRANT LEE BUFFALO
GODDESS ON A HIGHWAY: MERCURY REV
THE LIGHT 3000: SCHNEIDER TM
EVERYONE HAS SEX APPEAL FOR SOMEONE: RONALD FRANKAU
THE LONELY SEA: THE BEACH BOYS

Pattabhi Jois arrives in the Big Apple in July of 2000 to teach a weeklong series of morning ashtanga yoga classes at the Puck Building, a landmark location on the corner of Houston and Lafayette streets. The New York yoga community greets the event with rapture, and several hundred of the country's bendiest and most committed practitioners flock to the Puck just to be in the same room with the man they call Guruji and sweat under his guidance. In the course of my two-year yoga immersion, I've grown used to the idea that this man, who sparked the yoga movement in the Western world and thus my own personal renaissance, is, if not divine, at least wise and compassionate, and has something to teach me. It'll be a scene, and I'll get to see what all the fuss is about.

Sessions take place in the aptly named Skylight Ballroom, which runs the length of a city block. I attend several. In his youth, Jois had a boxer's build, but now he has a belly that projects outward from his black Calvin Klein boxer briefs. He speaks little English, calls out the postures in Sanskrit, and acts as a sort of benevolent drill instructor. Counting at a maddeningly slow pace, he forces you to hold these poses far longer than usual, and the earliness of the hour only adds to the effort required. Restricting himself to the rows of people at the front of the room, Jois stops seemingly at random to make hands-on adjustments, or even body-on adjustments, sometimes leaning his entire bulk upon a supine woman. This kind of personal attention is greatly desired by the faithful, who set up in front for that very reason, although it's probably feared a bit as well. He's not gentle.

I find a place on the outer periphery, in the back row, far from the main action. Halfway through, Jois's eldest son, Manju, comes up behind me and presses down softly on my back while I'm in a seated forward fold, helping me to extend my reach and clasp my big toe. I hold on for a few seconds before losing my grip. On the last day of the residency, I set up in front where Jois holds court. He's around me throughout the class and even gives me a verbal direction, but I can't understand what he says, and he moves on.

After every class, a long queue forms as people await a turn with him. Still in his boxers but wearing a tank top, Jois sits in a folding chair. When you reach him, you're expected to bow down. Some kiss his feet. Some bring flowers. Some hold up infants for him to lay hands on.

I'm not a kneeler. I've never been taken by the mysticism of India. And if my grandma were here to see what I'm now contemplating, she would plotz. What swayed me to finally get in line and assume my current state of genuflection at the feet of the guru is David Life himself. As he and I stood watching the people on line, I told him I wanted to meet Guruji but was unsure about the bowing business because "bowing seems to imply subservience."

I can't remember the exact words David used in his reply, but oddly enough—and by this I mean *odd as hell*, a description of our conversation exists in a scholarly article by a prominent Christian apologist named Robert Bowman Jr., titled "Does Yoga Conflict with Christianity?" Either David recounted this moment in a subsequent class that Bowman happened to attend (unlikely) or Bowman read about it in the blog portion of the Jivamukti website, where David's account of the event in New York mentions our discussion.

> When one of Life's students expressed uneasiness about bowing down to the guru, Life told him, "Don't bow down to just a man... instead bow down to your own Self that you recognize inside him. Then bowing down to him is no different than bowing down before your own higher nature." The student complied, apparently

deciding that he didn't have a problem worshiping himself. After all, according to the pantheistic philosophy he was taught, we are all one divine Self.

Well, how was Robert Bowman Jr. to know that as I touched (not kissed) the feet of K. Pattabhi Jois, I recited a short, self-composed ecumenical prayer under my breath: *"This is not meant in any sort of creepy subservient way or to imply that you are a holy being. Amen."*

On my way to the elevator I run into Jennifer, a friend from junior high in Tenafly who is now a Brooklyn restaurateur, a mother, and a diligent yogi. We aren't close friends exactly, but we've become reacquainted through shared classes, and that coupled with our common Jersey provenance makes for a happy lack of self-consciousness in our dealings. So, without giving it much thought, I express something that's been on my mind, something I wouldn't necessarily mention to my teacher friends.

"Guruji sure seems to spend a lot of time with women. Did you notice that? And he seems to adjust their poses in ways that he doesn't with men. Like, really pressing up against them. Is it just me?"

"Oh, are you kidding?" she says. "He just felt me up."

"What? Like, copped a feel?"

"No, I mean, I was in plow pose [that's the one where you're on your back hinged at the waist with your feet behind your head] and he places his hand on my crotch and just kind of... keeps it there."

"What the hell?"

"I don't know. I guess that's just... his way? I wasn't the only one."

I have no idea what to do with this information. Could a man so revered be as low as this? It's beyond belief. That would call everything into question. I file it away. I'm too pleased with the newer, healthier me that's emerging to dwell on it. Hell, Jennifer relates the story with a shrug—she hasn't lost faith, so why should I? I refuse to allow this cognitive dissonance to dent my ardor for the practice, for the scene, for my new friends, even for the inscrutable Guruji. In an email to a work confidante, I gush about the old man who recently cupped my friend Jennifer's crotch in the name of therapeutic adjustment: "You really have never seen such a happy wise smiling old face." My friend writes back to say she hopes I'm not turning into a religious wack job.

Months go by before I see Piper again. She's been working on a film in Vienna all summer. We meet for Tibetan food on Ninth Street, then we hit this little nook of a wine bar on Second Avenue she knows of. We share some red wine on a small couch at the back of the place, and our faces are closer than they've ever been before. Afterward, I walk her home, and she says, "Why not come up for a drink?" A few minutes later, she's pulling my boots off.

In the morning, with springtime light filtering through her Zen East Village kitchen, Piper makes perfect coffee in one of those classic aluminum espresso makers, completely naked, as if nakedness were her natural state.

"Let's get together soon," she says.

The next day, there's a message on my answering machine from Piper, asking if we can meet for brunch at Veselka. This sets off a few alarm bells—despite how much I love Veselka. I'm actually looking forward to having a few days to process recent developments, and isn't not rushing things one of the keys to a successful romance? The dating bible du jour, *The Rules*, confirms that a sudden request for brunch is a major breach.

And so, over pierogies and blintzes, Piper tells me a family friend molested her when she was young, and so now, when she has sex, she experiences it as rape. Those are her words. She also mentions something about her thyroid medication. In any case, we've crossed the Rubicon.

In class, I make sure to find a spot as far from hers as possible and pretend to be meditating heavily. Then one day I feel her hand graze my shoulder and I look up. She wants to know if I'm OK. I tell her not to worry, I'm not suicidal or anything.

"Well," she says, "that's… fortunate."

And I can't help but crack a smile. And in time, the sting of rejection wears off and the idea of Piper and me as a real couple starts to look like sheer folly. Eventually, Sharon and David cross the Rubicon themselves.

They issue an edict basically demanding fealty from the forty or so teachers they employ, and a contest of wills is set in motion. At issue is the fact that many of these teachers choose a different studio for their own daily ashtanga yoga practice. Sharon and David won't have it. Practicing at another studio, they insist, sends the wrong message to students like me.

Ashtanga is a set series of demanding asanas that lasts ninety minutes or more. You perform the series each morning before the sun comes up, with one day off for every twenty-eight. Many people never make it past level one. Gwyneth Paltrow has been working on the intermediate series for over a year. Then there's the third series, and the fourth—and the fifth. Maybe one person on Earth can do the sixth. Ashtanga, in other words, is for the hardcore, the lifers, and while Jivamukti offers its own versions of these classes, those who are really into it practice with Eddie Stern at the small, unflashy Patanjali Yoga Shala in SoHo, where there is no neon "Om" sign in sight.

Seeing their teachers opt for Stern, a former busboy at Life Cafe, over them, really grinds their gears. David, who can still recall this pale ginger dude struggling to balance a tray of Life Cafe's famous fifty-cent chili, is thinking, What in the accursed abode of Yama is going on here? I'm being usurped by *this* putz? On top of that, many of the big names who helped put Jivamukti on the map have jumped ship. Not everyone, mind you. Mike D of the Beastie Boys still shows up occasionally, and Russell Simmons is as regular as I am. (As men, we're forced to change out of our drenched clothing in the same tiny, barely curtained-off space; this is how I know Russell is an Arrid Extra Dry man.) But Gwyneth and Madonna are long gone, and they've been trumpeting the next-level thrills of Eddie Stern—like suddenly Jivamukti is AOL and Eddie's Gmail.

While David and Sharon can't do much about the whims of celebrities, they *can* demand that their own people bend the knee. But the strong-arm technique doesn't work. The teachers like it at Eddie's. Maybe they don't want to live half their lives at Jivamukti, and it's their own free time and free choice, right? So a diaspora occurs, and the first wave of teacher-trainees scatters across the city and beyond. Many set up their own studios. One of them, the Shala, across from the Strand Bookstore, becomes my new home.

Not long thereafter, I cross paths with Sharon and David one last time, on a Friday afternoon, at the corner of Lafayette Street and Astor Place. They're in a shiny black SUV, waiting for the light to change, and they don't seem to notice me. The light turns green, and I watch them pull away northward, destination Woodstock, looking every bit the successful New York couple headed off to their second home and getting a good jump on weekend traffic.

In eight years or so, multiple women will come forward and accuse Patthabhi Jois of the kind of groping my friend Jennifer described to me. Others will recount being "adjusted" by him so forcefully that their bones broke. By then, Jois will have already left his body, as the yogis say. Still, all is coming.

In 2016, "Lady Ruth" is named in a sexual harassment suit brought by a teacher-trainee she had mentored. Also named in the suit: Sharon, David, and the center's loyal office manager. Three years later, the New York center shuts down and Life and Gannon retire from teaching. They remain loyal to Jois to the end.

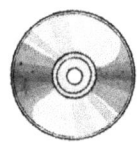

Chapter 27

Alice Something with an H

Being in desperate need of lodgings is a familiar situation by now, but this time I know a guy. Tommy Morgan has just taken over a two-bedroom apartment that has passed through his two sisters. Christina, the more recent tenant, has been making out very well of late, renting out the smaller of the apartment's two bedrooms, and even the fold-out couch in the living room, to a string of NYU students armed with Mom-and-Dad money. But Christina's moving on up, into Max's pleasure palace on East End Avenue, and 300 Mercer has fallen into Tommy's giddy clutches.

Undistinguished, ungainly, girded in scaffolding at least half the year, the Hillary Gardens is a thirty-five-story rent-controlled property in a mostly co-op neighborhood. It looms over adjacent buildings at the northern terminus of Mercer and Eighth Street, bounded by a busy section of Broadway to the east. I pay six hundred a month to occupy the much smaller room—and I'm not complaining. I have a door I can shut, a window and a bathroom and everything. Privacy, self-respect even.

The immediate neighborhood has nothing to offer really—it's lacked any venue of cultural importance since the closing of the Cookery, a jazz club on the corner of University and Eighth that's now a BBQ joint and typical of the "cheap eats for college kids" vibe in this bastion of NYU. Still, I'm minutes from the record shops of St. Mark's Place, the bars of Second Avenue, and several key subways. There's even a pool on the roof. I'm not official or anything, but for all intents and purposes, I live here. Even the surliest of the uniformed doormen acknowledges me.

Tommy and I have it good. He's gotten sober and found a vibrant community of like-minded others. Now he's attending daily A.A. meetings, focusing on building a business, and mentoring others in the Program. Tommy's life changes don't get in the way of our friendship though. He's not judgmental, doesn't care if I come home a little sloppy, never suggests I should examine my life or find God or join him and Stephen Mailer during intermission at the Grateful Dead show, when they meet up at a particular gate with an organization of sober Deadheads called the Wharf Rats, bolstering their resolve to stay clean amid an atmosphere blooming with blotter acid and nitrous balloons. If we're both home at eleven, we watch a *Honeymooners* rerun together, me out in the living room on the couch, him in his room with the door open, our laughter resounding in stereo all around the apartment. Like pals do.

Tommy's type is the girl at the party who stands out for her comely feminine allure—soft-voiced, somewhere between shy and aloof. He always wants *that one*. Despite having provided a fellowship and a genuine appreciation for sensory existence unmuddied by intoxicants, the Program has not yielded him any dates. In fact, you're not supposed to get serious with a fellow member until you both have, like, ten thousand days of sobriety each.

Tommy's at the party of a business associate when he catches sight of Francesca, who's on her third glass of Chardonnay and doesn't mind Tommy's direct approach. With effort, her Aussie/South Africa inflections have melded to a point where she sounds vaguely British, at least to the untrained American ear, and while not necessarily soft-voiced and comely, she's striking and poised and... *a ballet dancer*. Tommy is smitten. I watch it all unfold from the sidelines, from the night he first spots her, to the first time she spends the night, to her first time staying the weekend, to she's moving in. Of course, a few modifications will need to be made.

It only takes two days of IKEA construction, interior detailing, and junk removal to eliminate any trace of pre-Francesca Tommy. It's goodbye, dorm-room Picasso poster, hello, Patrick Nagel print; farewell, *Daily News* obituary of New York Giants quarterback Y.A. Tittle, greetings, gaudily framed studio portrait of Francesca en pointe. These changes surely qualify as an aesthetic improvement, but I'll miss the glorious shamble of the original decor—where a charcoal sketch of a woman's torso, bought from an artist on Astor Place, was thumbtacked with pride between a framed Arabian thoroughbred in three-quarter profile and a vintage Notre Dame pennant. At least it was *him*. Seething at the change in apartment dynamics, I take my woes to the bar, but the Petes have no sympathy whatsoever.

"Wot you whinging about, Dave? *You* should be grateful he doesn't just toss you out on your ear, mate. That's wot I would do," says Manchester Pete, and Sneaky Pete concurs. And they do have a point. Plenty of people who *aren't* barstool curmudgeons would say the same thing: "Sorry, pal, I've found the love of my life. You'll have to make other living arrangements." This is the law of the jungle, and it's been wreaking havoc on best-friend-hood for centuries. But to his eternal credit—out of basic loyalty, basic decency, and who knows, maybe a trace of special dispensation for the pain he caused me as a result of a childhood accident that occurred almost exactly twenty years ago—Tommy keeps me on. Even as our household friction refuses to dissipate and his bond with Francesca grows ever tighter, he remains the Switzerland between our two warring nations.

Somehow the spiritual aspect of Tommy's twelve-step program has softened him up to the point where he's open to religious notions far beyond the traditional Catholicism he grew up with. Like the popular Course in Miracles mind-training seminar, which he and Francesca attend together. Based on a 1976 book whose author claimed Jesus dictated the text word for word, the two-day retreat is actually not that Christ–y. Instead, participants are immersed in discussions and presentations like "Coming to Consistent Peace of Mind," "Getting Rid of Fear," and "Learning to Trust the Higher Self."

When Tommy announces out of nowhere that he's moving to Brazil to fulfil his dream of starting an import/export business, Francesca is just as blindsided as I am. She starts to cry, and they retreat to his room. Eventually Tommy sits us down. "Come on," he says, "you're both great people. My favorite people. I love you both. Don't tell me you can't get along without killing each other." Neither of us wants to disappoint him, so Francesca and I take a deep breath and vow to give it a shot. But the minute he walks out the door, the scene is set for a standoff.

Francesca is still auditioning for stage work while studying for her real estate license, so to maintain her weight she's living principally on microwave popcorn doused with no-cal ranch dressing. Even in my room with the door firmly shut, that cloying synthetic oleo scent seeps in and nestles beneath my nostrils, taunting me like a cartoon finger and rendering me a human rage bomb. My fuming response to this thrice-daily event is purely Pavlovian. Tommy tries to referee from South America, but when a yelling match ends with me bellowing, "Go to your room!" like a total dickhead, Francesca calls up Tommy's buddy Jared Stiegenthaler, who shows up in a beige North Face parka, all Curtis Sliwa, wanting to know what the problem is—he heard there was some kind of problem.

When Francesca finally does move out, once I've cavorted naked around the apartment to the strains of Karl Denver's insane version of "Wimoweh," I head straight to my local watering hole to find a new tenant. Enter: Pete the Greek, better known as Bubble.[14]

BUBBLE
Hobbies: Stella, Jägermeister, pulling the birds
Football team: Arsenal
Favorite band: Radiohead
Favorite insult: Tosser
Other favorite insult: Complete wanker
Favorite superlative: Mental
Favorite superlative for an attractive woman: Fit as a butcher's dog

Bubble may not be the ideal roommate, but he's a friendly sort, at least. Calls everyone "geez." *Awroight, geez?* And he's steadily employed as a graphic designer in the fashion industry. How can that not be an improvement over the popcorn queen? True, he never cleans a dish and has to be chased down to pay his share of the bills. When I'm out of town, he'll let his friend crash in my bed and the friend will throw up in it. But we weather the storms. It's only after a few years that Bubble finally bails. A rent increase that brings his share up to $900 proves the sticking point.

"Sorry, Dave," he says, writing out the final check. "It physically pains me to do this each month." Not unwisely, he moves to Brooklyn.

And where do I go? Why, back to the bar. Fool me twice—*please.*

Roomie No. 2 comes courtesy of a friend of Manchester Pete—a British woman who skips out on me after two months of awkward cohabitation. No less awkward is our forced reunion before an arbitrator at Manhattan's Small Claims Court, where monetary justice is dispensed daily along with a heaping dollop of schadenfreude at no extra charge.

With the Telephone Bar no longer looking like such a hot option, I place an ad in the *Village Voice*. Somehow, I land another Brit. Gary lives to crank the thirty-two-minute unexpurgated version of "Dig It" from some treasured, idi-

---

14. "Bubble and squeak" is Cockney rhyming slang for "Greek." (Bubble and squeak is a traditional fried British dish consisting of leftover cabbage, mashed potatoes, eggs, and any other veggies that might be lying around.)

otic Beatles bootleg. Next comes Rachel, my ex-roommate Dave's cousin from Lawn Guyland. We almost come to blows over the air conditioner, which she insists must be kept on all day even though we're both off elsewhere working. Hey, it costs money! Vlad, a Russian law student at NYU who loves his techno, is by far the neatest. And then there's the summer I take in my brother, who's no longer living large in London and needs a place to crash—which lasts two years. Or feels like it anyway.

In May of 2000, midway into her ninth decade, my beloved maternal grandmother, Ethel Horowitz, dies. Grandma's fade is mercifully brief, but it hits me hard. Our love was pure and uncomplicated. You might even call it unconditional, a concept Mom has always rejected. "The minute a mother sits a kid down on the toilet and says, 'Do your business,' the relationship is conditional." That was Mom's heartfelt belief—she voiced it more than once—and she was blunt on other matters too.

For the first few months of my life, Mom was convinced she'd birthed an ugly kid, a *meeskite*, in the Yiddish, and she was genuinely concerned. My older brother, while unsoothable in temperament, was golden blond and cherubic. In my case, the faded black-and-white pictures that survive seem to attest to Mom's recollection that I looked like a little chimp. She'll relate this with a chuckle, framed as praise for the punim she now approves of, the one her own mother had assured her would be *gorgeous*.

Well, bless Grandma for having faith. It was not Mom's strong suit. Somewhere around the three-month mark, in Mom's telling, Grandma's prediction started to look more plausible. But had I remained simian in appearance? Things could have gotten ugly.

Grandma and I often spoke on the phone, and she'd always ask, "Do you need a little money?" And I'd say yes, because I always did, and she'd say, "I'll send you a little something to tide you over. Don't tell Mother."

In her will, Grandma leaves me (and my siblings) a not insubstantial amount of stock, in a pharmaceutical company where Dad once worked. Just like that, I can afford to pull the plug on the roommate parade. The timing could not be better. My station in life is at an all-time high. I'm a health-minded, spiritually centered guy with a "good job" as an online editor at the Princeton Review. And now, thanks to Grandma, I can come home from work, slide my key in the door, give it a little push, and find only Meema—a tortoiseshell tabby taken in by Tommy and airlifted from Brazil to a life of ease in the Village. To all appearances, I've righted the ship. Grandma would be pleased.

Step 1 in the twelve-step recovery process so highly prized by Tommy is to acknowledge that you have a problem. At nearly forty, I'm giving serious thought to the idea that I have a problem. No, not with drugs or alcohol. I like them both, but they aren't tripping me up in any way that I can see. My problem, the thing holding me back and the reason I don't have the relationship I desire, is that I'm too critical of people. Various friends and family members have suggested this, and it makes objective sense. I was, after all, forged in a cauldron of critique at 5 Sherwood. Maybe I *have* been demanding too much from the nearly decade-long string of sharp, artistic, slightly neurotic women I've discovered, to my repeated surprise, I'm not in love with.

Not that I'm immune to having the same pain inflicted on me. "Ghosting" isn't a term in common usage yet, but more than once, someone I find really enticing just swiftly and inexorably pulls back after a promising beginning, and it leaves me in pieces. During these low periods, I discover my unsuitability as a drinker to excess. Even when determined to get righteously drunk out of self-pity, I feel so hellish the next day, or even by the end of the night, that all I want is to be compos mentis again.

My leap into the online dating pool in June 2001 is like fifteen years of my dating life condensed into a three-week stretch: a couple of no-shows, a visibly disappointed manic pixie dream girl, an episode of enthusiastic couch sex, a rail-thin blond who shows me her fresh lipo scars and calls me a homo after I chat amiably with the male bartender... Oh, and Mindy—who shows up on Rollerblades, snuggles with Meema in spite of a known cat allergy, and skates off minutes later with swollen lips and an unforgettable parting cry:

"It was nice meeting you! My friends call me the disaster magnet!"

Before long, I'm in the familiar position of being entangled with a woman who is great and everything, but just Not the One. Despite knowing this with absolute certainty, I accept an invitation to have dinner at her apartment on a Saturday night. Because maybe I *am* being too critical. Maybe tonight I'll start to see past my superficial, picky Klein-ian objections and appreciate her for who she is: a clever, savvy, independent New York gal who just wants to see where all this is going. So she'd said in a recent, impeccably spelled email.

That's tonight. Today is Alison, who suggested meeting at the Strand Bookstore, in the H section, in honor of her favorite author, Alice... something with an H. Clover smoking clove ciggies seemed like an affectation, but I read nothing into Alison's favorite author being named Alice. She's a reader; that's what counts. Still, none of my mid-afternoon coffee dates have led anywhere, and I admit to a slight sense of disappointment that she's opted for a nooner.

Post-work rendezvous, under the balm of bar lighting and with the lubricant of alcohol, have yielded the more interesting results thus far.

In her match.com profile picture she wears a red corduroy shirt tucked into loose jeans held in place by a belt. Taken in a playground or a park, from six feet away, the photo doesn't tell you what she looks-like looks like, only that she's smiling. I wonder about this as our email communications begin to get a little flirty. But the moment I see her, it's clear that Alison's blurry photo on match.com is just a ploy to keep the bad eggs away, to conceal, or at least taste-fully obfuscate, the plain fact that she is Renaissance-painting beautiful.

In a montage sequence, we stroll out of the Strand together, closely and in step, pausing to kiss on East 12th and Third, lolling on a slope of grass in Tompkins Square Park, lunching under red maple boughs in the garden behind Yaffa Cafe, and spreading out across a bench in front of St. Mark's Church just as the sun nudges past the tree line. When we get to parting at the Astor Place subway, I'm about to ask if she's busy later, but a voice inside tells me to hang back, play the game a little. Don't be *too* available. Give the girl some space and time to process it all. This is a wise tactical move, I figure. It also gives me the chance to deal in good faith with that entanglement I mentioned earlier, which had completely slipped my mind.

We've only known each other for a few weeks, and even though she is Not the One, and even though I have just *found* The One, ending things with a phone call feels cold. This evening, as she envisions it, will entail the consumption of assorted delicacies and interesting beers from Citarella, the upscale food purveyor that's something of an Upper West Side institution. From there, we have several DVDs to choose from—she's leaning toward *Nurse Betty* but isn't married to it. This would almost certainly be a sleepover situation had I not just fallen deeply, madly, and permanently in love with someone else.

On the train uptown, I consider what words I'll use. Eventually I settle on a phrase that strikes me as reasonable. Perhaps prefaced by a sigh, my plan is to explain that "when you and I met, I should have said, there was someone else in the picture." As if my sin was in neglecting to include an important detail—frightfully sorry for the oversight. I figure we'll still go through with dinner and a movie, or at least I'll be met with something other than immediate banishment from the premises. Instead, she weeps, and Kevin, her Italian greyhound, won't stop furiously humping my leg. She finally has to pull him away, like, don't waste your doggie affections on this shit-heel.

What can I say? My friends call me the disaster magnet.

On the street, I spot a pay phone and fish out a quarter. (I still refuse to purchase the cellular kind.) This is tactically a major blunder, just the kind of thing that if it all goes south, I'll look back and say *this* was the moment when I blew it. But I'm ready to drop a dime. If calling too soon makes me look desperate and ruins the whole thing, so be it. Membership in the What the Hell School of Thought is a lifetime commitment, like being a Mason.

As it turns out, The One has much in common with Not the One. Both are dog owners, both work at nonprofits, and they live within a few blocks of each other on the Upper West Side. Kevin and Minerva (Alison's pooch) might even be on friendly sniffing terms.

I'm happy to report that "My plans fell through" succeeds where "There was someone else in the picture" failed, and in minutes I spot Alison moving in my direction, her hound in tow, and when she reaches me and our bodies meet in an easy embrace, I feel a little clench.

We traipse and gambol through the slowly fading dusk of a balmy July evening, and then we drop Minerva off at Alison's apartment and find a cozy little Italian joint, and then we go back to her place…

and…

and…

and…

When you know, you know.

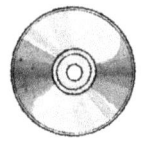

Chapter 28

Lotus Land

It's a little early for the Jesus & Mary Chain, truth be told, but whoever's cranking *Psychocandy*, I like the cut of their jib. I'm pushing my twin sons around the block in a double stroller on a crisp, bright Saturday morning so Alison can get some undisturbed slumber. The caustic auditory spray emanates from Lotus, a café-bar with big windows on the southwest corner of Stanton and Clinton. We're new to the Lower East Side, and I've just found my local. Just in time, too.

The dot-com boom has dried up, taking my respectable-sounding job with it. And with my master's degree in early childhood and elementary education as my lone viable credential, I'm back to teaching. Only, the New York City private school demimonde has undergone a paradigm shift. Progressive educators still give lip service to the idea that kids should get to be kids, but private schools are businesses supported by paying customers, and New York City parents circa 2005 want results. They aren't paying 30K a year so little JoJo can learn experientially. They could give a crap about the paint-blob thing. Can the kid tally a ledger sheet?

The emphasis is on constant skills acquisition, even for five-year-olds—kids who are still young enough to have an imaginary friend and sleep with a special blankie. The school treats this protocol with an infuriating gravity. There are meetings upon meetings: with learning specialists, supervisors, assistants—as if constantly discussing what we're doing is the only way to produce greater outcomes. Full-staff meetings, where the longest-serving faculty deliver jeremiads as others sit in respectful silence or, maddeningly, crochet and sip over-fragrant tea, are my midweek nightmare.

My descent is swift. All it takes is some flailing attempts to make my class-room camera-ready for the first day of school for my supervisor, Denise, to experience an extreme case of buyer's remorse. I now have to show up at her office every Monday morning with a spreadsheet outlining what I plan to cover during the week and how much time I plan to devote to each "unit." Denise is really not into me. It's humiliating.

Bookending my schooldays is a nerve-jangling commute-by-bike along several treacherous Manhattan thoroughfares, from the Lower East Side to the far reaches of the West Village and back again. Add in the ever-present stresses of life with a pair of fascinating if unsynchronized toddler boys, and you can see why the vision of a late-afternoon lager at Lotus beckons at the end of the working day.

This move of ours has finalized my split from the Telephone Bar, and it almost feels like a divorce. The prospect of a new place with a new crowd and new vibes is enticing. And new streets! Thanks to the endless hours of double-stroller pushing I've put in over the past year, I have no desire to ever walk through my old neighborhood again. Plus, I now possess an acute under-standing of the pang-filled paternal ennui that a Stockholm writer named Karl Ove Knaussgaard is experiencing at the very same moment, and is poised to alchemize into literary gold.

The Lower East Side geography almost counts as exotic to me. Even as a vet-eran New Yorker, I've spent precious little time down here. When I did venture south of Houston, for a particularly tempting party invitation or an art open-ing, I'd steel myself for those long, ominously underlit blocks between Houston and Delancey on high alert—eyes peeled for brigands. Now this is where we live. Block-long stretches once dominated by hole-in-the-wall travel agencies, hair salons, and mylar-balloon emporia now boast the likes of Clinton Street Baking Co., where weekend customers queue up for the legendary blueberry pancakes, and wd~50, Wylie Dufresne's molecular gastronomy workshop, where newly christened "foodies" and urban trend followers alike dine on aerated foie gras and kaffir lime leaf churros. Bars pop up like fungi—from swanky cocktail lounges fronted by lab-coat-wearing mixologists to micro-scopic six-stool affairs that only open at midnight every other Saturday.

Nobody thinks twice about crossing Houston Street anymore, but the area's rough edges haven't completely disappeared. A few months ago, a young woman out on the town with some friends was accosted in the pre-dawn hours on Clinton Street, just around the block from our apartment. She challenged the robber who had just pistol-whipped her fiancé and was shot dead.

Without aspiring to the already despised "hipster bar" status, Lotus plays its role in the zeitgeist as corner bars have always served as incubators for art and culture. Lotus just happens to play that role in an era where the no-frills corner bar, the daily newspaper, and other hallowed institutions are about to experience a major correction. Still, for the moment we have Lotus, where a would-be writer named Mick Madison-Park, whose given name is nothing like Mick Madison-Park, came in recently after bingeing on concert footage of the Clash all afternoon, and announced to all within earshot that there's this thing called YouTube where you can watch *any fucking video that's ever been made*. Mick is very serious about the Clash. The volume knob of a Vox AC 30 amp that Paul Simenon *might* have played bass through hangs from a shoelace he wears around his neck.

Also at the bar to take in the good news about YouTube: Full-of-Shit Ken, who knows everybody and has done everything; Manuel, a surly Nuyorican poet, long past his former glory, who pounds PBRs and rum shots all day and makes inappropriate remarks to the female servers; *New York Times* reporter Colin Moynihan, who covers the Lower East Side beat and is a ubiquitous presence on his bike around these streets, always in a Carhartt coat and blue button-down; Matt Roberts, a *Daily News* photographer fresh from a stakeout at Manhattan Criminal Court, and a few stoners from Def Jux Records, the alternative hip-hop label, who've started releasing their own music and design T-shirts for side projects and no longer use email. You can also count on a cohort of free-wi-fi hogs who hunch at nearby tables, nursing single cups of coffee for an entire afternoon and grousing about connectivity.

Lotus's resident Jesus & Mary Chain fan is a guy named Ivan, who has Bob Dylan's hair circa *Blonde on Blonde*, a rapid low-volume speaking style, and a deep and abiding love for the Velvets, Iggy, and Nick Cave. Doubtless, his habit of playing emphatic air drums with his back turned does not please the customers, who are just trying to order coffee and a scone, for chrissake, but he's unfailingly polite once you get his attention. Following his promotion from daytime café worker to afternoon bartender, our feverish late-afternoon music conversations become a regular thing that I look forward to. Ivan sees a lot for twenty-one, and he's willing to point that high-powered perception at himself. When the place is dead, he'll blast anything—the latest demo by his band, the Royal Chains, *Dusty in Memphis*, the Brian Jonestown Massacre, *Pet Sounds, Loveless* ... twice in a row, if necessary. We have a saying: "When in doubt, play the greatest record ever made." Which means either the Stone Roses' self-titled or *Ocean Rain* by Echo & the Bunnymen.

Like my previous hangout, Lotus is no slouch in the sociopath department. Every bar worth its salt needs one, I guess. Omni, an opiate enthusiast who lives on a leaky houseboat docked in the Brooklyn marina, speaks with a fake Australian accent and never takes off his sunglasses, on account of, according to Ivan, having eyes like two piss-holes in the snow. In November of '07, when Omni is arrested for committing his eighteenth armed robbery in a two-month period, we find out his real name is Herbert Rodriguez—soon to be rechristened "the Untalented Mr. Ripley."

Stopping in for a quick beer is a nascent music writer named Klingman, who writes funny, incisive dispatches on bands I've never heard of, for an MP3 blog cobbled together by his college pals—goofily named Merry Swankster by the one who'd first thought to start one. After fewer shared beers than you might think, Klingman hooks me up with a "writing column" at Merry Swankster.

The timing here is crucial; we're in the brief window of a purer Internet where everyone aspires to influence, but there's no easy way for the suits to commodify it. And just like that: *a column of my own*. Suddenly, my most passionate feelings and thoughts on the subject I'd been studying all my life have a place in the world—and an audience. It's exhilarating, and it also stirs up a kind of long-simmering resentment. Music reviewers have shat all over my tastes for years and made me feel stupid for liking Jethro Tull and late-period Hüsker Dü—guys like Robert Christgau, who pontificate via epigrammatic put-downs and never tell you what the damn thing sounds like, and trash records and artists with the assurance of biblical truth tellers. Not to mention older brothers who sniff, "What the hell is this shit?" if the song playing in your apartment happens to contain a cheesy lyric.

My column—wherein I extol the likes of the Volcano Suns and Willie "Loco" Alexander for an audience of just-under-the-wire Gen Xers who have never bought a single LP on Homestead Records—is called Obscurer Than Thou. Aimed at punks who've just spent years gorging on Napster-pirated album downloads enabled by shared university modems, this is no light claim.

One afternoon, I roll up to Lotus, existentially parched, and Ivan's out in front in the little recess at the bar's main entrance. He's smoking cigarettes with a petite dark-haired girl in white sunglasses wearing an American Apparel onesie. A rectangular road case that's practically her size, containing some kind of keyboard, is propped up against the glass within arm's reach. Ivan introduces her as Stef and says she's playing gigs around town under the name Lady Gaga.

I bum a smoke and listen as they talk about David Bowie. Ivan, ever the proselytizer, is trying to sell Stef on portions of D.B's nineties output, but she doesn't seem to be buying it. I'm itching for an opening to tell my Tony Visconti story, or better yet, how the one time Bowie and I were in the same room was when he was fronting Tin Machine at the Academy, but Gaga has got to get going. She hands us some flyers for her upcoming performance at the Bitter End before lugging her keyboard to the corner and hailing a cab. I have no time for gigs these days, but even if I did—the Bitter End?

"Pffft. That Bleecker Street stretch of clubs has always been the lowest echelon of the New York City music performance circuit," I say sagely, once her cab takes off.

"She's actually really talented," says Ivan. "Sings, plays a bunch of instruments, writes her own songs. I started chatting her up one day, played her a few Royal Chains demos on MySpace, like, aren't I cool? And then she played me a few of hers."

"MySpace?"

"Yep. Where else are you gonna go?"

"Good stuff?"

"Put it this way. I think she'll go places."

"Well damn, son, if she's playing the Bitter End, she's got nowhere to go but up."

Back inside, Ivan cues up a song from the most recent CD mix I'd made for him, saying, "This is the one that really jumped out at me." Hearing the opening synth pulse of Anna Domino's "88," I give him the "Wise choice, Grasshopper" nod of approval. Of course Ivan picked up on its greatness.

"I mean, if Lady Gaga ever does anything to match this, she'll have succeeded. Because seriously, this has gotta be... well, the ultimate #88 song of all time."

In retrospect, this was a rash remark. Had I paused for even a second, surely "Rocket 88" by Jackie Brenston & His Delta Cats (one of perhaps a half-dozen songs regularly cited as the first rock 'n' roll song) or the droll "88 Lines About 44 Women" by eighties synth-poppers the Nails would have sprung to mind, and I might have qualified the statement. But my mind is already in overdrive.

"Hey, think of it. Ivan. There has to be, like, a definitive number song for every number—not to infinity but, say, to a hundred—where a song so *owns* a number that it's like an athlete whose number has been retired. A Hall of Fame song. That's it, the number song Hall of Fame. Like, the Brothers Johnson's

'Strawberry Letter #23.'" That's gotta own the #23 slot, right? Can you think of a better #23 song?"

"Not off the top of my head, but I think I see where you're going with this," he says. "So, like, get your kicks on Route 66?"

"Exactly. 'Route 66' would seem like a no-doubter," I say, taking a quick gulp. "Alice Cooper—'I'm Eighteen.' Another no-doubter."

" '24 Hours,' he volleys back. "Joy Division."

"Good one! Can't think of another #24 song but there must be a bunch of others. What about 'Eight Days a Week'? Ooh, or 'Eight Miles High'? Tough call there. Cage match."

"19th Nervous Breakdown."

"Well played, Squire. I'll see your '19th Nervous Breakdown' and raise you '96 Tears'"...

By dusk, I've filled up three or four slightly damp bar napkins with song titles.

A journey of a thousand miles begins with a single step. Mine began that night, in the shadow of the Streit's Matzo factory. Minerva had paused to do her business, and not wanting to block the narrow sidewalk, I took a step backward and gazed imploringly at the star-betwinkled sky. Right then, as my sole sank into a fresh pile of dogshit, it came to me.

I was going to write a book—the one that legendary producer Tony Visconti wondered why I hadn't written yet. On a subject that has never been studied—number songs. A genuine first-time-given gift for music obsessives that even Sara would appreciate. I would start at the beginning, at #1, and just keep climbing. And I knew I would see it through because now I understood something about commitment.

Why number songs? Songs with a number in their title comprise a mini-genre unto themselves. There are others like that, of course. Love songs, for example. But love songs are too general—where would it end? Likewise, you'd never run out of drinking songs or breakup songs, but that would grow tedious after a while—you'd just be compiling an endless list. Numbers, and hence number songs, are different somehow. The singularity of each number means that each one—at least those from 1 through 99—seems to occupy its own little fiefdom in a way that letters, or even words, do not. Songs that share a number, especially an offbeat one, are often united in a very specific way. You can't really generalize about songs that begin with the letter R, or even songs that have the same word in them, but after examining the major #17 songs out there, you can determine with some degree of certainty that many of them are about adolescent girls. I knew #18 had a certain rebellious flavor, thanks to Alice Cooper, and #16 had a "sweet little" connotation, courtesy of Chuck Berry. But what was #34 like? Was there even an #83 song—a good one? No one had ever chronicled the numerical strands running through pop music. I would be the one to do it.

Lotus was living on borrowed time. First the beer ran out, then the place shuttered, then it reopened near Peter Luger's in Brooklyn for a brief final run. Supplanting Lotus on the corner of Stanton and Clinton was a pseudo-Irish bar called Donnybrook with an inscription near the entrance proclaiming "*Home to lively debate and raucous revelry*" in fancy cursive. In short, not the type of place where you can play *Loveless* all the way through.

Early in 2008, the same year Lady Gaga releases her six-times-Platinum debut album, *The Fame*, Alison receives an offer to run the financial aid office at Duke University in Durham, North Carolina. It takes some time to wrap my brain around the idea of leaving the city, but living and working in the same smallish apartment can get pretty claustrophobic, and when it comes time to pull up stakes, the prospect of a home that has a yard where my kids can play kickball is looking better and better.

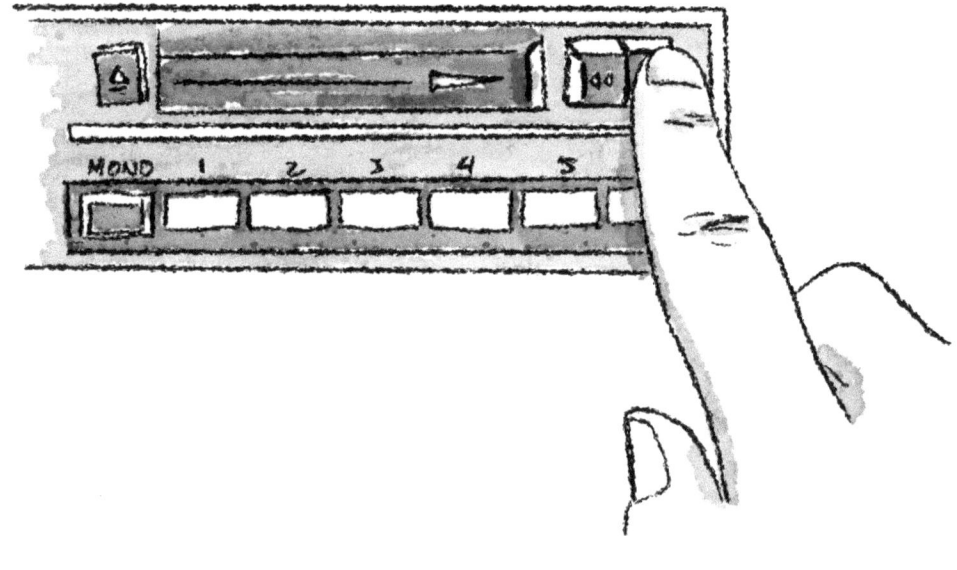

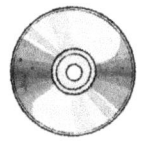

Chapter 29

Sham On

Our household is a strictly G-rated affair. I attribute this to Alison, whose family prohibited the use of "shut up" and "stupid"—words that were not the least bit eyebrow-raising in my own childhood home and sometimes were even the preferred terminology. Thus, for my seven-and-a-half-year-old sons, there are two S-words: the SH-word and the ST-word. The other S-word (the one recognized by the rest of the world) doesn't even have a name. That's how taboo it is. One Sunday afternoon, as I'm tooling along Roxboro Road toward the farm in Rougemont, North Carolina, (pop. 1,000 or so) where Nathan and Daniel ride horses named Bandit and Tommy, an unexpected turn of the iPod creates a conundrum.

Earlier that morning, I had put together a CD mix for the ride out to Rougemont and happened to include "Rockin' the Suburbs" by Ben Folds Five. The boys know the song from *Over the Hedge*, an animated film about a conniving raccoon and cohort of charming woodland animals. They were once obsessed with the movie, but they've moved on, and the song disappeared into the iTunes ether. I included it on the mix figuring they would receive it as a sort of golden oldie. Sure enough, when those crunchy opening chords hit, followed by that ear-worm synth hook, they start bouncing up and down like cartoon headbangers. But hang on—something's different. This is not the version that plays over the end credits of *Over the Hedge*.

As it turns out, I had downloaded the original Limp Bizkit-baiting riff-rocker from the band's 2001 album, which features a half-dozen words that are verboten in most households with grade-school-age children. With my finger hovering over the FF button, I do some quick mental math. My first exposure to songs containing bad words was in 1967, thanks to the original cast recording of the off-Broadway production of *Hair*. Side 1 began with "Ain't Got No," which wasted no time in dropping the real S-word ("Ain't got no smokes / *Shit!*"), followed by "I Got Life," which included several others you still can't say on broadcast TV.

I was five. Nathan and Daniel are pushing eight. I figure it's time.

> *Lemme tell y'all what it's like / being male, middle-class and white*
> *It's a bitch if you don't believe / listen up to my new CD, sham on!*

They pretty much gasp in unison. Not because they've never heard these words before, but because Dad is here and he's letting it happen.

"Hey, guys?" I shout over my shoulder, once Ben Folds drops an S-bomb in the second verse. "Guys, we don't want to *say* these words. But *sometimes*, like in a song like this, it's OK to *hear* them."

In the rearview, their expressions turn into mischievous grins, followed by a flurry of movement as my boys return to headbanging.